NEW ZEALAND'S FIRST AIRLINE
HOKI TO HAAST

RICHARD WAUGH

Dedication

Reverend Jean Mary Waugh
1927 – 2009

A pilot's wife, who like many others, prayed and looked for the safe return of the de Havilland biplanes from South Westland

FRONT COVER: Bert Mercer's original DH83 Fox Moth ZK-ADI flies up the coast from Haast to Hokitika in February 1997. This was soon after its return to New Zealand by new owner Gerald Grocott. The pilot is Rod Hall-Jones. (John King)

FRONT COVER INSERT: Pioneer pilots Bert Mercer (left) and Jim Hewett at Franz Josef Airfield (Waiho) in the early summer of 1936 with Fox Moths ZK-AEK and ZK-ADI. (Mercer Collection)

REAR COVER: At Milford Sound Airfield in August 1961, Brian Waugh rests his hand on the port propeller of West Coast Airways' DH89 Dominie ZK-AKT, after a scenic flight from Hokitika. While at Milford, Waugh often met his pilot friend Brian Chadwick who in February 1962 went missing, never to be found, on a flight to this scenic region in Mercer's former Dragonfly ZK-AFB. (Geoffrey Houston via Noeline Watson)

REAR COVER INSERT: Brian Waugh flying a Dominie near Haast in 1960. Note the central turn and bank dial indicating a slight left turn and, at right, the morse code operating key. (Waugh Collection)

Published by The Kynaston Charitable Trust in conjunction with Craig Printing Company Limited, PO Box 99, Invercargill 9840, New Zealand.

© 2009 Richard J. Waugh

The right of Richard Waugh to be identified as the author of this work in terms of section 96 of the Copyright Act 1994 is hereby asserted.

This book is copyright.
Except for the purposes of fair reviewing, no part of this publication may be reproduced or transmitted in any form or by any means without permission in writing from the publisher. All the photographs in this book are genuine and have not been altered other than some cleaning and minor digital enhancements.

ISBN 978-0-473-15936-8

Printed by Craig Printing Company Limited,
122 Yarrow Street, PO Box 99, Invercargill 9840, New Zealand.
Email: sales@craigprint.co.nz Website: www.craigprint.co.nz

122599

Foreword

GOVERNMENT HOUSE
New Zealand

GREETINGS, Kia Ora, Kia Orana, Fakalofa Lahi Atu, Taloha Ni.

As Governor-General of New Zealand, it gives me great pleasure to provide a foreword to *Hoki to Haast - New Zealand's first Airline*.

A book such as this serves several purposes. It is a timely reminder that the age of safe and comfortable travel in high speed passenger aircraft is a relatively recent phenomenon. It is little more than a century since the first aeroplane flights and just 60 years since the first jet airliner took to the skies.

This book takes us back to a time when air travel was still in its infancy and reminds us that for those services to be established, someone had to go first. Despite its isolation, New Zealand has had its fair share of aviation pioneers including Vivian and Leo Walsh, George Bolt and Jean Batten to name but a few.

Another of those pioneers was Captain J.C. 'Bert' Mercer. While Chief Flying Instructor for the Canterbury Aero Club, he recognised the potential for an airline on the West Coast to service scattered and isolated settlements where roads were patchy or, in South Westland, non-existent.

And so it was that Mercer's airline, Air Travel (NZ) Ltd was the first to start licensed scheduled air services in New Zealand when he flew the company's de Havilland Fox Moth from Hokitika on 18 December 1934. The airline was a hit with the locals, expanding to five aircraft by 1938 and operating flights to Nelson during and after the Second World War.

Not long after Mercer's tragic death from injuries in a crash in 1944, his airline was nationalised and the service continued to be operated by NAC under senior route pilots Norm Suttie and Frank Molloy, and later by West Coast Airways under chief pilot Brian Waugh. Indeed, the sturdy fabric-covered, wooden and wire de Havilland biplanes continued flying until 1967 when the impact of the new Haast Highway rendered the air service redundant.

I wish to congratulate aviation historian Richard Waugh QSM for writing such a comprehensive book, and to all those who assisted him. Reverend Waugh's book provides a fascinating window on a pioneering saga in New Zealand aviation and highlights its significant role in the development of our country.

No reira, tēnā koutou, tēnā koutou, kia ora, kia kaha, tēnā koutou katoa.

Hon Sir Anand Satyanand, GNZM, QSO
Governor-General of New Zealand

Westland
District Council

WESTLAND'S HISTORY has been a colourful one with many local characters making their mark on the pages of New Zealand's history. None more so, than those personalities associated with the establishment of the first licensed scheduled air service in New Zealand – pioneered by Air Travel (NZ) Ltd. The company was born out of a vision for tourism opportunities and an economic passenger, freight and mail service to the "far-downers" who lived in the harsh, yet awe-inspiring and remote areas of South Westland.

Captain Bert Mercer recognised the opportunities that lay untapped and quickly encouraged investment in this new enterprise. The original shareholders were determined to open up the West Coast and did so by creating a valuable and economic new air transport business, unprecedented at the time in New Zealand. Fully funded by private capital, mostly local, the company thrived, quickly expanding from one de Havilland Fox Moth in 1934 to five Fox Moth and Dragonfly aircraft by 1938, servicing a growing customer base. The isolation of South Westlanders was at an end and new opportunities presented themselves.

In the 1930s and 1940s the people of Hokitika and South Westland were the most air-minded in the country, becoming reliant on the air service for exporting and importing produce, mail and people. The scenic wonders of South Westland were now there for all to see from the wonderful vantage point of a Fox Moth, Dragonfly or Dominie cabin. Aircraft and flying became a part of everyday West Coast life, long before most other people in the country.

Reverend Richard Waugh (son of the last pilot, Brian Waugh) has a great passion for New Zealand's aviation history. Richard and the many people who have helped him, especially Graeme McConnell, are to be commended for unearthing rare photographs, many interesting stories, facts and statistics about Air Travel (NZ) Ltd, NAC and West Coast Airways Ltd. *Hoki to Haast – New Zealand's first Airline* is an accurate and creatively produced book that takes us on a journey into what has become a legendary part of New Zealand's transport and social history.

This book will be launched as part of the 75th anniversary celebrations of New Zealand's first licensed scheduled air service. It will be an enduring record of the foresight, skill, ingenuity, and hard work of the many people who made the air service an unrivalled success.

Maureen Pugh J.P.
Mayor, Westland District Council

Acknowledgements

BERT MERCER and the early years of the South Westland air service were first recorded by Leo White in his 1941 book *Wingspread*. During the halcyon days of the late 1930s White, a friend of Mercer, demonstrated how to take great photographs and Mercer knew how to pose and take advantage of the resulting publicity.

From the early 1970s John King revived interest in Mercer's exploits, publishing various articles and photographs. Des Nolan and Bill Cropp worked on the local scene to keep memories alive and Jim Jamieson also gathered important material. Like these enthusiasts, I too had been collecting photographs and associated material about the early West Coast airlines from the late 1970s. However, my interest focused on the entire South Westland air service period, including the neglected NAC and West Coast Airways years. In 1994 I took the initiative which lead to the organising of the 60th anniversary celebrations of New Zealand's first licensed scheduled air service, which culminated in a range of memorable events attracting national attention. John King, Paul Beauchamp Legg and I wrote *When the Coast is Clear* which placed the three airline periods together, telling the whole thirty-three year history of the air service.

Why do I have an abiding interest in the South Westland air service? When I recall flying as a boy in the Dominie it was all rather intoxicating; various aromas in the airy cabin, the Gipsy Queen engines and their throaty roar, the smell of hot oil and 73 octane petrol, cameras furiously clicking, stunning views through the wing bracing wires, and many fascinating characters who flew the service. Especially memorable was my Dad in the snug Dominie cockpit, turning and beckoning me to come forward, lean in and take over the controls for some gentle manoeuvres. While I attended Hokitika Primary School, my father flew overhead in the Dominie, sparking much excited conversation among us boys about flying and planes.

As a youngster I experienced the final years of the South Westland air service but I did not appreciate anything of its historical significance. In 1969 the West Coast Airways advertising sign was still on the hospital hill near the main road into Hokitika. I remember my father saying, "I must talk to Des Wright about getting that old sign down". As I had contemplated rescuing the sign myself, those were probably my first inklings of an interest in history. At the same time I remember Frank Molloy as our school caretaker. Dad told me he had been a local pilot but I had no appreciation of his distinguished South Westland flying career.

Over the years I met and interviewed a number of people closely connected with the air service including; Billee Douglas (Mercer), Marie Lindsay (Mercer), John Neave, Ron Kirkup, Jim Kennedy, Dick Ferguson, Ross Grant, Margaret McKenzie (Penman), Doug Lister, Jock McLernon, Shem Dowd, Des Holden, Jack Humphries, Paul Beauchamp Legg, Des Wright and Dave McDonald. Later I had the privilege of leading funeral services for John Neave, Ron Kirkup, Jim Kennedy and Billee Douglas.

With the 75th anniversary in 2009, there is further opportunity to publish newly researched material. There has been much information and many photographs discovered since 1994 and significant developments regarding a variety of historic de Havilland aircraft connected with the air service — prominent among them the return to New Zealand of historic DH83 Fox Moth ZK-ADI.

For this book special thanks are due to Graeme McConnell, Nelson's aviation historian, for his willing and helpful assistance to me with photographic selection work, some graphic design, editing and important primary research at National Archives and at the Canterbury Museum. Without his specialised help this book would not have been ready in time. In 1994 Graeme, with his elderly father Hec McConnell, built the Kawatiri Junction aviation memorial commemorating the 50th anniversary of the tragic accident of DH84 Dragon ZK-AHT in which Bert Mercer died. Pam McConnell – thank you for your support of Graeme in this work. Bruce Gavin did the research and writing of the appendix history of West Coast airlines, assisted by Father Steve Lowe, and Peter Layne has done all the index work. Their contributions have added considerable value to this book.

Many willing people from throughout New Zealand have helped with research and supply of information including family, friends, aviation historian colleagues, and those keen about West Coast aviation. I thank them all including: Fletcher Anderson, Kevin and Sandra Anderson, Ron Ark of the Canterbury Aero Club, Spencer Barnard, the late Charlie Barnhill, Paul Beauchamp Legg, Norm Bishop, Murray Bowes, Bruce Broady (England), Allan Brown, Bede Brown, Jack Browne (Custodian of the D.A. Walker Photographic Collection), Peter Carmine, Hazel Chan of East City Wesleyan Church, Jim Chapman, Ian Coates, Chris Coll, Mike Condon, Gavin Conroy, Allan Cron, Lyall Delore of the Hokitika-Westland branch of the RSA, Paul Dimery (England), Brian Doig, Dorothy Dowell, Max Dowell, Joyce Eden, Simon Eden, Kerry Eggeling, Roger Eggeling, Lydia Feld, Noel Finch, Dorothy Fletcher, Damon Forsyth, Ron Fulstow, Brian Gauld, John Gavin, Patricia Gavin, Dave Grantham, George Greenhill, Gavin Grimmer, Gerald Grocott, Anne Hancock, Tony Hewett, June Hodgkinson, Jamie Houston, Drew Howat, Jack Humphries, Helen Hutchison, Jim Jamieson, Cliff Jenks, Mike Keenan of Westland District Council, Pat Keenan, Mike Kelly (D.D. Kelly Collection), Alan Kennedy, the late Jim Kennedy, Jeanette King, John King, the late Ross King, Thora King, Stephanie Layne, Peter Lewis, Marie Lindsay, Robert Lindsay, Philip Lister, Dave McDonald, Norm McKelvey of the Museum of Transport and Technology, Jimmy McLaren, Les McKenzie, Margaret McKenzie, Kaye McNabb, Paul Madgwick, Geoffrey Markland, Errol Martyn, Alan Mayne, Susan Minehan, June Molloy, Alison Morgan, Gerard Morris, Terry and Rosie Moyle of Contour Creative, Pat Nancekivell, Richard Neave, Don Noble, the late Des Nolan, Fay O'Callaghan, Warren Openshaw, Garth and Kathleen Paganini, Don Perry, Margaret Phillips, Delwyn Preston, John Pugh, Pat Pugh, Sue Pugh, Jerry Savage, Peter Scaife, Gina Schroder, Jacqui Stevenson, Jack Renton,

Diana Rhodes, Peter Robertson, Mary Rooney of the West Coast Historical Museum, Suzanne Scott (Fiji), Elaine Simmons, Colin and Maeva Smith of the Croydon Aviation Heritage Trust, Royce Smith, Ryan Southam of Croydon Aircraft Company, John Suttie, Matt Syron, Les Taylor, Gordon Thompson, Alan Tunnicliffe of the Airmail Society of New Zealand, Bert Waghorn, Francis and Brian Ward, Noeline Watson, Alec Waugh, the late Jean Waugh, Jean Wells, Pat Wells, Cyril Whitaker, Murray Whitehead, Richard Williams, Megan Wilson, Megan Wishart and Allan Rudge of Museum of Transport and Technology Library, Jocelyn Worrall, Dave Worthington, Kevin Worthington, Buster Wright, Raeoni Wright, and the staff and resources of National Archives, Wellington and Christchurch, and the Canterbury Museum.

I am especially grateful to John King for giving permission to use his excellent photographs of Fox Moths ZK-ADI and ZK-AEK and Dominie ZK-AKY – all in their natural South Westland habitat. Dorothy Fletcher and Paul Beauchamp Legg shared their valuable photographic collections and Ron Fulstow allowed me to reproduce several of his de Havilland drawings.

The forewords by the Governor-General of New Zealand, Sir Anand Satyanand, and Mayor of Westland District Council, Maureen Pugh, clearly articulate the national historical significance of the South Westland air service.

Thank you to Air New Zealand and Pacific Blue who assisted with research travel and to the Renton family of Hokitika.

Once again it has been a pleasure to work with Ellen van Empel and the team at Craig Printing Company Limited who have produced another high quality New Zealand history book.

My aviation work would be impossible without the loving support and patience of my wife Jane and our children Simon, Theresa and Kristie. Thank you,

Rev Richard J. Waugh QSM
Howick
Auckland
October 2009

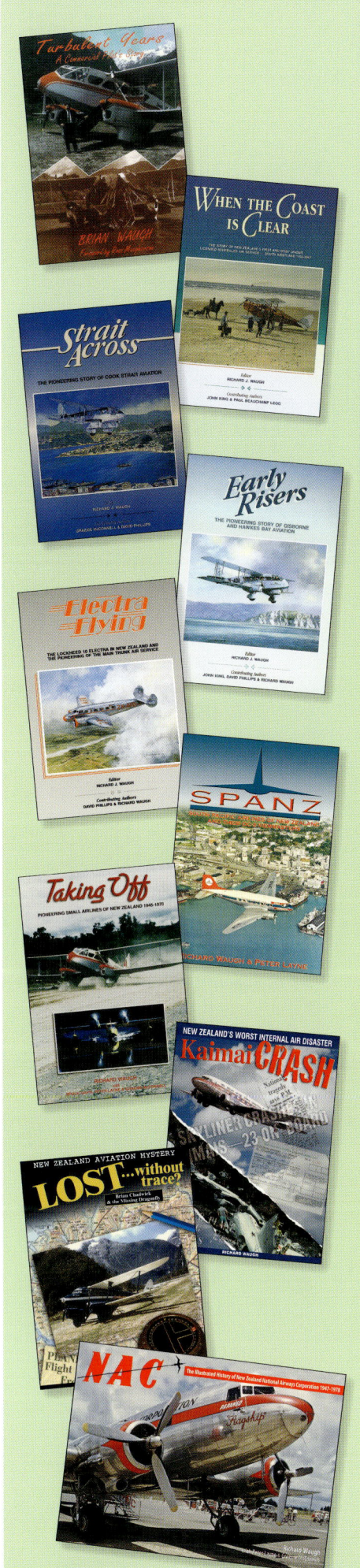

Companion New Zealand aviation books from the Waugh Collection

Turbulent Years
A Commercial Pilot's Story
By Brian Waugh, edited by Richard Waugh
Christchurch, Hazard Press 1991
(Reprinted 1992 and 1997)

When the Coast is Clear
The story of New Zealand's first and most unique Licensed Scheduled Air Service – South Westland 1934-1967
Edited by Richard J. Waugh
Contributing authors John King,
Paul Beauchamp Legg and Richard Waugh
Invercargill, Craig Printing Company Limited, 1994
(Reprinted 1996 and 2000)

Strait Across
The pioneering story of Cook Strait Aviation
Edited by Richard J. Waugh
Contributing authors Graeme McConnell,
David Phillips and Richard Waugh
Invercargill, Craig Printing Company Limited, 1995

Early Risers
The pioneering story of Gisborne and Hawkes Bay Aviation
Edited by Richard J. Waugh
Contributing authors John King,
David Phillips and Richard Waugh
Invercargill, Craig Printing Company Limited, 1997

Electra Flying
The Lockheed 10 Electra in New Zealand and the pioneering of the Main Trunk Air Service
Edited by Richard J. Waugh
Contributing authors David Phillips and Richard Waugh
Invercargill, Craig Printing Company Limited, 1998

SPANZ
South Pacific Airlines of New Zealand and their DC-3 Viewmasters
By Richard Waugh and Peter Layne
Invercargill, Craig Printing Company Limited, 2000

Taking Off
Pioneering Small Airlines of New Zealand 1945-1970
By Richard Waugh with Bruce Gavin,
Peter Layne & Graeme McConnell
Invercargill, Craig Printing Company Limited, 2003

Kaimai Crash
New Zealand's worst internal air disaster
By Richard Waugh
Invercargill, Craig Printing Company Limited, 2003

LOST...without trace?
Brian Chadwick and the missing Dragonfly
By Richard Waugh
Invercargill, Craig Printing Company Limited, 2005

NAC
The Illustrated History of New Zealand National Airways Corporation 1947-1978
By Richard Waugh with Peter Layne and Graeme McConnell
Invercargill, Craig Printing Company Limited, 2007
(Reprinted 2008)

These books are available from Craig Printing Company Limited. See contact details on page 2.

For further information and sample pages of these books see: www.nzairlineresearch.co.nz

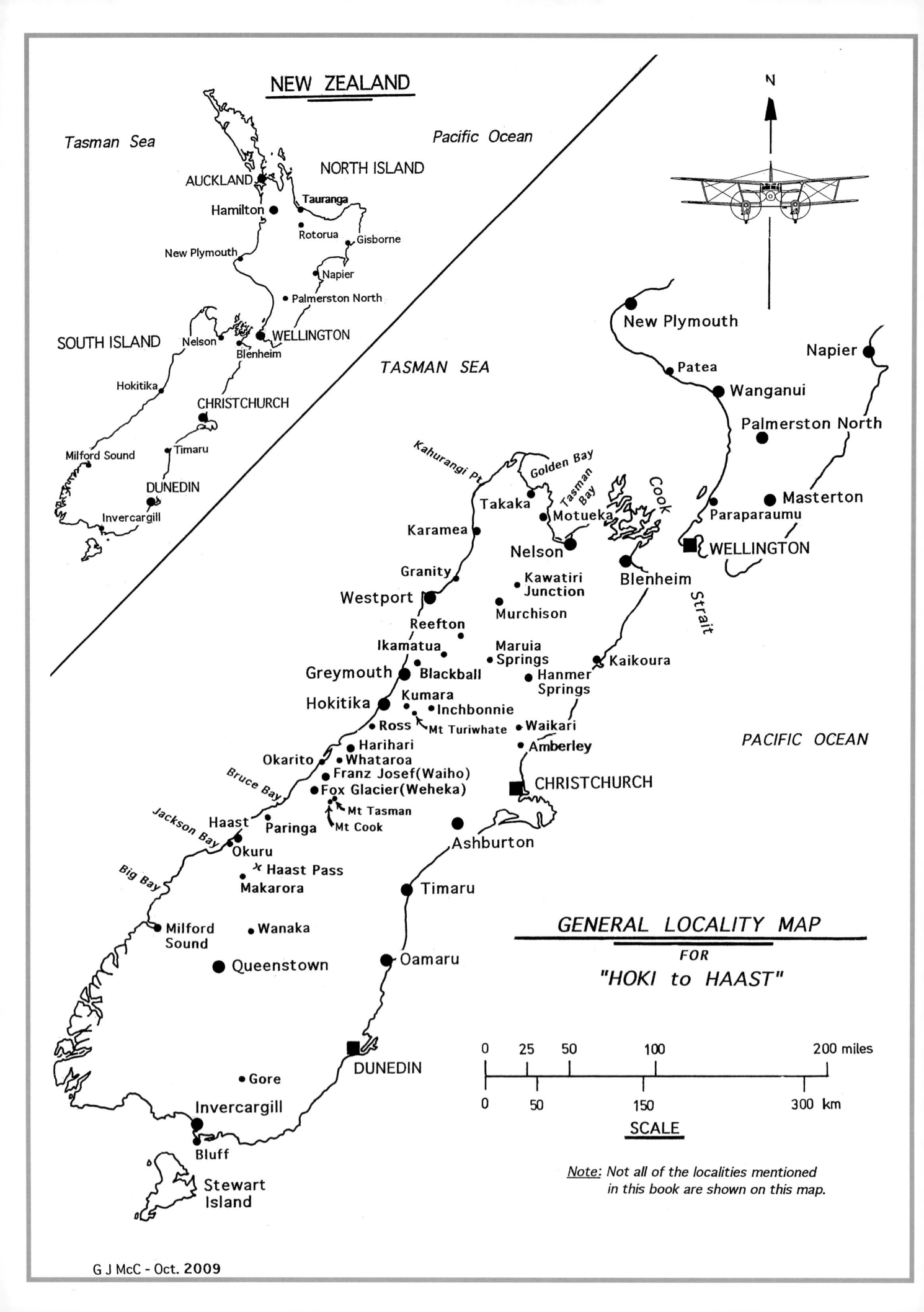

NEW ZEALAND

GENERAL LOCALITY MAP
FOR
"HOKI to HAAST"

Note: Not all of the localities mentioned in this book are shown on this map.

G J McC - Oct. 2009

Contents

DEDICATION 2

FOREWORDS BY: Sir Anand Satyanand,
Governor-General of New Zealand 3
Maureen Pugh,
Mayor of Westland District Council 3

ACKNOWLEDGEMENTS 4

LOCALITY MAP by Graeme McConnell 6

1 **PIONEER BEGINNINGS** First aeroplanes on the West Coast 8

2 **HALCYON DAYS** Air Travel (NZ) Ltd 1934 -1939 24

3 **CHANGE AND STRUGGLE** Air Travel (NZ) Ltd 1940 -1947 52

4 **NATIONALISATION** NAC 1947-1956 74

5 **VERSATILITY RETURNS** West Coast Airways 1956 -1967 90

6 **GONE, BUT NOT FORGOTTEN** Remembering the air service 115

Appendices

1 **South Westland air service staff** *by Richard Waugh* 129

2 **Airlines operating on the West Coast** *by Bruce Gavin* 131

BIBLIOGRAPHY *by Richard Waugh* 144

INDEX *by Peter Layne* 150

The Blazing Arrow H 5241 (G-NZAO) being loaded onto a pontoon at Okarito ready to be taken across the lagoon to a better take-off site. Note the Arrow Aviation Company name on the port side of the fusealage.
(Havelock Williams via Diana Rhodes)

LEFT: *A starboard view from the* Blazing Arrow *on the first flight to South Westland on 22 January 1924. Photographer Havelock Williams wrote on the back of this print, 'Over Moltke Spur – bad weather'.*
(Havelock Williams via Diana Rhodes)

1
Pioneer Beginnings
First aeroplanes on the West Coast

"MOUNTAINS, GLACIERS, LAKES, RIVERS AND FORESTS." This was signwritten on the nose of Bert Mercer's Dragonfly aircraft in the 1930s. It is still an accurate description of the scenic wonderland of South Westland on the West Coast of the South Island. One of the world's most remote locations, it has been designated a World Heritage Area because of its diverse, pristine and unique landscape.

The South Westland region has always been sparsely populated, hemmed in on one side by the majestic Southern Alps, and on the other by the turbulent Tasman Sea. Julius von Haast, a geologist-explorer, crossed the Haast Pass from Otago in 1863 and was likely the first Pakeha to make the arduous trek. Since the beginning of organised settlement in the 1870s the farming families of the Haast region, or "far-downers" as more northern residents sometimes called them, were among the most isolated New Zealanders with Hokitika 180 miles (290km) away and Wanaka 90 miles (145km) away, and no road connection until 1960. Supplies were brought in by coastal shipping and when there was a medical emergency, men and horses were needed to make the arduous two or three day trip to the nearest doctor and hospital. Because of this isolation it is easy to see why South Westland features so prominently in the pioneering story of New Zealand aviation.

On the beach at Hokitika in January 1924 is Arrow Aviation Company's Avro 504K H 5241 (G-NZAO) Blazing Arrow, *the first aircraft to visit the area. Situated opposite Batchelor's Paddock, North Revell Street, and surrounded by many interested people of all ages the aircraft is being readied for another 'joy-ride'. Mechanic Bill Harrington is up on the engine cowl while pilot Maurice Buckley already has a fare-paying passenger aboard. The Abattoir building can be seen in the background. (Havelock Williams via Whites Aviation via Jim Jamieson)*

Doctor E. Teichelmann reports on the first flight to South Westland and the Franz Josef Glacier as a passenger in the *Blazing Arrow* H 5241 on 22 January 1924:

"All the time from the coast to the Okarito Lagoon, the Franz Josef Glacier became more and more a prominent feature, and from an elevation of 6200ft the steep descent of the great river of ice became noticeable. It was a grand sight, and one can only imagine how much grander it would have appeared had the atmosphere been clearer. For a time we passed through light flying clouds, and, as we were now directly above Graham's Hotel, I attempted to drop a little parachute intended for Mr Graham. It first got caught on the tail, but as we turned it dropped off, and its fate is still unknown. At an elevation of 6200ft we crossed the lower spurs of Mount Moltke and the snout of the glacier making back directly to Okarito.

"There seems something mean about inspecting country from the air. It is like taking the roof off a house and watching the performances from above. I should say that to the experienced eye it would yield up most of its secrets. I felt that I could almost tell the nature of the soil of the different parts of the country passed over. Heavy timber, light timber, flax swamp, pakihi and lagoons could all be quite easily picked out. Nothing was more distinct than the desolation produced in the sawmill areas that have been cut and subsequently fired – such as between Hokitika and Ross and around Lake Mahinapua. On the other hand, the patches of clean grassed country about the Totara Stream, near Ross, and around Ferguson's homestead, were a delight to the eye. The aeroplane, coupled with photography, should save the Survey Department much expenditure."

(*Lyttelton Times* 24 January 1924)

Guy Menzies' Avro Sports Avian G-ABCF Southern Cross Junior *in the La Fountaine Swamp, near Harihari, soon after its trans-Tasman flight on 7 January1931. This aircraft had previously been flown by Charles Kingsford-Smith from England to Australia. In spite of the determination and fortitude of Menzies in making the historic solo flight some suggested the registration really stood for "Australian Bastards Can't Fly!"* (via Jim Jamieson)

Ironically the first aircraft on the West Coast did not fly south but rather more westerly, to Westport. On 14 December 1921 pilot Maurice Buckley and mechanic Bill Harrington flew Canterbury (N.Z.) Aviation Company's Avro 504K (H1970) from Tahunanui, Nelson, for a landing at Westport. After they circled the town and attracted much attention, they flew to the nearby prearranged landing site, the abattoir paddock known as Bullock Island. The large crowd gathered was shocked to hear the Avro's 110 hp Le Rhone engine cut out on final approach and the aircraft crash-land just short of the landing area. Fortunately pilot and passenger escaped with only lacerations and bruises, but just ten minutes after they left the scene for medical attention, a careless spectator dropped a match and the smashed aircraft was burnt out.

The impetus for the second aviation foray to the West Coast was the British and Inter-Colonial Exhibition held at Hokitika from December 1923 to February 1924. This time Buckley and Harrington were better prepared with their own Arrow Aviation Company and the loan of another Avro 504K, G-NZAO (H5241), named appropriately for a trailblazer, *Blazing Arrow*. Railed to Hokitika, they first flew the Avro over the town on 30 December 1923.

Buckley and Harrington stayed on the coast for more than five months, giving aerial displays and much joy-riding at Hokitika and Greymouth and as far north as Karamea. Among the *Blazing Arrow's* significant achievements was the first flight to South Westland and over the Franz Josef Glacier on 22 January 1924, the first aerial photographs, and on 4 June the first aircraft to fly over the Southern Alps when it returned to Christchurch. Buckley was very enthusiastic about the commercial future of aviation and even talked at this time of his plans for a permanent air service on the West Coast.

Simmonds Spartan ZK-ABU of New Zealand Airways Ltd at Mussel Point, South Westland on Monday 10 August 1931. This was the first aircraft to land in South Westland. A large group attended including from left; Kevin Nolan, Bill Nolan, Dini Nolan, John Cron, Robbie Nolan, Eddie Nolan, Captain T.W 'Tiny' White, Johanna Nolan, Maria Nolan, Mary Nolan, Nora Cron, Reg Cron, Ann Nolan and Myrtle Cron. The passenger on this historic flight was Horatio Mackay, Managing Director of New Zealand Airways Ltd.
(via Roger Eggeling)

On the shingle of the Hokitika riverbed, Hamilton Airways Ltd Gipsy Moth ZK-AAS is inspected by locals in 1930, with the Kortegast Brewery buildings in the background. Flown by Malcolm 'Mad Mac' McGregor (standing at rear) the Gipsy Moth was on a pioneering cross-country flight. (via Jim Jamieson)

ZK-ABU with a large admiring crowd after the first landing at Hokitika's Southside Airfield, on 20 January 1932. Pilot 'Mad Mac' McGregor had brought the first airmail from Wellington to the new airfield which had only just been opened, thanks to the work of the Renton family (their home in the background) who made their property available plus some adjoining Government land. (via Jim Jamieson)

Gipsy Moths ZK-AAI, ZK-AAH, ZK-AAW, ZK-ABQ of the Canterbury Aero Club parked alongside the clubrooms at Wigram, Christchurch, about 1933. Bert Mercer served as Chief Flying Instructor from 1929 until he started Air Travel (NZ) Ltd in late 1934. It was from this base at Wigram that the Gipsy Moths set off on their pioneering trans-alpine flights to the West Coast.
(Mercer Collection)

Aviation throughout New Zealand fell into the doldrums in the mid 1920s and it was another five years before the West Coast saw its next aerial visitor. Two DH60 Gipsy Moths of the New Zealand Permanent Air Force were tasked in June 1929 with aerial survey work and message carrying between Westport and Karamea following the Murchison Earthquake. Maurice Buckley was again one of the pilots, along with H.B. 'Sam' Burrell.

Another early aircraft to come to the West Coast, on 7 January 1931, was Avro Sports Avian G-ABCF *Southern Cross Junior* flown by 21 year-old pilot Guy Menzies, all the way from Sydney, Australia. The ambitious pilot was the first to fly solo across the Tasman Sea but mistook the La Fontaine swamp near Harihari for a suitable landing place. The Avro turned over in the rough landing, leaving Menzies hanging upside down and some of his personal belongings tumbling into the underlying swamp. While Menzies made no commercial contribution to aviation on the West Coast he did add glamour and excitement, and attracted helpful publicity including much international interest.

This map of Hokitika Aerodrome was published in Wings *of November 1932. It was one of an early aerodrome map series sponsored by the Shell Oil Company of New Zealand Ltd.*

The first West Coast pilot, Jack Renton, with Gipsy Moth ZK-AAI at Wigram, about 1933. Renton was a young and enthusiastic advocate of the benefits of aviation for the West Coast. (Hugh Preston Collection via Dorothy Dowell)

– 12 –

A rare pre-war colour photograph of Simmonds Spartan ZK-ABU likely taken at Greymouth about 1936. Imported into New Zealand in 1931 it flew a one day mail flight from Invercargill to Auckland on 12 November that year. The aircraft pioneered many a West Coast route and strip before Bert Mercer. It is shown here back in a two seater configuration and operated by the West Coast United Aero Club. It was cancelled from the register in March 1939.
(D.D. Kelly Collection via Mike Kelly)

Arthur Nancekivell (left) and Jack Renton (right) made the first landing at Mussel Point in ZK-ABU on 28 September 1932. They carried the first airmail to Okuru and the experimental airmail flight demonstrated the benefits a regular air service would bring.
(via Pat Nancekivell)

Canterbury Aero Club's Gipsy Moths ZK-AAW and ZK-AAH, taken from ZK-AAI, while on a charter to Hokitika and South Westland in 1933. (via Paul Beauchamp Legg)

Simmonds Spartan ZK-ABU at the time of an early landing at Waiho (Franz Josef) on 28 September 1932. The Spartan, flown by Arthur Nancekivell and Jack Renton, also brought the first experimental airmail from Hokitika. Nancekivell is standing to the right of the cockpit wearing his flying suit. The glacier is visible in the distance. (A.C. Graham Collection via Dorothy Fletcher)

Taken from another Canterbury Aero Club Gipsy Moth, ZK-AAI is on a southern excursion flight passing Mount Aspiring. The club's Gipsy Moths first flew across the Southern Alps in early 1933. (Mercer Collection)

During the early 1930s aviation gained an increasing public profile on the West Coast, helped by Jack Renton of Hokitika, having gained his pilot's licence. The work done by him and many others helped prepare for the establishment of local aero clubs and landing grounds, especially at Southside, Hokitika. Occasional visiting aircraft also created continuing public excitement and encouragement to local aviation enthusiasts.

On 10 August 1931 Trevor 'Tiny' White and Horatio Mackay landed Simmonds Spartan ZK-ABU on the newly prepared Mussel Point airstrip near the mouth of the Okuru River on land owned by the Eggeling Brothers. Des Nolan later recalled, "With bulldozers and front-end loaders unheard of in those days, most of the local farmers converged on the site with their horses and drays. Picks, shovels and grubbers were the tools used. Being near the sea, it was sandy type soil and easy to work with – about three such days saw the strip in readiness… all of a sudden there was a roar which could only mean one thing. The aircraft did a pass over the strip, then banked eastwards, passing right over us. We viewed the very first landing of a plane in South Westland."

The new Southside Aerodrome at Hokitika, established by the Renton family and using their land and some adjacent Government land, was first used by Malcolm "Mac" McGregor when he landed Simmonds Spartan ZK-ABU on 20 January 1932. This was just three weeks after the cross fences had been removed. A direct result of this visit was the formation of the Hokitika Aero Club. The aerodrome was licensed for light aircraft and was gradually improved by the assistance of the unemployed. It was built using horses, carts, picks and shovels.

Captain Bert Mercer and his trusty camera alongside Gipsy Moth ZK-ABQ, after landing on the Haast Riverbed in 1933 during one of his early flights south.
(via Roger Eggeling)

BELOW: *Canterbury Aero Club's Gipsy Moths at Hokitika's Southside Aerodrome in 1933. From left, ZK-AAH being refuelled by Jack Renton, ZK-AAW and the ill-fated ZK-AAI.* (The Auckland Weekly News)

RIGHT: *At Mussel Point in 1933 Gipsy Moth ZK-ABQ with from left: Norman Dickie, Dick and Dorothy Eggeling, Captain Mercer and unidentified.* (via Roger Eggeling)

Peter Graham, Doll McBride and Captain Mercer before leaving on an early charter flight from Franz Josef about 1933. Doll was flying to Christchurch for medical advice and had been warned she could take very little luggage in the Gipsy Moth. It was later discovered she was wearing three sets of underclothes!
(A.C. Graham Collection via Dorothy Fletcher)

With the Spartan ZK-ABU being purchased in May 1932 for West Coast flight training and charter work by local hotelier Arthur Nancekivell, Hokitika had its first locally owned aircraft. It was reported in December 1932 that five pupils had already been trained and had received their "A" Licences. These were: Rev Father McKay, Arthur Nancekivell, Horace Parry, Hugh Preston and Jack Stuart. There were three others who came down from Greymouth at weekends; Ivan Finny, Dick Shallcrass and Frank Molloy.

The early 1930s were a time of advance for aviation in the Hokitika district as Nancekivell was a driving force and the Spartan ZK-ABU became well known on the West Coast for flight training and a range of versatile charter flights. This flying was not without incident, such as the 'prang' on 23 August 1932 when ZK-ABU collided with telegraph wires and crashed on take-off from Hokitika. Repairs were soon complete and the resilient biplane took to the air again.

CONTINUED ON PAGE 20

The name of Mercer's original airline was to be Tourist Air Travel and Transport Service Ltd. His initial promotional letter and brochure were distributed from 10 October 1933.

Phone 30-816

5 Korari Street,
Riccarton,
10th October, 1933.

Dear Sir or Madam,

It is my intention in the near future to promote an Air Transport Company to develop Aerial Tourist Traffic, and the carriage of mails and goods in the South Island, especially on the West Coast.

With this object in view and with the intention of interesting those who wish to bring the scenic beauties of this Island before the travelling public, thus stimulating business generally and bringing the South Island more prominently before Tourists, I am giving a Lecture on Tuesday, October 17th, at 8 p.m. in the Canterbury Automobile Association Rooms, 151 Worcester St., in order to demonstrate the advisability of early action in this direction and I cordially invite you to attend.

I feel sure you will be interested as with the assistance of lantern slides I will demonstrate how some of the most beautiful scenery in the world can be seen from an angle that the cleverest mountaineer cannot hope to attain.

I will also endeavour to point out to you :-

1. The enormous factor such a Company would be in advertising the South Island, thereby encouraging Tourist Traffic to the advantage of business generally.

2. The great saving for those who have only limited time in which to spend on holiday making.

3. The practicability of my scheme from a financial and profit making point of view.

In the meantime, I would like an opportunity of discussing the matter with you, and would appreciate a ring from you at my house (No. 30-816) should you care for an opportunity of going into this interesting proposition.

Yours faithfully,

J.C. Mercer

TOURIST AIR TRAVEL AND TRANSPORT SERVICE LTD.

All photographs reproduced on the other side of this leaflet were taken from the air.

Wonderful panoramic views of mountain grandeur, beautiful bush scenery and the lakes and fiord land of the South Island were obtained over the week-end by Mr. J. C. Mercer and Mr.———— of Christchurch, in a round aerial trip of seven hundred miles, which embraced Hokitika, the Franz Josef Glacier, Okuru, Mt. Aspiring, Lake Wanaka, Hawea and Wakitipu.

Apart from anything else, the excursion which was enjoyed by both pilot and passenger, demonstrated the possibilities of short tourist flights for those who cannot afford leisurely trips to remote parts by land.

Christchurch "Times"—14/3/33.

At the Landing Ground, Franz Josef Glacier; Waiho Gorge.

— 16 —

JACK BERTRAM RENTON – *Pioneer Flyer*

THE FIRST WEST COASTER to obtain a New Zealand pilot's licence, Jack Renton became interested in the potential of aviation, and began flying lessons with the Canterbury Aero Club in late 1929, being taught by flying instructor Bert Mercer. With his "A" licence granted in April 1931 he became a territorial pilot officer with No.4 Squadron of the New Zealand Air Force.

Born on 10 November 1909, Jack was the second son to Paul and Mary Renton, a prominent Hokitika couple, whose family had been involved in the local hardware business since 1874. Always mechanically minded he worked with his father in the sales, installation and servicing of milking equipment, machinery, pumps and engines.

With youthful energy, mechanical aptitude and financial support, Renton was the influential aviator on the West Coast in the early 1930s. His friendship with Mercer encouraged the Canterbury Aero Club to arrange regular trips across the Southern Alps and down to the glaciers.

As well as continuing links to the Canterbury Aero Club, Renton worked with his father to establish the Westland Aero Club (later the Hokitika Aero Club) and became its first secretary. He also visited many small settlements in South Westland, encouraging locals to make suitable landing grounds for the aircraft that would soon come to the area.

With another early West Coast pilot, Arthur Nancekivell, he flew extensively around the South Westland region. On 12 June 1932 Renton and Robert Matheson, after a 50 minute flight from Hokitika, made the first landing at Waiho (Franz Josef Glacier) in Spartan ZK-ABU and were greeted by a welcoming crowd. On 28 September 1932 Renton and Nancekivell shared the flying and flew an experimental air mail of 1483 letters and packets in the Spartan from Hokitika to Waiho and down to Okuru. Earlier in May 1932 Renton had gone down to Okuru by local steamer and helped choose the landing site at Mussel Point. All these flights attracted much public attention.

Renton was planning to work with Nancekivell in further developing a West Coast airline initiative. On Labour Day 1933 he joined Bert Mercer and Jack Busch in the first three aircraft round trip flight from Hokitika via Cromwell, Oamaru and Timaru. At this time Renton had about 100 flying hours and was considered one of the most promising young airmen in the South Island.

A few weeks later, he set out in the Canterbury Aero Club's Gipsy Moth ZK-AAI, on an extensive flight with passenger J.D. 'Jimmy' Lynch, a former Greymouth mayor and well known West Coast businessman. They left Christchurch on Saturday 18 November 1933 and passed over Picton and Blenheim, and flew to Nelson and stayed the night. On Sunday they flew from Nelson to Hokitika for another overnight stay. At 2pm on Monday 20 November they took off from the Southside Aerodrome to return to Christchurch. At the aerodrome saying goodbye was his older brother Paul, his mother and Dr Ebenezer Teichelmann. Paul Renton later wrote, "When Jack passed over Hokitika at 2.05pm that day, the clouds were low and there was a slight N.W. wind on the ground. There did not seem to be much wind at all up above as the clouds we saw were practically stationary. There was a bright opening to the N.E. which Jack made for and I saw him go through it at about 3000 feet."

The Gipsy Moth did not arrive at Wigram Aerodrome as expected after 3pm. Anxiety mounted by late afternoon, heightened by a report from the Turiwhate area, nine

Jack Renton, the first West Coaster to learn to fly, with young Ted Andrews, signing up for an aero club flight at Hokitika's Southside Aerodrome in 1932. (Renton Family Collection)

miles from Dillmanstown (near Kumara), that the noise of a plane had been heard at 2.30pm, followed by the sound of a crash.

Search parties from Turiwhate, Hokitika and Kumara went out that afternoon, but the rain and fog hampered their best efforts to locate the missing aircraft. From what locals heard it was suspected the aircraft had struck Mount Turiwhate (4488 ft). A more intensive search began the following day, Tuesday, with more than fifty well-equipped and experienced bushmen and mountaineers taking part. Five teams were arranged led by locals M. Treacy, T. Teen, W. Neame, A. Straight, and also C. Morrison from the Lands and Survey Department, Hokitika. Dr Fraser from Greymouth Hospital and Constable Drummond from Hokitika accompanied the searchers. Rain and fog made for very poor conditions. Many locals helped with support services including food and drink.

Bert Mercer left Wigram on Tuesday morning to take part in the search. He flew to the West Coast by way of Nelson and Collingwood and arrived at Hokitika at 11.30am. He then flew low over the Grey River and then made for Taramakau but found conditions so bad he was forced to return to Hokitika. Instead he soon joined the ground search. In the early afternoon searchers found the wrecked Gipsy Moth about 200 ft from the summit of Mount Turiwhate. W. Neame and G. George were in the party that first sighted the crumpled silver wings. The engine was rammed back by the force of the impact and both occupants had been killed instantly. In spite of wet and muddy conditions, search parties were able to bring the bodies down the mountain. Mercer and others carefully inspected the wreckage, removing key parts before setting it on fire.

The Director of Air Services, Mr T.M. Wilkes, was reported as saying no good would be served by holding an inquiry as both the pilot and passenger had been killed. Mercer later commented that it was hard to state the cause of the accident but he thought Renton had been above the clouds but had not been sufficiently high above them. He said, "I think that the pilot was above the clouds all right, but owing to the atmospheric conditions prevailing that day he was really trapped."

This early flying tragedy made a deep impression on many West Coasters. The loss of two prominent citizens alerted people to the dangers of flying in fickle West Coast weather. The Mayor of Hokitika, Mr G. A. Perry, requested all shops to be closed for the funerals. A Presbyterian service was held at Southside in the Renton home and a Roman Catholic Requiem Mass held at St Marys for Mr Lynch. The combined cortege to the Hokitika Cemetery was more than half a mile long and was attended by one of the largest crowds ever seen in the town. At the conclusion of the grave-side services a number of Maori women from Arahura Pa chanted a wail over the graves and upon each a posy of wild flowers from Mount Turiwhate was laid.

The Mount Turiwhate tragedy had an ongoing influence. Renton's older brother, Paul, took over his late brother's role as secretary of the aero club and the following year he became a foundation director and shareholder of Mercer's Air Travel (NZ) Ltd airline. Support for this new pioneering airline was a fitting tribute to Jack Renton, the young pioneering airman of the West Coast.

Searchers surround the wreckage of Canterbury Aero Club's Gipsy Moth ZK-AAI near the summit of Mount Turiwhate (4488ft). Jack Renton and Jimmy Lynch were both killed in the crash on 20 November 1933. Bert Mercer supervised removal of salvageable parts before setting fire to the wreckage. (The Auckland Weekly News)

The Memorial Cairn near the summit of Mt Turiwhate in memory of J.B. Renton and J.D. Lynch. The Mountaineering Club discovered the remains of the wreckage in 1939 and a few months later made a second trip with sand, cement and stones and built the cairn. Charlie Barnhill made the plaque from a piece of crumpled wing and in 1940 Charlie and Jean Barnhill, with Paul Renton and Dick Thomas, climbed and placed the plaque on site. This is one of the earliest aviation memorials in New Zealand. (Charlie Barnhill via Renton Collection)

A view of Cron's homestead at Haast, about 1934. The landing strip is further to the right, out of the photograph. The house became, over the years, a well-known landmark for pilots landing at the Haast Aerodrome. Note the Fox Moth flying in the distance. (Whites Aviation via Canterbury Aero Club)

At the Waltham Railway yards, Christchurch in March 1934 Bert Mercer (left) and Bill Brazier unpack the Canterbury Aero Club's new DH83 Fox Moth ZK-ADH after its long sea voyage from England. The Fox Moth was to be influential in shaping Mercer's plans for a regular West Coast service. (Arthur Brazier Collection)

Make Use of that Small Field

REDWING

Safety Aeroplanes Side-by-Side—Two-Seater.

Landing Speed 30 m.p.h.   Cruising Speed 30 m.p.h.
Landing Run 60 yds.   Max. Speed 90 m.p.h.
Take-off Run 60 yards   Petrol Con. 20 m.p.g.

H. T. PARRY
N.Z. Rep., HOKITIKA.

This Robinson Redwing ZK-ADD arrived at Hokitika in September 1933 for private owner Horace Parry. Powered by a five cylinder Genet radial it was the second aircraft owned on the West Coast and was distinctive in having side-by-side seating for two people. The Redwing flew all over the West Coast and is seen in a rare pre-war colour photograph at Karoro Aerodrome, Greymouth, about 1937.
(D.D. Kelly Collection via Mike Kelly)

On 31 March 1934 Mercer flew the new Fox Moth ZK-ADH to Hokitika and Waiho for first time. Here it is at Waiho with tent accommodation for the adventurous travellers. (A.C. Graham Collection via Dorothy Fletcher)

Perhaps more than any other region in New Zealand, there was significant aviation consciousness on the West Coast with small aero clubs established at Greymouth, Westport, Reefton, Ikamatua, Karamea, South Westland (Ross) and Whataroa. Federation of these aero clubs was achieved in 1933. Landing strips began to be formed, especially in South Westland – all were practical demonstrations of a commitment to end isolation. In September 1933 Horace Parry of Hokitika bought a small Redwing aircraft ZK-ADD, the second privately owned aircraft on the West Coast. It had a radial Armstrong-Siddeley Genet IIA engine, was economical to fly and was seen all over the coast on flight training, and sight-seeing flights.

ARTHUR NANCEKIVELL – *Pioneer Charter Pilot*

ARTHUR HAROLD NANCEKIVELL, a Hokitika publican, became interested in aeronautical matters after local business experience with taxis and trucks. He later wrote: "In late 1931 I could see great possibilities for the future of aviation on the West Coast of the South Island, especially between Hokitika and South Westland, where shipping was greatly restricted, and no overland transport was available. I was very keen to take up flying as a career and I approached Jack Renton of Hokitika with the idea of forming an Aero Club in the district. We decided to call a meeting of the residents of the surrounding districts, and this meeting was held at my hotel, the Railway. Quite a number of lads attended who were anxious to take up flying."

The Canterbury Aero Club was approached to supply an aircraft and instructor, but they eventually declined due to the risks involved of continual flying over the Southern Alps. Nancekivell therefore purchased Simmonds Spartan ZK-ABU *Lovebird* on 11 May 1932, which became the first aircraft to be based on the West Coast. His commitment was considerable as he also funded the appointment of an instructor, Bob Matheson, and John Flynn as ground engineer.

Nancekivell later remembered, "I decided that I would learn to fly as quickly as possible. Before long I received my "A" licence, my "A endorsed", and finally my "B" licence [13 May 1933] for commercial flying – the latter being obtained in record time. I was entitled to fly for hire and reward, and I immediately took up the duties of pilot and commenced taxi trips throughout the surrounding districts. It was surprising to me how quickly the people of the West Coast became air-minded, owing, I think, to the fact they were continually seeing the 'plane overhead and those were the days when people looked up when an aeroplane was overhead."

On 20 September 1932 Nancekivell made the first flight from Franz Josef Glacier to Christchurch and continued to do much local joy-riding and many charter flights. During this time he made plans for further expansion and years later reminisced, "I began to prepare for increased business. I approached a friend, Mr W. Stopforth, who I knew would give thought to any future possibilities, and he agreed that there was a great future for aviation on the West Coast. We immediately decided to form a limited company, which was called West Coast Airways."

In 1933 ZK-ABU was modified by New Zealand Airways at Timaru with a new Hermes II engine and accommodation for two passengers with an enclosed canopy. It was purchased by West Coast Airways Ltd which had been registered on 23 August 1933 with share capital of £700. Its object was "to establish air services and to foster aviation". Shareholders were listed as: J. Johnston, G.W. Kelly, J.A. Murdoch, J.J. McIntosh, J.A. McCallum, A.H. Nancekivell, H.T. Parry, H.B. Preston, S.J. Preston, W.H.A Stopforth, T. Seddon, J.L. Turner and Dr E. Teichelmann.

Nancekivell was appointed pilot for West Coast Airways and on 30 August 1933 undertook the first aerial ambulance flight on the West Coast when he flew Sir Houghton Cameron from Okuru to Hokitika on a hospital board emergency charter. A stretcher was able to be fitted in the front modified cockpit after the seats were removed. Another air ambulance flight was made on 6 December with patient J. Cowan.

On 10 February 1934 ZK-ABU crashed at Te Kinga, necessitating repairs at New Zealand Airways Timaru hangar. But the Spartan was soon back in the air and Nancekivell made the first landing at Bruce Bay on 12 March with passenger S.K. De Castro. Another first was on 25 July when Nancekivell landed at Upper Okuru (Nolans) for the first time. Des Nolan remembered, "Whether it was an emergency or otherwise, the arrival of Nancekivell's Spartan *Lovebird* never failed to create a buzz of excitement in the district. As school kids, we had several half holidays over to the landing strip to greet him, not forgetting the

Pioneer pilot Arthur Nancekivell in the Simmonds Spartan, ZK-ABU, which he flew all over the West Coast in the early 1930s. (via Pat Nancekivell)

– 21 –

time we bolted class at the sound of his motor, to be scolded back in by an irate teacher. To us aeroplanes were just something out of this world and the men that flew them were folk heroes."

Aircraft incidents abounded in those pioneering days. Nancekivell had a forced landing in ZK-ABU on 14 April 1934 when over Marshland, Christchurch, following a crossing from Hokitika via Lewis Pass. The propeller became detached but fortunately Nancekivell and passenger A. J. McDowell were able to land safely on a nearby paddock. The Spartan was taken by truck to Wigram for repairs. Another air ambulance flight was made on 5 August from Hokitika to Haast and return.

The end of West Coast Airways came on 2 November 1934 while ZK-ABU was on a Hokitika to Christchurch flight, flown by Nancekivell with passenger A.B. Beban. It suffered engine failure due to a throttle control working loose and force-landed on the east bank of the Bealey River. The aircraft overturned and although badly damaged, was later repaired and continued to fly up until 1939. There were attempts to make arrangements with New Zealand Airways to carry on air-taxi services and continue the charter airline, but this did not eventuate. The company also needed to update to a newer and more practical aircraft so it was decided to cease operations.

Nancekivell was a true pioneer West Coast pilot and aviation promoter. In the mid 1930s he moved to Australia but returned to New Zealand on several occasions, including for the Haast Highway opening in 1965. Nancekivell died in Australia at the age of 91 years in 1988.

Early aero club pilot Hugh Preston with West Coast Airways Simmonds Spartan ZK-ABU at Hokitika, in 1934. The front cockpit has been enlarged to take two passengers and fitted with a canopy. (Hugh Preston Collection via Dorothy Dowell)

It was into this busy and exciting environment that J.C. 'Bert' Mercer, from the Canterbury Aero Club, entered the West Coast aviation scene. He was already recognised as a man of considerable aeronautical experience and maturity, aged in his mid 40s. Mercer was encouraged to fly across the Southern Alps and visit the West Coast on various charter flights. His first flight over to Hokitika was on 4 January 1933 in Moth ZK-ABQ, in a flight time of one hour and 35 minutes and then a flight to Waiho of one hour and 10 minutes. On 11 March 1933, he flew with two other aero club aircraft, piloted by Jack Renton and Jack Busch, on a Wigram-Hokitika-Franz Josef -Mt Cook-Franz Josef charter, and the pilots and passengers stayed the night at the Graham's Glacier Hotel at Franz Josef.

Allan Cron, from Haast, was learning to fly at the Canterbury Aero Club and invited Bert Mercer to accompany him home to South Westland on 20 August 1933 in Moth ZK-AAI. They landed at Haast and this was the beginning of Mercer's remarkable links to this remote region. At the same time it was reported in the media in August and September 1933 that, "Tourist Aerial Travel and Transport Service Ltd may be the name of a new company which is being formed to work an aeroplane service for tourists and sportsmen on the West Coast. Canterbury, West Coast, Otago and Southland men are interested in the company, which Mr J.C. Mercer, instructor to the Canterbury Aero Club, has taken a prominent part in promoting." It was further reported that de Havilland Fox Moth aircraft were intended to be used and that Mr Mercer had made exhaustive aerial surveys of the landing grounds to be possibly used by the new company. On 4 September Mercer reported in something of a prophetic manner, "We have wonderfully fine country in the South Island, that should be world-renowned, but it is necessary to have air transport to see it."

On 14 September 1933 Mercer flew Mr Lincoln Ellsworth, the American Antarctic explorer from Wigram Aerodrome to Waiho and over the Franz Josef Glacier. Ellsworth was preparing for an Antarctic expedition later in the year and his visit created much interest and publicity which also helped Mercer's endeavours. On 10 October Mercer flew ZK-AAH from Wigram to Okuru with Mrs Eggeling, the first resident to travel by air from and back to Okuru. At this time he sent out circular letters to interested people from his residence in Korari Street, Riccarton. It said in part, "It is my intention in the near future to promote an Air Transport Company to develop Aerial Tourist Traffic, and the carriage of mails and goods in the South Island, especially on the West Coast." As part of this promotion he gave a well attended lecture and lantern slide presentation on 17 October at the Canterbury Automobile Association Rooms in Worcester Street.

Over the Christmas season of 1933 and early summer of 1934 Mercer flew many charter flights to the West Coast and brought his family to stay at Waiho for several weeks. While based there he took more than ninety tourists on sight-seeing flights over the glaciers and Mount Cook in ZK-ABQ. One media story quoted Mercer as saying, "After drinking in the rare vistas, we landed at Graham's Hotel. That is the right way to do it and much better than drinking in Graham's Hotel and landing in the vistas!"

From late March 1934 Mercer flew the Canterbury Aero Club's new Fox Moth ZK-ADH and made the first Fox Moth flight to Hokitika and Franz Josef on 31 March. On the following day he took eleven passengers for local scenic flights. The enclosed passenger cabin brought many advantages, not least of which was room for three or even four paying passengers. By this time Mercer had already developed an enduring affinity with many of the people of South Westland.

WHAT TO SEE TODAY

Guy Menzies Historic Trans-Tasman Sea Flight Memorials

At Harihari in South Westland are several excellent commemorations to the pioneering trans-Tasman flight of young Guy Menzies on 7 January 1931. On the main highway in the middle of the town, is a memorial park and display building which contains a full size replica of Avro Sports Avian G-ABCF Southern Cross Junior. This was dedicated during the 75th anniversary celebrations in January 2006, along with a bronze plaque, information display panels and a large pylon marker at the actual landing site, about 12km toward the coast from the town. See page 126.

Mount Turiwhate Memorial Cairn

On the northern face, near the summit of the mountain are the remains of the original 1939/1940 memorial cairn for the November 1933 Gipsy Moth accident in which pioneering pilot Jack Renton and passenger J.D. 'Jimmy' Lynch died. These were the first aviation fatalities on the West Coast. A wheel from the Gipsy Moth is also on display at the Hokitika Aero Club. The cairn is one of the earliest aviation memorials in New Zealand. Access to this area of difficult terrain is via Grahams Creek to the marked but un-maintained mountain track and crosses private property and Department of Conservation land.

In February 1935, soon after the pioneering air service had begun, Fox Moth ZK-ADH is ready for a mail and freight flight to South Westland. As well as mail bags for specific locations, there is a hand operated waterpump, parcels and a bundle of axe handles ready for loading at Hokitika.
(via Canterbury Aero Club)

2

Halcyon Days
Air Travel (NZ) Ltd 1934 -1939

"NEW AIR SERVICE" WAS THE HEADLINE IN LATE 1934 as Captain J.C. 'Bert' Mercer's plans for a new West Coast airline came to fruition. For two years he had been working on a myriad of tasks and gathering financial support to operate a licensed airline under the new transport legislation. The name of "Air Travel (NZ) Ltd" had only just been confirmed in October – a much shorter name than "Tourist Air Travel and Transport Service Ltd," used in all the fundraising brochures and previous publicity material.

Incorporated on 14 May 1934 the new airline company had a capital of £3000 with original subscribers being; James Cuthbert Mercer, Aviator, Christchurch; Paul Edmond Louis Renton, Merchant, Hokitika; Henry Worrall, Company

Is this New Zealand's most iconic aviation photograph? On the beach at Bruce Bay in September 1935, Captain Bert Mercer has just climbed down from the cockpit of Fox Moth ZK-ADI after a flight from Hokitika and is greeted by locals. From left: Jack Condon with young daughter Fay riding Fairy *the horse, Alex McEwan with suitcases, Pat Mahuika, Jimmy McLaren, Cyril McEwan, Letti McEwan and her youngest child Margaret, Captain Bert Mercer, unidentified small girl and Iris Wilson. Off shore, the Government steamer S.S* Hinemoa *has arrived from Bluff with supplies, including stud Hereford bulls for the Condons. Jack Condon has his dogs ready to muster the bulls away from the aircraft when they swim ashore from the steamer.* (Whites Aviation)

ZK-ADI flying along the coast to Haast with Bert Mercer at the controls. This was the last production Fox Moth from the British de Havilland factory and flew the inaugural flights on 18 December 1934. (via Jim Hewett Collection)

Manager, Christchurch; Rose Graham, Hotel Keeper, Franz Josef; Peter Graham, Alpine Guide, Franz Josef; Alexander Carter Graham, Alpine Guide, Franz Josef; and James Richard Delahunty, Jeweller, Christchurch. Directors were named as: Mercer (Managing Director), Worrall (Chairman of Directors), Renton and H.C. Newman. Other early shareholders were the Cron, Nolan and Hende families of South Westland, and many Canterbury subscribers, including *The Press* newspaper.

Mercer resigned as Chief Instructor of the Canterbury Aero Club on 30 November 1934 and kept busy successfully applying for a temporary licence for the air service and then overseeing the assembly of a new Fox Moth aircraft which had just arrived on the *Port Fairy* from England. Also confirmed was a tender for the airmail contract on the Hokitika - Bruce Bay - Haast - Okuru route. On 15 December Mercer flew Fox Moth ZK-ADI across the Southern Alps to Hokitika for the first time to a welcome by locals and flew a number of charter flights, including one to Okuru on 16 December with passenger S.J. Conradson.

Surprisingly, only modest fanfare greeted the inaugural flight on Tuesday 18 December 1934. Mercer began a regular passenger service from Inchbonnie, about 10 miles west of Otira, with passengers from the trans-alpine train, taking them to Hokitika and Franz Josef Glacier and return. On the first scheduled flight in the Fox Moth he picked up Harry Worrall and Hume Christie at Inchbonnie at 3.20pm and flew them to Hokitika and then over the Franz Josef Glacier, arriving at Waiho at 4.50pm. Afternoon tea was enjoyed at the hotel and the aircraft then retraced its way to Hokitika and Inchbonnie in time for the two passengers to catch the train back to Christchurch. A newspaper report said, "The trip was an excellent one in every way, the machine proving particularly comfortable, and one of the passengers, with hardly any previous experience, enjoyed the sensation of flying perfectly. From the point of view of scenic attraction the trip is without parallel in New Zealand."

Creating more public interest was the inauguration of air mail services on 31 December 1934. This new contract to South Westland replaced a pack horse service which had taken four days each way. The new air mail service

Bert Mercer delivering The Weekly News *to the Cron family at Haast in September 1935. From left Allan Cron, Reg Cron, Jack Cron and Nora Cron.* (Whites Aviation via MOTAT)

Fox Moth ZK-ADH at the old Weheka (Fox Glacier) Airfield with some scenic passengers in the winter of 1935. This was soon after Mercer had his crash with ZK-ADI at the same airfield and the Canterbury Aero Club aircraft was then hired for Air Travel (NZ) Ltd services.
(via Des Nolan Collection)

At the newly established Arawata campsite in early 1935, Fox Moth ZK-ADH has just flown in from Waiho with supplies for this first mountaineering trip using the support of aircraft.
(H.E.Newton via Dorothy Fletcher)

-27-

Waiho Aerodrome (Franz Josef) in 1935 showing the Air Travel hangar with Fox Moth parked outside, the nearby name of the aerodrome laid out in white painted stones and at right the Public Works Department camp. (Mercer Collection via A.C. Graham Collection)

Look what variety of things you can get into a Fox Moth! Allan Cron, pet fawn and cats with supplies for a hunting trip including rifles, food and tramping boots. (A.C. Graham Collection via Dorothy Fletcher)

Fox Moth taxiing into Waiho with a waiting group of scenic flight customers. Note the single bay hangar that later in 1935 was doubled in size. The hotel is in the background. (Mercer Collection via A.C. Graham Collection)

Fox Moth ZK-ADH at Nolan's homestead at Upper Okuru. From left: Mary Nolan, Jim O'Brien MP, Dini Nolan and Robbie Nolan. (Mercer Collection via A.C. Graham Collection)

At Upper Okuru in 1935 farmer Dini Nolan, a strong advocate and shareholder in Air Travel (NZ) Ltd, stands by the wingtip of the Fox Moth waiting for the team of Clydesdale horses to pass by while working to improve the airstrip surface. (via Paul Beauchamp Legg)

was important; the first unsubsidised air mail in New Zealand and probably the first air mail in the British Empire to carry all classes of mail. Ironically, at the same time the Duke of Gloucester was touring New Zealand and he received the first airmail to travel between England and New Zealand. On the first airmail flight Fox Moth ZK-ADI left Hokitika with 3600 letters amounting to 161 pounds of mail. At Okuru the aircraft had to wait for a quantity of mail to be stamped for the return journey. Passengers on the return flight to Hokitika were Mr and Mrs Jack Cron of Haast. The Fox Moth landed at Southside at 3.45pm to a waiting crowd who welcomed Mercer and the Crons with hearty cheers. Mr T. E. Y. Seddon, son of the famous Prime Minister, Sir Richard John Seddon, was among dignitaries present, and said if all South Westland people were like the Crons, Captain Mercer should have plenty of passengers. He commented, "I think you people here are more air-minded than in any other place of its size in this country and are taking a keen interest in aviation."

It didn't take long from the establishment of the air service for most South Westland people to begin to realise the social and communication revolution of the new air service. Just weeks later

```
Telegrams: "Airtravel,"                    Phone 134 S.,
         Hokitika.                              Hokitika.

AIR TRAVEL (N.Z.) LTD.
    J. C. MERCER, Managing Director, and Chief Pilot,
Southside Aerodrome    ::    HOKITIKA

ROYAL MAIL SERVICE—Hokitika — Bruce Bay—
    Haast—Okuru.

PASSENGER SERVICE—Inchbonnie—Hokitika—Franz
    Josef Glacier—Fox Glacier.

Rail Passengers from Christchurch can connect with 'planes at
Inchbonnie (near Otira) and arrive at Glaciers for afternoon tea
                     same day.

AIR TAXIS TO ALL PARTS OF NEW ZEALAND.
        All Fares Extremely Moderate.

          Full particulars from
N.Z. GOVERNNEMT TOURIST BUREAUX
   N.Z. RAILWAYS BOOKING OFFICES
 AIR TRAVEL (N.Z.) LTD., HOKITIKA.
```

BELOW: *Haast Aerodrome from the north in the mid 1930s at the time Air Travel (NZ) was pioneering air services.* (Whites Aviation via Des Nolan Collection)

The new landing ground at Mussel Point (Lower Okuru). A Fox Moth is parked near the farmhouse.
(via Jim Hewett Collection)

RIGHT: *At Mussel Point in 1937 C.W.F 'Bill' Hamilton (wearing black beret) arrives to supervise improvements to the airfield. Troubles had been experienced operating the mechanical scoop in the sandy conditions. Bill Robertson had been sent by Hamilton's contracting business to sort out the difficulties and Hamilton also called to inspect progress. Hamilton did other work in South Westland, including improvements to the Haast Aerodrome.*
(Bill Robertson via Peter Robertson)

on 30 January 1935 a *Press* reporter wrote, "A month ago, a young Christchurch man, a prospector, left Hokitika to travel by motor, by pack-horse and on foot to Okuru in South Westland. It took him three weeks to get there. He suffered delays and privations unbelievable. On Monday he left Okuru at 1.30pm and was in Hokitika at 4pm, after making three stops on the way. On the second occasion he travelled the 170 miles by aeroplane. And every week scores of men and women are following his example and using the same aeroplane to annihilate distance and break down in that short journey the terrible isolation which has been the drawback to life in the south for 60 years."

JAMES CUTHBERT MERCER – *Legendary Pilot*

BORN AT CAVERSHAM on 16 September 1886, Mercer was educated for a time in Australia and in Dunedin and began his working life with an apprenticeship in a bicycle shop. He moved to working on cars in garages at Invercargill and Dunedin, and then at Ashburton in mid Canterbury and at Amberley and Waikari in North Canterbury. He participated in early Automobile Association reliability trials and had a long association with Hupmobile cars.

In 1908 Mercer had a ride in a gas balloon in Invercargill constructed by Mr Bob Murie, and this began his life-long interest in aeronautical matters. He married Eleanor Jane Trethewey at the Baring Square Methodist Church, Ashburton, on 21 May 1913 and they had two daughters, Marie and Billee Jean.

During the early years of World War One Mercer had been registered for service overseas, but when the authorities reduced the upper age limit, he was ineligible. This did not stop him joining the Canterbury (N.Z.) Aviation Company Ltd flying school at Sockburn as a mechanic, with a more important plan to learn to fly and work as an instructor. He passed the examination for a pilot's certificate and was issued with the Royal Aero Club's aviator certificate No. 5438 on 28 August 1917. His excellent progress was reported in the newspapers which said he had achieved his certificate after completing nineteen days of tuition and three hours of flying. Major J.L. Sleeman, the examiner, especially commended Mercer on his good flying skills and performance, noting he was the seventh certified pilot from the school. Mercer went on to be assistant instructor for the school and did extensive flying on the Caudrons and with chief instructor Cecil Hill, who taught him to fly, trained nearly 200 pupils in a short period.

On 17 February 1918 Mercer was sent by Hill to help a lost student, Colin Fyfe, who, while carrying out a portion of his flying examination test, became enveloped in a heavy mist near Lake Ellesmere and found it impossible to locate the aerodrome. The situation was precarious and difficult owing to the rain and heavy mist. Mercer gained contact with the pupil and helped guide him back to a safe landing at Sockburn. The following day Major Sleeman wrote a letter of commendation for Mercer's rescue flight.

Bert Mercer with a Caudron biplane of the Canterbury (N.Z) Aviation Company Ltd at Sockburn at the time he gained an aviator certificate on 28 August 1917. (J.N. Taylor via Mercer Collection)

Following the war, the Canterbury (N.Z.) Aviation Company's activities were scaled down and Mercer resigned in June 1920 to join Rodolph Wigley's New Zealand Aero Transport Company at Timaru. Expansionist plans to grow civil airline work in New Zealand had not come to fruition at this time, so instead the Timaru company did extensive charter and special long distance flights. On 1 December 1920, Mercer and Captain Maurice Buckley made the first flight to Mount Cook, carrying two passengers and taking aerial photographs of the historic flight. On 25 October 1921 Mercer flew de Havilland DH9 D3139 from Timaru to Auckland, setting a new one-day distance record and giving him national prominence. He obtained his ground engineer's licence on 1 December 1921.

The Timaru company, along with all other private aviation companies, was forced to discontinue flying activities by 1924, and Mercer was compelled to re-enter the motor trade in Christchurch. He joined the NZAF on 18 January 1924. However throughout the 1920s he continued with regular flying refresher courses at Wigram and on 14 February 1927 was promoted to the rank of Captain. By this time he had accumulated 850 flying hours.

A national aero club movement began forming throughout New

Zealand in the late 1920s and this gave Mercer the opportunity he needed. The Canterbury Aero Club, based at Wigram, was formed in 1928 and engaged him as the first pilot-instructor from 8 April 1929. On 18 April two aero club Gipsy Moths, one flown by Mercer, and the other by Captain James Findlay, flew from Wigram to Auckland for the Auckland Aero Club pageant, a record trip for Moths. In May it was reported Mercer had nine pupils. One of his early pupils was Aroha Clifford, the first club trained woman pilot in New Zealand.

Over the next few years at the Canterbury Aero Club Mercer became the best known pilot in the South Island and flew extensive charter flights to all regions, including the scenic West Coast. His title at the club changed to chief pilot from September 1934 and it is estimated he trained about seventy pilots before he relinquished his instructing duties on 30 November 1934 to concentrate on his own Air Travel (NZ) Ltd airline.

Kingsford-Smith's Fokker Southern Cross VH-USU is led into the parking area by Bert Mercer at Wigram in 1933. (Mercer Collection)

RIGHT: Captain Mercer (left) talking to an English tourist couple with Fox Moth ZK-AEK at Waiho (Franz Josef) on 27 November 1936. During his bicycle tour of New Zealand, Elmer Grantham stayed at Franz Josef and dined with Captain Mercer and other guests. On this day he recorded in his diary, "Heard an Englishman and wife were going up in the plane so asked if I could join them. Went over Franz Josef Glacier , a bit too bumpy, went down to Gillespies Beach and saw Fox Glacier. Captain Mercer saw some Rata for first time which he showed us. Saw Tasman but not Cook. Good value for one pound for a 40 minute flight." (Elmer Grantham via Dave Grantham)

– 32 –

Unfortunately Mercer experienced a mishap soon after the service started. While at Weheka (Fox Glacier) on Friday 8 February, taking short scenic flights, the Fox Moth was charged by some frightened cattle and over-turned leaving Mercer and his passenger, S.J. Conradson, hanging upside down! Fortunately Conradson's injuries were not serious but the near new aircraft was badly damaged. Mercer took immediate steps to charter the Canterbury Aero Club's Fox Moth ZK-ADH for an extended period and in an early branding lease had the Air Travel name and details signwritten on the engine cowling.

A five year licence for the new South Westland airline was confirmed by the Transport Co-ordination Board and this further demonstrated confidence in a growing future for aviation in the region. For the three months of operations, up to 31 March 1935 Air Travel carried 595 passengers, 1841lbs of mail and 2637lbs of freight. The Fox Moth carried everything from household supplies to farm equipment, including live poultry, ducks and dogs. This exceeded expectations and Mercer announced plans for the purchase of a second Fox Moth. However Fox Moths were no longer being made (ZK-ADI was the last production aircraft) so a used example with an interesting history was procured. *The Press* on 29 May announced the identify of its recent owner, *"Prince of Wales' Aeroplane - Purchase for New Zealand"*. This Fox Moth had been used by the Prince of Wales, later King Edward VIII, and still wore the Royal Blue and Scarlet colours of the Brigade of Guards Flying Club.

Licensed Aerodromes and Landing Grounds

These aerodromes were on a list issued by the Civil Aviation Branch of the Defence Department as at 1 December 1936:

- **Landsborough Aerodrome**: Location, on south bank of Clark River, one mile below Clark-Landsborough Junction, 27 miles from Haast River mouth; category and class, temporary light aircraft; controlled by Air Travel (NZ) Ltd; expires on 8/1/36.
- **Cron's (Haast P.O.) Aerodrome**: Location; 1½ miles from Haast River mouth on south bank; category and class, restricted; controlled by Air Travel (NZ) Ltd; expires on 14/3/36.
- **Waiho (Franz Josef) Aerodrome**: Location, in Waiho Gorge, between old river channel and Waiho River; category and class, restricted; controlled by Waiho Gorge Domain Board; expires on 14/3/36.
- **Inchbonnie Aerodrome**: Location, 2¼ miles south of Lake Brunner, 3 miles north-north-west of Inchbonnie railway station; category and class, restricted; controlled by Air Travel (NZ) Ltd; expires on 14/3/36.
- **Upper Okuru (Nolan's) Aerodrome**: Location, on south side of Okuru River, 2 miles east of river bank; category and class, restricted; controlled by Air Travel (NZ) Ltd; expires on 14/3/36.
- **Mahitahi River Mouth Aerodrome**: Location, south of Bruce Bay, 1¼ miles from mouth of Mahitahi River, on east bank; category and class, restricted; controlled by Air Travel (NZ) Ltd; expires on 8/4/36.
- **Weheka (Fox River) Aerodrome**: Location, between Clearwater and Fox Rivers, east of junction of Cook and Fox Rivers, category and class, restricted; controlled by Air Travel (NZ) Ltd; expires on 8/4/36.
- **Arawata Aerodrome**: Location, 24 miles from Arawata River mouth, ½ mile above Eros Creek; category and class, restricted; controlled by Air Travel (NZ) Ltd; expires on 12/4/36.
- **Hokitika (Southside) Aerodrome**: Location, 1 mile south-west of Hokitika; category and class, public, light aircraft; controlled by Westland Aero Club; expires on 20/6/36.
- **Mussel Point (Lower Okuru) Aerodrome**: Location, between Hapuka River and Tasman Sea and ¼ mile south of Okuru River mouth; category and class, public, light aircraft; controlled by Air Travel (NZ) Ltd; expires on 14/9/36.

Sitting on the Fox Moth wing, an Okuru resident reads his mail soon after the aircraft had arrived.
(Whites Aviation via MOTAT)

In late 1935 ZK-ADI at the new Jackson Bay airstrip situated about two and a half miles from the proposed wharf site. Manual work progresses in the background.
(Mercer Collection)

In late July the rebuilding of ZK-ADI was complete and ZK-ADH was returned to Christchurch after a total hire cost of £611. Mercer soon after reported to the Transport Co-ordination Board at its sitting at Wellington, applying for the right to use a second machine, that all traffic had exceeded expectations. He had estimated 100 pounds of mail a week. In the first quarter, however, the machine had carried 1800 pounds, in the second 3600 pounds, and in the third 4200 pounds. In nine months the company had made 1045 flights, carried 1100 passengers, 6225 pounds of goods and 9568 pounds of mail.

Canterbury Education Board School Inspectors J. Wyn-Irwin and A. Lake were flown by Fox Moth ZK-ADI to Franz Josef and Fox Glacier on 8 November 1935, probably the first such aerial education visit made in New Zealand, The following day they were flown to Bruce Bay and Okuru. Ambulance flights had been regularly flown from South Westland, even prior to Mercer starting his airline, and the last recorded for 1935 was on 30 December when Mercer flew to Fox Glacier to pick up young Jim Sullivan, who was suffering from appendicitis, and brought him and his parents to Westland Hospital at Hokitika where he made a quick recovery.

With the arrival of the "Royal" Fox Moth ZK-AEK, Mercer made overtures to employ a second experienced pilot. Captain Jim Hewett agreed, but his starting time was delayed some weeks as Mercer had made a forced landing in ZK-ADI, due to a fuel blockage, and knocked off the undercarriage.

Hewett had a flying career even more extensive than Mercer. Born 18 January 1891 at Te Awamutu he enlisted in the army from 1911. He went on active service from 1915 and transferred to the Royal Flying Corps as a 2nd

Lieutenant from April 1916 and began flying the same year. He served with the both the Royal Flying Corps and the Royal Air Force and achieved over 1000 flying hours in this time. In 1917 he was posted to No.23 Fighter Squadron, France, gaining distinction in the Ypres and Somme areas and after promotion to Captain was decorated in 1918 with the Croix de Guerre Avec Palme (Fr) with the citation, "Has brilliantly engaged in numerous combats

At Hokitika's Southside Aerodrome in early 1936, Bert Mercer (in the cabin) and Jim Hewett load Fox Moth ZK-ADI with mail and freight for a flight south.
(Whites Aviation via Jim Hewett Collection)

Fox Moths ZK-ADI (left) and ZK-AEK at Franz Josef with Hewett and Mercer doing maintenance work early in the morning. Hewett tops up oil and ZK-ADI's wings are still folded after being pushed out of the hangar. Mercer is ready to sort out the Castrol oil supplies. Franz Josef was a busy location for Air Travel (NZ) Ltd tourist flying.
(Jim Hewett Collection)

'Joy-riding' Flights at Franz Josef

At the Waiho (Franz Josef) aerodrome Air Travel (NZ) Ltd kept a large hard cover log book recording most flights from August 1935 to January 1938. In addition to name and address there were "Yes" and "No" columns for "First Flight?" and a "Remarks" column. The majority wrote "Yes" in the first column and the written remarks column was always descriptive.

Some examples:

"I felt on top of the world"

"It's quite safe"

"The scene from below is magnificent; the scene from the air is incomparably impressive"

"Second best thrill of my life"

"Well worth the money – a perfect flight"

"Never thought I would go up – just wonderful"

"Glad to have lived to do this"

"A wonderful trip with a splendid pilot – scenery of remarkable grandeur –
actually saw the chamois in its native haunts – no visitor to the Franz Josef should miss this thrilling experience."

"First aerial experience – a great thrill"

"Best quid I ever spent"

"We'll do our best to 'tell the world'"

"This is God's own country"

"Never thought I would have the nerve to fly – delightful"

"Steady as a rock, no need to be nervous with Captain Mercer"

"Thrilling – liked the air pockets"

"Why live on earth?"

"Most marvellous panorama I have ever seen! Absolutely magnificent"

"Seeing is believing"

"Thank God for it all"

"Everyone should take advantage of this flight. Many thanks to Pilot Hewett"

Alternative transport for the Mercers! During a rare recreational break from flying duties, Bert Mercer and his wife Jane are about to set off on a horse trek from the Graham's Glacier Hotel on 13 January 1937. Jane Mercer is riding Jenny *and Bert on* Midget. *They are being seen off by their daughter Marie, who worked in the Air Travel (NZ) Ltd office for several years.*
(Mark Lysons via A.C. Graham Collection via Dorothy Fletcher)

BELOW: *Fox Moth ZK-ADI flying over Makawhio Point, formerly known as Jacobs Bluff, a prominent coastal feature near Bruce Bay. Mount Cook and Mount Tasman are prominent in the background.*
(Whites Aviation via Mercer Collection)

Bert Mercer talks to local boys at the Bruce Bay settlement, a regular landing place on the South Westland service, 1936. Note the limp windsock at right among the flax bushes. From left: Ronnie Clark, Noel Andrews, Archie McLaren, Ben Mahuika, Pat Mahuika and Jimmy McLaren.
(Whites Aviation via Mercer Collection)

BELOW: Famous aviatrix Jean Batten visits Hokitika in December 1936 and calls at Southside to meet Captain Mercer and see the Air Travel (NZ) Ltd base.
(D. Stevenson via Jim Hewett Collection)

with enemy aircraft over the French front, bringing many of them down in our lines."

Following the war, Hewett served with the RAF in India, on the North-Western Frontier, operating with the Waziristan Field Force. He resigned his commission in 1921 and returned to New Zealand joining the New Zealand Permanent Air Force in 1925, being promoted in 1934 to Squadron Leader. In 1928 he took up commercial aviation with the Goodwin-Chichester Aviation Company. Hewett then established his own Falcon Airways air taxi business with Gipsy Moth ZK-AAR. He gained national prominence when he flew the Gipsy Moth on the first Dunedin to Auckland non-stop flight on 15 March 1930, a distance of over 800 miles, in ten hours flying. Soon after, Falcon Airways based at Orakei in Auckland and Hewett became well known with charter flying around the North Island.

A participant in the famous 1934 MacRobertson Air Race from London to Melbourne, Hewett flew de Havilland DH89 Rapide ZK-ACO *Tainui* to a commendable fifth in the handicap section. After the race he flew the Rapide across the Tasman Sea on 14 November in nine hours and forty five minutes establishing three important 'firsts'; the first aircraft to fly from England to New Zealand, the first twin

- 37 -

Seeing to the Full
AERIAL IMPRESSIONS OF SOUTHERN SCENERY

Not to have flown over the bush, glacier, mountain, lake and river scenery of the south is not to have used the gift of sight to the full, according to Miss M. McGovern, of Rongotai Terrace, Wellington, who has just returned from an aerial visit to South Westland.

From Hokitika the Fox Moth machine formerly owned by the King and now flown by Flight Lieutenant J.C. Mercer was used. A feature was that there was warm air supply in the cabin for high flying over the mountains.

"The scenery on this flight is almost indescribable," said Miss McGovern. "As you fly down the coast dense bush gives place to flat lagoons, with the blue sea breaking along the shore in lacy scallops as far as the eye can see. The flat lagoons are soon replaced by sheer cliffs, still covered with bush, and, flying alongside these for miles you see one waterfall after another. I counted at least 20. We saw Mount Cook and the range of the Southern Alps as we neared Waiho, but the greatest thrill was flying straight up the Franz Josef Glacier between bushed valley sides rising to snow-capped mountain giants above, with foamy fairy-like waterfalls cascading from the mountain crests through the bush to the glacier's edge.

"Franz Josef Glacier is a great sheet of white, though not the pictured white, but white glorified with tints ranging from pale blue to deep blue and even jade green. The sun's rays stain the mountain tops a brilliant orange red, making a striking kaleidoscope of colouring. Waiho River, caked in parts with blocks of ice, pours from the ice cave of the glacier."

Up the valley of the Arawata River the plane flew between great hills covered with bush. "The hills glow with the ruby red of autumn-tinted birch," said Miss McGovern. "The fields are a golden yellow, and crowning the head of this valley of delight are Five Fingers Mountains, Andy's Glacier and the Cascade Waterfall. The valley seems alive with tuis, pigeons, paradise and blue duck, and on the return journey, swooping down, we startled from peaceful reverie on the lagoons scores of grey ducks and black swans."

(Excerpts from *The Dominion* 24 April 1936)

Haast Aerodrome with the Fox Moths ZK-ADI and ZK-AEK sitting in the sun before a return flight to Hokitika. The pilots and passengers are likely having a cup of tea and hot scones at the Cron homestead. Mosquito Hill in the background.
(via Des Nolan Collection)

BELOW: *Jim Hewett with ZK-ADI on the Paringa riverbed with whitebaiters Dick McIntrye and (at right) Bill Duthwaite. This was a typical flight to pick up bait and deliver other freight, including the regular aerial delivery of newspapers.* (Whites Aviation via Jim Hewett Collection)

engine aircraft to cross the Tasman Sea, and in so doing Hewett, Cyril Kay and Frank Stewart became the first all New Zealand born aircrew to fly the Tasman.

Hewett made his first flights with Air Travel on 8 January 1936, ready for the busy summer tourist season. He and his wife and daughter took up residence at Waiho and his main aircraft was primarily Fox Moth ZK-AEK doing scheduled, scenic and freight flying. The Hewetts stayed at Franz Josef for four years until moving to Hokitika in December 1939. At the same time Hewett began flying, Owen Templeton, an assistant ground engineer, was employed at Hokitika and worked with Mercer on all the pre-war aircraft.

Both Mercer and Hewett, like most of their contemporaries had military flying experience. Hewett was the first former operational war pilot on the South Westland air service but not the last with a number of others such as Frank Molloy, Jock McLernon, Jack Humphries and Brian Waugh being pilots during World War II.

In mid July 1936 both Fox Moths were used by local body delegates for viewing the proposed line of the road over the Haast Pass – a portent of things to come.

The new Dragonfly ZK-AFB soon after its arrival at Southside on 29 October 1937. Directors, shareholders and other interested people gather including (at left) Paul Renton and Marie Mercer and (at right) Dr Ebenezer Teichelmann wearing Plus Fours. The Dragonfly was the first twin engine aircraft based on the West Coast. Teichelmann, born in Australia, had arrived 40 years before as Surgeon Superintendent of Westland Hospital. His mountaineering achievements in the years 1899 to 1921 established him as one of New Zealand's foremost climbers.
(Jim Hewett Collection)

At Neils Beach in the late 1930s, Parata Pita Kere (aka Friday Kelly) and Taane (Dan) Te Koeti with Dragonfly ZK-AFB. These men carried the mail to Haast and Jackson Bay for 43 years. Note the plywood monocoque structure of the Dragonfly fuselage which made for a clean and streamlined finish.
(Mercer Collection via Des Nolan Collection)

LEFT: *Gordon Bowman working the Hokitika Aeradio, call sign ZMP, on 4 August 1937. The Aeradio office was originally based in an annex of the Air Travel hangar but later moved to its own nearby separate building.*
(Arthur Orchard via Gordon Bowman Collection)

Fox Moth ZK-ADI circling before landing at Okuru. The Whitebait factory is the largest building and in front a row of Public Works Department tents. (Whites Aviation via Des Nolan Collection)

In the 5 September 1936 *Wings* magazine it was announced, "In view of the decision to undertake the Haast Pass road construction, Air Travel (NZ) Ltd, has decided to extend operations to the Haast Valley. To that end landing grounds have been selected at the foot of Haast Pass, and when workmen are employed, urgent supplies, mails and parcels can be delivered at regular intervals, instead of waiting days for the packhorse service. The aeroplane service will also be invaluable in cases of sickness, accident or other emergency among the workmen."

Government officials also used the air service in early February 1937 when a ministerial party spent over four hours airborne in South Westland. In July members of the Westland County Council, the largest in New Zealand at the time with 4419 square miles, inspected their southern region from the comfort of Fox Moth cabins. The late 1930s were a time of

FOX MOTH ZK-ADI

THE LAST NEW DH83 FOX MOTH produced by de Havillands in England carried constructors number 4097 and was built as a Speed Model with a warranty being issued on 22 October 1934. It arrived in Lyttleton on board the *Port Fairy* on 8 December 1934 and was assembled soon after at Wigram and flown to Hokitika by Bert Mercer. On 18 December it earned its place in New Zealand history by inaugurating the first licensed scheduled air service and on 31 December the first unsubsidised air mail service.

On 8 February 1935 it was involved in an accident at Weheka (Fox Glacier) and was badly damaged. Repairs took six months before the aircraft returned to West Coast service. Throughout the late 1930s and the early war years ZK-ADI was a familiar sight in South Westland, transporting thousands of passengers, much freight and air mail and undertaking many air-ambulance and scenic flights. A new engine was fitted in November 1939, and Mercer test flew the aircraft at Hokitika on 1 December. ZK-ADI made one of a number of forced landings at Whataroa on 8 April 1939 and was involved in an accident at Jackson Bay on 10 February 1940. By October 1940 it was reported the Fox Moth had flown 2740 hours.

While the wartime patrols of Air Travel (NZ) Ltd were usually flown by the Dragonflies, on 3 May 1942 Mercer carried out one such patrol in ZK-ADI. On 12 April 1943 ZK-ADI was impressed into RNZAF service as NZ566. Air Travel (NZ) Ltd was compensated £1300 for the aircraft. During its early air force service it was fully camouflaged but later was painted silver overall. It spent time with the Communications Flight at Rongotai which later became No.42 Squadron. One recorded wartime flight of NZ566 was on 8 March 1944 when Flying Officer Cliff Lewis flew mail from Napier to Wairoa during serious flooding in the district.

Post war the Fox Moth was modified for aerial fire patrol duties and was stationed at Rotorua during the summer season of 1945-1946 and the following two summers. The aircraft was demobilised in 1948, allocated the registration ZK-ASP and sold to the New Zealand National Airways Corporation (NAC) on 16 July. It was named *Mimiro* (North Island Tomtit) and continued to be flown on the South Westland air service until withdrawn from service in 1953. Sold to Keith Wakeman it was then owned by a succession of eight owners, including Air Contracts of Masterton, Alex Blechynden, R.N. Rae and S.M. Marker. John Switzer purchased the aircraft in 1961 and restored it over the following two years, then made extensive tours throughout New Zealand before selling it to A.J. Evans in the late 1960s. A forced landing during take-off from Ardmore on 30 July 1968 considerably damaged the aircraft. David Lilico purchased it in April 1971 and set about restoration. This work was followed by several nostalgic flights, including a visit to South Westland in July 1972, in conjunction with the 25th anniversary of NAC. John King accompanied this flight and did much to revive interest in the history of the South Westland air service. The Fox Moth was then sold to Myles Robertson who took it to the United States in April 1974 where it was registered N83DH on 23 September 1975. In 1984 it was sold to Brian Woodford in the United Kingdom and operated by Wessex Aviation as G-ADHA, painted to represent a Royal Flight Fox Moth.

Gerald Grocott, a New Zealander flying for Swissair, became interested in the Fox Moth because of its historic New Zealand heritage, and made a trip to England in 1994 to see if a purchase deal could be struck but Woodford was away overseas. It was a year later on Christmas Day 1995 that Grocott and Woodford discussed the possible sale and a deal was settled soon afterwards. Grocott returned the Fox Moth to New Zealand to be based at the Croydon Aircraft Company at Old Mandeville Airfield, near Gore. After some refurbishment and a return to Air Travel's original colour scheme it took to the air in early 1997. It made a nostalgic return to South Westland, landing at Big Bay and Hokitika, flown by Rod Hall-Jones and was displayed at the February 1997 Westport Air Show. The Croydon Aviation Heritage Trust eventually purchased ZK-ADI and operates it with a transport licence. How fortunate New Zealand's first airliner continues to fly into the twentieth first century as a special tribute to the pioneering work of Captain Bert Mercer, Air Travel (NZ) Ltd and the South Westland air service.

John Neave in the pilot's seat of ZK-ADI on a South Westland flight.
(Jim Hewett Collection)

Jackson Bay in 1937 showing the Public Works Department and Rope Construction Company camp at the time of the wharf construction being completed. The Post Office and Aeradio building are among the buildings at centre.
(Gordon Bowman Collection)

Sometimes there was hardly any room for passengers! Here the cabin of Fox Moth ZK-AEK is being shared with mail and freight.
(via Des Nolan Collection)

transport expansion and for the West Coast the opening of the Lewis Pass Road in 1937 further reduced the isolation of the region from its near neighbour, Canterbury.

Along with increasing passengers and freight, there was a noticeable increase in tourist numbers, helped by Mercer and his marketing of the scenic wonderland of South Westland. Mention was often made that the West Coast offered more scenic attractions in 400 miles than any other place in the world; in fact a bold claim was sometimes made that to see the same range of scenery elsewhere you would likely have to travel 4000 miles! As a consequence of increased air traffic, Mercer explored the possibility of purchasing both DH84 Dragons from East Coast Airways. However the Air Travel directors eventually decided to purchase a new twin engine aircraft and announced on 19 May 1937 an order for a de Havilland DH90A Dragonfly. With Gipsy Major engines, like those used in the Fox Moths, there was mechanical commonality and already proven experience with de Havilland biplanes on the South Westland air service. Capital was increased from £3000 to £10,000 to facilitate purchase of the new aircraft.

FOX MOTH ZK-AEK

WELL KNOWN IN NEW ZEALAND in the 1930s as the former Prince of Wales aircraft, this Fox Moth, c/n 4033, was produced in late 1932 and registered G-ACAJ to Flt Lt E.H. Fielden of Hendon, as nominee for HRH The Prince of Wales (later King Edward VIII), but soon changed to G-ACDD. The Prince only used the aircraft briefly before it was replaced by DH84 Dragon G-ACGG and sold in June 1933 to Guy Hansez in Belgium as OO-ENC. In Hansez's ownership the Fox Moth flew many international flights including to Egypt and the Belgian Congo.

In 1935 it was returned to the de Havilland factory, re-registered as G-ACDD and sold to Air Travel (NZ) Ltd. The aircraft arrived at Hokitika still in its British markings and Royal colour scheme and was assembled at Hokitika under Bert Mercer's supervision. Registered ZK-AEK on 18 October 1935, it was mainly used in the new year by Jim Hewett and based at Franz Josef. Early operations were eventful with a forced landing on the beach at Haast on 5 November 1935 and then soon after on 3 December in the Arahura Riverbed, which damaged the undercarriage and split the propeller.

Like the other Fox Moths, ZK-AEK operated extensively all over the West Coast, until another accident on 3 February 1940. While landing at Jackson Bay it was caught by a gust of wind, skidded and collided with a log. John Neave, the pilot, and two passengers were unhurt. It returned to Hokitika aboard the *Gael* for repairs, only to be damaged again after being charged by a bull while taking off from Haast on 6 July. At this time it had flown 2929 hours since new.

Its most famous accident occurred on 29 October 1943 when it force landed on the Franz Josef Glacier. Pilot O.D. "Ozzie" Openshaw and four WAAF passengers survived the crash and were soon rescued by a team of mountaineers. Salvaged in a large and difficult operation about a month later it was eventually rebuilt by the de Havilland factory at Rongotai, Wellington, and returned to flying. Interestingly one piece of the engine cowling eventually came to light at the face of the glacier in May 1950, practically unmarked!

ZK-AEK returned to Hokitika on 21 May 1944 sporting a new fuselage. NAC took it over from 1 October 1947 and named it *Mohua* (Yellowhead) and it was finally withdrawn from service in March 1953 and sold to Keith Wakeman. It crashed at Craigieburn on 22 December that year when it had flown a total of 8112 hours. After repairs, ownership passed to C.A.Wornall who named the Fox Moth *Duke,* then to Ray Sweney of Hokitika. Sweney financed sending it to Fiji on the *M.V.Tofua* in March 1957 where Bryan McCook was to operate it on a freight service. It was registered VH-FAT in Fiji but was eventually cancelled. The aircraft badly deteriorated in the tropical conditions and the engine, propeller and a range of fittings, including the windscreen and cockpit canopy, were brought back to New Zealand by Don Nairn in September 1959.

In early 1990 Nairn mentioned to Colin Smith of the Croydon Aircraft Company that he had some Fox Moth "bits" and were they of any use? Roger Fiennes, an Englishman, visiting New Zealand became interested in the prospect of a rebuild of c/n 4033, because of its special history and an agreement was reached to rebuild the famous Fox Moth using as many of the original fittings as possible. Civil Aviation authorities agreed that sufficient original parts remained for the aircraft's identity to be reinstated. Colin Smith commented, "Roger believed I could capture the right effect and atmosphere of his aeroplane. It was a gamble at first because Croydon had never produced a complete project at that time."

The complete rebuild restoration came to fruition with a first test flight on 5 May 1993 by Neil Robertson. Registered G-ACDD, it flew throughout the South Island, including a trip up the West Coast and a visit to Hokitika, before being shipped to the USA for display at the Oshkosh air show and then shipped on to Great Britain. The following year the Fox Moth was purchased by Sir Tim Wallis of the Alpine Deer Group Ltd of Wanaka, whose family had a strong affinity to the type from its days on the West Coast. It flew again in the South Island in early 1994 and in December of that year was a prominent feature at the 60th anniversary of the South Westland air service at Hokitika. In 2007 ZK-AEK was sold to Canada and remains airworthy as C-FYPM at Vintage Wings of Canada, a private foundation at Gatineau Airport, Ottawa.

ZK-AEK on one of the basic South Westland landing grounds in the late 1930s.
(M.C.Lysons via Jim Hewett Collection)

FOX MOTH ZK-AGM

THIS AIRCRAFT, carrying constructors number T/S 2810, was built in 1938 with an interesting history. The basic fuselage had been built by apprentices of the de Havilland Technical School during the years the Fox Moth was in production, and was then stored. In the late 1930s Air Travel (NZ) Ltd was keen to add another Fox Moth to its fleet. But when inquiries were made to de Havilland none were available, only the training fuselage. This was eventually offered and accepted by Bert Mercer. At the same time Mercer purchased the remains of Fox Moth ZK-ADH (c/n 4085), formerly owned by the Canterbury Aero Club, which had crashed on 7 June 1936 near Wigram, and been written off.

The training fuselage, plus many parts salvaged from ZK-ADH, as well as new replacement parts, were all put together at Hokitika in 1938 with a first flight test on 10 June. The "new" Fox Moth was registered ZK-AGM and soon went into busy West Coast service as No.4 of the Air Travel (NZ) Ltd fleet. It was mostly flown by the younger pilots as Mercer concentrated on Dragonfly flying but Mercer did record 129 flying hours with ZK-AGM over the next six years.

Its activities were typical of the era; on 30 January 1942 it flew an ambulance flight to Weheka, on 20 September 1943 a flight to Paringa to inspect the landing ground there and also a check for new pilot Norm Suttie. A final Air Travel (NZ) Ltd incident occurred on 14 August 1947 when ZK-AGM made a forced landing at Haast with water in the petrol tank. From October of that year the Fox Moth flew in NAC service as *Matuhi* (Bush Wren). With improvements to the aerodrome at Franz Josef, which made it more sutiable for DH89 Dominie use, the days of the Fox Moths were numbered. ZK-AGM had the distinction of flying the last official Fox Moth service on 28 February 1954 from Hokitika to South Westland, although it was retained for occasional use over the next eighteen months.

Wanganui Aero Work Ltd purchased the aircraft in February 1956 for communications work. On 28 October 1960 it was involved in a fatal accident when a bystander was struck and killed by the aircraft's propeller. At this time the aircraft had flown a total of 8405 hours. It was sold again and registered to new owner Terry Garnier in January 1963. On 27 April Garnier with passenger M.E. Reid flew into the West Wanaka area but due to spatial disorientation crashed in Minaret Creek. Reid was killed and fire broke out destroying much of the aircraft. However this was not to be the end of the Fox Moth as the engine and a number of useful parts were eventually recovered. In 2009 this veteran aircraft is in the ownership of New Zealander Bruce Broady at Hungerford, England, and is being restored. Latest reports are that the wings were being temporarily attached to trial rig it, before being covered. Broady plans to eventually return the Fox Moth to New Zealand.

ZK-AGM with pilot Jim Hewett and some of the Nolan family at their new Upper Okuru home. (Jim Hewett Collection)

A rare pre-war colour photograph of Fox Moth ZK-ADI at Greymouth. The orange and silver colour scheme was designed to be distinctive against the bush and mountains of South Westland.
(D.D. Kelly Collection via Mike Kelly)

Dragonfly ZK-AFB (c/n 7560) was assembled by Mercer and Templeton at Wigram. Mercer taught himself to fly the twin but in the process did incur a particularly hard landing which broke an engine bearer arm. On 29 October 1937 Mercer flew across the Alps to Hokitika and a large welcoming crowd. ZK-AFB was the first twin engine aircraft based on the West Coast and cost the fledgling airline about £5000. It was a significant gesture of confidence in the airline's future. With fleet 'No.3' painted on its nose, along with the routes flown, the Dragonfly was quickly put to work and for a number of years did frequent beach landings as well as at the usual remote air strips throughout South Westland. The following month a third pilot, Cliff Lewis, was engaged by the airline.

The Public Works Department supplied much business

Relaxing during a rare occasion of no flying on a sunny day! From left, Jim Hewett, Mrs Linda Hewett, Bert Mercer and Alec Graham aboard the Graham's Hotel launch on Lake Mapourika. (M.C. Lysons via Jim Hewett Collection)

LEFT: *A happy group at the Mahitahi River mouth airstrip, near Bruce Bay, after returning from a Franz Josef sports meeting in Dragonfly ZK-AFB.* (via Des Nolan Collection)

Hokitika's Southside Aerodrome in the mid 1930s soon after the cross runways were developed. Close to town, access was across the long combined road and rail bridge.
(M.C.Lysons via A.C. Graham Collection via Dorothy Fletcher)

to Air Travel in the 1930s, and for many more years. On 10 January 1938 ZK-ADI and ZK-AEK flew seventy men returning after their Christmas holidays from Hokitika and Waiho to camps at Bruce Bay and Jackson Bay. All mail for the large Jackson Bay camp was carried by the Fox Moth and delivered to Okuru and then picked up by a launch from the camp. Figures for the period 1 January to 31 March 1938 were; 2000lb of mail to and from Okuru, and during the first three weeks of April, the mail weighed 1200lb. Cliff Lewis recalled some years later, "We used to fly the aircraft onto beaches, riverbeds and private paddocks – anything we could use as landing places. The Fox Moth was beautiful to handle and her ability to carry her own weight was stupendous for the time." Also recorded was the consistently high regularity maintained by Air Travel (NZ) Ltd on its South Westland air services with 99.1% of flights being maintained for the first quarter in 1938. Considering the demanding weather on the West Coast this was a very satisfying result.

Two more aircraft were added to the Air Travel fleet in 1938. First, the damaged remains of Fox Moth ZK-ADH were purchased from the Canterbury Aero Club. A new fuselage was ordered from de Havillands and a specially made example by apprentices of the de Havilland Technical School, was shipped to New Zealand in early 1938. Assembly of the reusable parts of ZK-ADH, including the wings and tail unit, were matched to the new fuselage and the first flight of ZK-AGM was made on 10 June at Hokitika.

A new Dragonfly, registered ZK-AGP, was purchased later in the year, arriving from England on the *Rangitiki*. Assembled by Owen Templeton and Andrew Sutton of The Air Survey and Transport Co Ltd at Rongotai, it was flown by Mercer to Hokitika on 17 November 1938. With the Dragonfly operational, a special formation flight of all five company aircraft was made on 26 November from Hokitika to Westport and return to celebrate the arrival of the new aircraft and to commemorate four years operation by the pioneer airline. Pilots were Bert Mercer, Jim Hewett, Cliff Lewis, and recently employed John Neave and Arthur Baines.

Even prior to the introduction of the two additional aircraft the directors were able to report healthy growth for the year ended 30 June 1938 with 3411 flights, occupying 1655 hours flying, carrying 4719 passengers, with over 28 tons of mail and eight tons of freight. It was also noted that with the Westport air taxi service having recently commenced, the airline now operated all the way from Westport to Milford Sound.

Air travel from South Westland in the late 1930s helped reduce the severe isolation, but it also gave those who lived "far down" the West Coast a greater "airmindedness" and general experience of flying than any other region of New Zealand. The versatility of the air service permeated virtually every sphere of life. Freight efficiency, airmail, emergency air ambulance benefits, many visitors and tourists, but also the ability of South Westlanders (men, women and children) to have a heightened sense of perspective and awareness about where they lived. At a time when many Kiwis had not flown, most "far downers" were thoroughly familiar with the experience of viewing, from the air, the stunning landscape of

Some of the Air Travel (NZ) Ltd staff and visitors line up at Southside Aerodrome in 1937. From left: Irene White (wife of photographer Leo White), Captain Ron Kirkup (Cook Strait Airways), Billee Mercer, Owen Templeton, possibly Jack Carroll, Roy Markland, Jack Leslie (Post Office), Gordon Bowman (Aeradio), Dave Stevenson (Photographer) and Bert Mercer. (via Des Nolan Collection)

Fox Moth ZK-ADI on a scenic flight up the Franz Josef Glacier. Such alpine flying required experience and skill from the pilots with unexpected winds, turbulence and increasing high ground always a challenge. (Whites Aviation via Des Nolan Collection)

AIR TRAVEL (N.Z.) Ltd.
Air Service Inchbonnie, Hokitika, Franz Josef and Fox Glaciers
A 1713
SOUVENIR OF FLIGHT
From.......................
To............................
Passenger...............
Pilot......................... Date....................
Air Mail—Hokitika, Bruce Bay-Haast Okuru-Jackson's Bay

where they lived. Cooped up in the little Fox Moth cabin, they could see the mountains, glaciers, rivers, lakes and the great expanse of the Tasman Sea. As they flew from "Hoki to Haast" there was plenty of time to contemplate the scenic splendour and their place in that rugged and isolated part of New Zealand – a part that was still rugged, but because of the air service, no longer as isolated.

For the year ended 30 June 1939 Air Travel (NZ) Ltd statistics indicated a continuing increase in average monthly flying hours compared to the previous year. A useful summary of airline operations from commencement in December 1934 to June 1939 indicated 6537 flying hours, 13,577 flights, 15,570 passengers, 223,230 lb of mail and 80,243 lb of freight. In round figures the latter two items represented about 100 tons of mail and 36 tons of freight. At the same time it was reported the company suffered a small loss of £53 against the profits of £934 and £917 in the two preceding years. Directors reported repairs and maintenance of machines were heavy during the year, with two engines being practically rebuilt and a failure to obtain a revision of the mail contract rates.

Air Travel's Fox Moth ZK-ADI on a sandspit at Milford Sound during a southern charter flight. Note the Bowen Falls in the background. Arthur Bradshaw of Southland Airways was the first to land here on 17 November 1938. (Mercer Collection)

The information panels and commemorative plaque for the South Westland air service at the site of Hokitika's Southside Aerodrome. This display was unveiled and dedicated on 18 December 1994. In the background, at right, are farm sheds where the Air Travel (NZ) Ltd hangars used to be. In the distance, at centre, are the 1930s Aeradio masts, still in use. (John King)

Pilot Arthur Baines flies Fox Moth ZK-AEK past the Defiance Hut at an altitude of 2700ft on the Franz Josef Glacier, Christmas 1939. The photograph was taken from the doorway of the hut. (via Jean Prins)

With the declaration of war in September 1939 Air Travel was engaged by the Defence Department to do regular coastal patrols. The first flight was made on 9 September in Dragonfly ZK-AGP with Gordon Bowman accompanying Mercer on a Hokitika to Invercargill flight, via Milford Sound and Stewart Island, then on to Dunedin. The following day the Dragonfly flew back to Hokitika via Haast.

Aeronautical advances on the West Coast had been astonishingly rapid. The first aircraft to land in South Westland was in August 1931, Mercer started the regular service just three years later, two aircraft were operating by early 1936 and by late 1938 there was a fleet of five aircraft, including two twin-engine aircraft. All this in the space of a little over seven years! It was, unquestionably, the turning point for the people of South Westland, the key to early tourist development and the first phase of a remarkable air service that was unique in New Zealand history.

WHAT TO SEE TODAY

Southside Plaque Memorial and Information Panels

On State Highway 6 at the southern end of the main Hokitika River Bridge, near the site of the former Southside Aerodrome, is a large aviation memorial with a plaque and three information panels. These tell the significant aviation history of the site from 1932 to when the aerodrome was closed in 1951. The memorial plaque and information panels were unveiled during the 60th anniversary celebrations of the South Westland air service on 18 December 1994 and were generously funded by the Renton Family who had important links to the pioneer air service.

Fox Moth ZK-ADI Replica Aircraft, Plaque and Display Building

Situated adjacent to the Hokitika Airport Terminal, this full size replica Fox Moth, with an impressive mannequin of Captain Bert Mercer, is a popular attraction for airport visitors. This replica display and information panel are a fitting tribute to New Zealand's first licensed scheduled air service.

Fox Moth ZK-AEK Replica Aircraft

On display at Auckland's Museum of Transport and Technology, it was built in the late 1990s to commemorate the pioneering work of Air Travel (NZ) Ltd, and is positioned alongside DH89 Rapide ZK-AHS and Lockheed 10A Electra ZK-BUT. This replica aircraft is displayed in the unique combination colour scheme of ZK-AEK as flown on the West Coast in the late 1930s.

Bert Mercer Wing

This extension to the Hokitika Airport Terminal was opened as part of the 75th airline celebrations on 18 December 2009 and on display are some photographs of Captain Mercer and the historic South Westland air service.

AIR TRAVEL (NZ) LTD
Commenced operations on 18 December 1934
Based at Hokitika

EAST COAST AIRWAYS LTD
Commenced operations on 15 April 1935
Based at Gisborne

NZ NATIONAL AIRWAYS CORPORATION
Commenced operations on 1 April 1947
Based at Palmerston North

COOK STRAIT AIRWAYS LTD
Commenced operations on 30 December 1935
Based at Nelson

UNION AIRWAYS OF NZ LTD
Commenced operations on 16 January 1936
Based at Palmerston North

The 'wings' insignia of the three provincial licensed airline operators and the main trunk airline operator of the period between 1934 and 1947. East Coast Airways Ltd was taken over by Union Airways of NZ Ltd in 1938 and in 1947 the three airlines of that time were brought together to form NZ National Airways Corporation.
In 1978 NAC joined with the international airline Air New Zealand to form the present Air New Zealand.

GMcC

ABOVE: *Three of Air Travel's aircraft fleet at Nelson, in 1940, outside the empty Cook Strait Airways hangar. With the outbreak of war and Cook Strait Airways five DH89 Rapides being requisitioned for RNZAF service, Air Travel took over the northern route to Westport and Nelson, operating on the CSA licence. At left Union Airways Lockheed 10A Electra ZK-AFE* Kereru, *from Wellington, with Fox Moth ZK-AGM and Dragonflies ZK-AFB and ZK-AGP. The newly established grass and concrete apron indicate Nelson Airport having only been open about eighteen months.* (via Des Nolan Collection)

BELOW: *Hokitika's Southside Aerodrome about 1940. Note the double hangar built for the DH90 Dragonflies in late 1938 and the small Aeradio building between the two radio aerial masts. The name 'HOKITIKA' in large white-painted concrete letters, can be seen near the centre of the aerodrome. These letters were covered up in the early stages of the war for security reasons and briefly exposed again for the 60th anniversary in 1994.* (V.C.Browne via Des Nolan Collection).

3
Change and Struggle
Air Travel (NZ) Ltd 1940 -1947

THE OUTBREAK OF WORLD WAR II on 3 September 1939 brought immediate change to New Zealand's aviation scene. Private flying virtually ceased and the burgeoning airlines were compelled to change and retrench at the direction of the Government. Many aircraft were requisitioned, including all the aircraft fleet of Cook Strait Airways. Union Airways were left to operate with only four Lockheed 10A Electras. Air Travel (NZ) Ltd, because of its unique service on the West Coast, was able to retain its aircraft, but directed from 10 November 1939, by the Government, to expand its operations north to Nelson, assisted by a regular subsidy.

During this early part of the war most of the airline's pilots went into Air Force service. Jim Hewett left in March 1940, after more than four years service and many thousands of flying hours in South Westland. He became Officer Commanding RNZAF Communications Flight (later No.42 Squadron), Rongotai, where he personally flew many distinguished guests such as the Governor General, Prime Minister and Ministers of the Crown. Sadly, Hewett's son, trainee pilot J. D. Hewett, was killed in the mid air collision of Oxford NZ1243 with Oxford NZ1257 at RNZAF Woodbourne on 31 December 1941.

John Neave's last flight was on 12 November 1940, after 1109 flying hours. He went to be the test pilot at Wellington's de Havilland factory, and after the war, Chief Flying Instructor for the Canterbury Aero Club. Cliff Lewis continued on until April 1942 when he entered the Air Force. 56 year old Mercer then wrote in his work diary, "I am back to where I started 8 years ago – on my own again."

The struggle for Mercer and his directors was how to operate a small busy airline with severe constraints on pilot availability. The only option was to obtain regular air force pilots on short term loan. While this arrangement enabled the airline to continue with many temporary pilots coming and going, all wearing their RNZAF uniforms while flying, Mercer was over-worked and the additional northern services to Westport and Nelson, operating on the Cook Strait Airways licence, meant that some southern services had to be reduced.

Passenger demand during the five days of Easter 1940 had two Union Airways Lockheed Electras and an Air Travel Dragonfly make 96 trips between Wellington, Blenheim

– 53 –

Tribute to
Edward Roy Markland
PILOT OFFICER NZ414656
(1920 - 1943)
✞

Roy joined the staff of Air Travel (NZ) Ltd as engineer assistant at Hokitika in 1937. He was born at Chorley, Lancashire, England on 1 April 1920, the son of Edward and Esther Markland. With his family he emigrated to New Zealand as a child, and attended Hokitika Primary School and Hokitika District High School where he did well at sport and was a member of the 1st XV. He joined the RNZAF and began a pilot training course at Levin in August 1941, then was posted to No.3EFTS at Harewood the following month to start his flying instruction on de Havilland Tiger Moths. Soloing on 8 October, he completed the course in early November and graduated with his "Wings" on 6 January 1942. Markland commented in his diary, "My ambition realised!" With fifteen other pilots he then sailed to Britain and was posted in May to the RAF's No.6 Pilot's Advanced Flying Unit at Little Rissington, flying Airspeed Oxford aircraft for refresher training and familiarisation with local conditions.

In July 1942 Markland was posted to No.16 OTU for conversion to Vickers Wellington bombers. His first operational flight, as a 'freshman', was to Dusseldorf on 10 September 1942 as part of a five-hundred strong bomber raid. Soon after he qualified as a first pilot on Wellingtons and in late September went on a conversion course for Avro Lancaster heavy bombers with No.1654 Conversion Unit. In November he was posted to No.106 Squadron and flew his first operational mission on Lancasters. On 17 January 1943 his Lancaster R5611 was badly damaged over Kiel but made it back to England, and during the flight his crew shot down a Junkers Ju88. On his nineteenth operation, on 18/19 February 1943, Markland and his crew were lost when his Lancaster R5750 failed to return from an attack on the German submarine base at Wilhelmshaven.

Pilot Officer Roy Markland and four of his crew were initially buried at the local cemeteries at Wilhelmshaven and nearby Jever, but later all five were reinterred at the Sage War Cemetery near Oldenburg, Lower Saxony, Germany. Two members of his crew were never found and are commemorated on the Runnymede Memorial, Middlesex, England. A letter to his parents in Hampden Street, Hokitika, from Wing Commander Guy Gibson, commanding officer of Roy's squadron and later of 'Dambusters' fame, said in part, "We are all appreciative of the motives which brought him from New Zealand to help us in our great struggle, and I can assure you he will not soon be forgotten."

Air Travel apprentices Roy Markland (left) and Ted Toohey at Southside Aerodrome in 1939.

and Nelson, carrying 708 passengers. At Christmas that year it was reported one of the Dragonflies was flying many special trips between Wellington and Nelson helping clear a backlog of passengers.

Beginning in September 1939 a specialised task for the airline was a contract from the Defence Department for Air Travel to operate regular reconnaissance patrols from Hokitika. Sometimes these flights would be north but mostly south, as far as Stewart Island. The purpose was to report any unusual sightings, especially foreign ships in Fiordland. Mercer made the flights about every two weeks or so and often on Sundays, so as to minimise any disruption to scheduled services. With their economical engines the Dragonflies had the longest endurance range of any aircraft in New Zealand at the time so were well suited to the task. Mercer undertook an especially long flight on 4 January 1940. Flying alone, he flew Hokitika to Invercargill, via southern sounds, and return, in a remarkable flying time of thirteen hours and 55 minutes.

Ross King joined Air Travel as a young storeman straight from school in early 1941 and many years later recalled the patrol flights. "The Dragonfly required extra fuel tanks in addition to its usual 85 gallon capacity. With Captain Mercer flying solo, a 40 gallon extra tank was secured on top of the back seat and a four gallon drum tied down on the middle seat. Sometimes he had to pour this extra tank while flying, which was quite a feat!" At other times, a passenger like Gordon Bowman accompanied Mercer, to help with the refuelling task, as well as relieving the monotony of the long flights which often lasted ten hours or more.

From Mercer's logs some examples of these flights are: 20th patrol on 20 October 1940 – 11.5 hours flying Hokitika-Haast-Invercargill-Haast-Hokitika; 21st patrol on 31 October 1940 – 7.45 hours, flying Nelson-Westport-Hokitika-Invercargill; 22nd patrol on the following day was the return flight to Hokitika; 23rd patrol on 8 December 1940 – 5.35 hours, flying Hokitika-Haast-Hokitika, but returned due to deteriorating weather. From all accounts nothing of any significance was reported by Mercer during these patrol flights. On 10 March 1942 Mercer recorded in his diary, "Patrolled out to sea 25 miles from Hokitika. Reports were that a Cruiser was sighted – turned out to be the scow *Sea Gull* with sails up!"

While Mercer was flying a Nelson to Westport flight on 19 November 1941, in Dragonfly ZK-AGP, he achieved his 10,000th flying hour, the first pilot in New Zealand to achieve this milestone. The Air Travel directors planned a formal dinner at the Hotel Westland on 29 November with many invited guests from around the country. About 60 guests gathered, including the Hon. Fred Jones, Minister of Defence, and Mr James O'Brien, MP for Westland. Chaired by Mr George Chapman, Chairman of Directors of Air Travel (NZ) Ltd, the greetings of those who could not attend were read. These included Lady Agnes Wigram who sent a telegram saying, "Congratulations on your splendid record of air service. Am proud to think the Canterbury Aviation Company had the honour of training you. The best of good luck to you." Another veteran pilot, 'Tiny' White, telegraphed, "Please convey heartiest congratulations to guest of honour. Bert Mercer is undoubtedly the historical figure in the aviation history

A rare interior view of Dragonfly ZK-AFB, with a suitcase tied onto the right-hand seat by hemp-rope, and the pilot's jersey on his seat. In the cockpit the two prominent curved levers control the flaps (left) and elevator trim. Behind the pilot's seat is the HF radio unit and beside it the long trailing aerial on its reel ready to be deployed down the tube and out through the bottom of the fuselage. Air sickness bags are ready and available.
(M.C. Lysons via Des Nolan Collection)

Bert Mercer at the controls of his favourite aircraft, Dragonfly ZK-AFB, ready for one of his reconnaissance coastal patrol flights to Fiordland and Stewart Island. (Whites Aviation via MOTAT)

Tribute to Edward Wallace Toohey
WARRANT OFFICER NZ416672
(1922 - 1944)
✝

Ted joined Air Travel (NZ) Ltd as an engineer assistant in 1938, soon after Roy Markland. He was born in Hokitika on 4 June 1922, the son of Cornelius and Alexandra Toohey. The eldest of nine children, he attended St Mary's Catholic School and first worked as a porter at the hotel at Fox Glacier. His mechanical aptitude and aviation interests, however, soon led him to secure a job with Air Travel and every day he biked to work from the family home in Sewell Street, across the long combined road and rail bridge to Southside.

Toohey applied to join the RNZAF in 1940 but after initially being turned down was eventually accepted for training as a wireless operator/air gunner and entered camp at Levin in November 1941. He returned on brief leave to Hokitika in January 1942 before sailing for Canada. There he trained at No.3 Wireless School, Winnipeg, and in September was posted to No.8 Bombing and Gunnery School at Leithbridge, Alberta. Promoted to Sergeant on 26 October, he soon after went to No.34 Operational Training Unit at Pennfield Ridge, New Brunswick, where he converted onto Lockheed Ventura medium bombers.

Leaving Canada for Britain Toohey arrived at Brighton on 17 March 1943 and by May was serving with No.487 Squadron, RNZAF in Norfolk. Promoted to flight sergeant on 1 June, he was soon on his first operation when the squadron's Ventura bombers raided an armament factory in Cherbourg, France. Over subsequent months he continued flying combat missions in Vickers Wellington bombers and later, from March 1944, in Short Stirling heavy bombers. In May he was posted to No.3 Lancaster Finishing School for conversion to Avro Lancasters. On 1 June 1944 he was promoted to Warrant Officer and later in the month was posted to No.75 (NZ) Squadron at Mepal, near Ely, Cambridgeshire.

On the night of 15/16 June 1944 Flight Sergeant Roland Betley, RNZAF, and his crew, including Toohey and two other New Zealanders, Lawrence Hale and Peter Cook, took off in Lancaster LL888 for a raid on Valenciennes, France, but were shot down close to the target and crashed near Rieux, a small village about 9km from Cambrai. All seven crew were killed and are buried at the Rieux Communal Cemetery.

Both Roy Markland and Ted Toohey are honoured on the World War II Memorial at the Hokitika RSA where their names are inscribed.

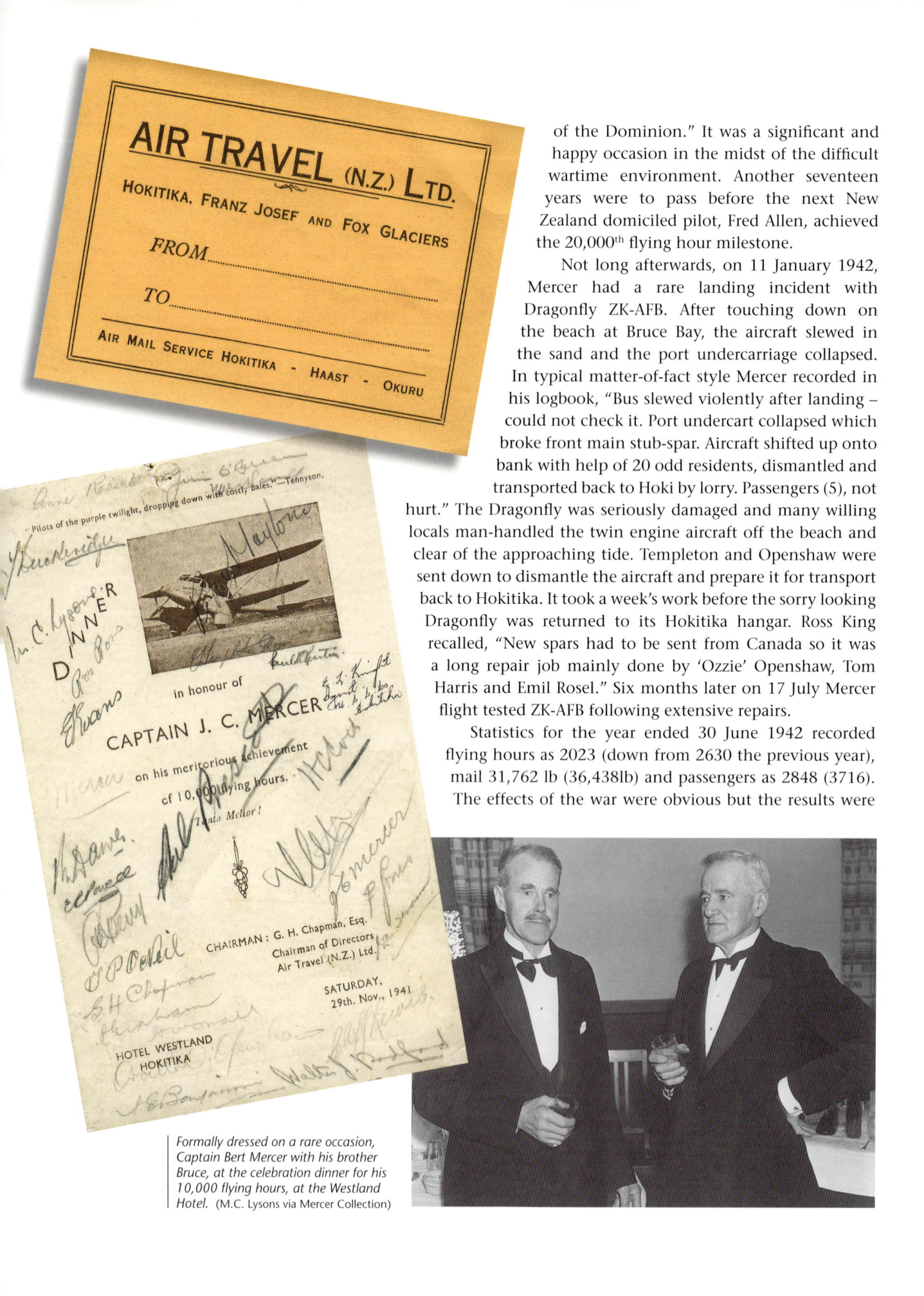

of the Dominion." It was a significant and happy occasion in the midst of the difficult wartime environment. Another seventeen years were to pass before the next New Zealand domiciled pilot, Fred Allen, achieved the 20,000th flying hour milestone.

Not long afterwards, on 11 January 1942, Mercer had a rare landing incident with Dragonfly ZK-AFB. After touching down on the beach at Bruce Bay, the aircraft slewed in the sand and the port undercarriage collapsed. In typical matter-of-fact style Mercer recorded in his logbook, "Bus slewed violently after landing – could not check it. Port undercart collapsed which broke front main stub-spar. Aircraft shifted up onto bank with help of 20 odd residents, dismantled and transported back to Hoki by lorry. Passengers (5), not hurt." The Dragonfly was seriously damaged and many willing locals man-handled the twin engine aircraft off the beach and clear of the approaching tide. Templeton and Openshaw were sent down to dismantle the aircraft and prepare it for transport back to Hokitika. It took a week's work before the sorry looking Dragonfly was returned to its Hokitika hangar. Ross King recalled, "New spars had to be sent from Canada so it was a long repair job mainly done by 'Ozzie' Openshaw, Tom Harris and Emil Rosel." Six months later on 17 July Mercer flight tested ZK-AFB following extensive repairs.

Statistics for the year ended 30 June 1942 recorded flying hours as 2023 (down from 2630 the previous year), mail 31,762 lb (36,438lb) and passengers as 2848 (3716). The effects of the war were obvious but the results were

Formally dressed on a rare occasion, Captain Bert Mercer with his brother Bruce, at the celebration dinner for his 10,000 flying hours, at the Westland Hotel. (M.C. Lysons via Mercer Collection)

ZK-AGP undergoing a major overhaul in the Southside hangar, 1940. (Bill Ward)

still respectable considering pilot constraints. Typical of the many RNZAF pilots who served Air Travel (NZ) Ltd on a short-term basis, usually about 400 flying hours, was Des Paterson who flew from 16 July to 19 September 1942. He assisted Mercer flying Fox Moth and Dragonfly aircraft on both the South Westland and northern routes. Paterson was a former Union Airways Lockheed co-pilot and came to Hokitika with about 3000 flying hours. He later served overseas and at the end of the war held the rank of Squadron Leader and had been awarded an OBE. A number of RNZAF pilots had reason to fly back to Hokitika after their West Coast service. Lloyd Parry (son of a local pilot) landed a Hudson, Arthur Baines an Oxford, and Jim Kennedy gave the Southside Aerodrome a real beat-up in a low flying Sunderland flying boat.

Ross King remembered the routine of the air service at this time. "Saturday was mail and freight day for South Westland. I had to go to the old Post Office in Sewell Street and after the mail was sorted it was weighed, the weights noted, a taxi rung and the mail taken to the drome. If it was an early take-off, I would load the Fox Moth with Jackson Bay mail in front of the front seat bar, Okuru on the floor, and Haast on top, with the bread loaded in the luggage compartment

An evocative scene with Air Travel (NZ) Ltd's original Fox Moth ZK-ADI on the firm sand of a South Westland beach. The Tasman Sea is very calm as a row boat comes ashore.
(Canterbury Aero Club Collection)

At Bruce Bay on 11 January 1942 Dragonfly ZK-AFB has slewed violently after landing, causing the port undercarriage to collapse, breaking the front main stub-spar and twisting the lower wing. An exciting occasion for local residents, especially small boys and dogs.
(Canterbury Aero Club Collection)

up the back. Sometimes the fully loaded Fox Moth was put in Parry's hangar and it was quite a struggle to get the loaded plane out on your own, through the sand at the hangar door, open the wings by yourself and then start the engine and warm it up ready for the pilot to walk out, get in, and take-off."

The busy wartime strain on Mercer was beginning to show. He took sick in September 1942, while at Franz Josef, and was flown home to bed and then transferred to hospital. He ended up staying in hospital for fourteen weeks. From the RNZAF, Flight Lieutenant's Colin Lewis and Arthur Baines maintained services. In early December Mercer returned to his home by the aerodrome but went immediately to work, recording in his diary for 7 December, "At home at Hokitika. Walking about. Legs very shaky. Weather good. Had fly today – went up and tested AFB". Five days later Baines and Lewis took a ministerial party to Franz Josef in the two Dragonflies.

Disaster struck the airline on Monday 21 December 1942. Mercer was still recuperating and working in the hangar when a message came through from Aeradio that Dragonfly ZK-AGP, piloted by Baines, was in trouble on a northern flight. Reported was the in-flight loss of the starboard propeller, with the aircraft returning to Westport. Very soon another report came through that the aircraft had not been able to make land and had ditched in the sea near Westport.

The scheduled service had left Hokitika at 8.25am that morning with passengers Albert Johnson from Hokitika and Albert Walters and Michael Hearty who had come up from Haast. Baines then flew to Westport and picked up Geoffrey McBride. The Dragonfly departed Westport for Nelson at 9.29am with McBride in the front seat next to the pilot, Hearty in the middle seat and Johnson

More than twenty Bruce Bay residents assist in jacking up the forlorn Dragonfly, and preparing to move it above high watermark. Note the major dislocation of the port wing and engine mounting, and the tube for deploying the aerial wire protruding from under the fuselage.
(Canterbury Aero Club Collection)

The Dragonfly returns to Hokitika by road after a week's work of dismantling by engineers Owen Templeton and 'Ozzie' Openshaw. The Dragonfly is on the back of a New Zealand Railways Road Services truck driven by A.J. Wall from Harihari, assisted by J.G. Wright.
(M.C. Lysons via A.C. Graham Collection via Dorothy Fletcher)

Dragonfly ZK-AGP flying south on a scheduled service from Westport to Greymouth, passing over Bullock Creek bridge. (M.C.Lysons via A. C. Graham Collection via Dorothy Fletcher)

AIR TRAVEL (NEW ZEALAND) LIMITED
HOKITIKA AND GLACIERS

NAME...
....194......
Enclosed ticket available for travel...............................a.m.
                                    at.........................p.m.
Car leaves office of..
Passengers proceeding privately to.............................a.m.
Aerodrome must report at Aerodrome Office not later than........p.m.

SEE 4000 MILES OF SCENERY IN 400 MILES

and Walters on the rear bench seat. By 9.42am the aircraft had gained about 4000ft of altitude over the sea and was breaking through cloud and turning to cross the mountains towards Nelson, when the starboard propeller came adrift from the aircraft with no warning. Baines throttled back and reported by radio the loss of the propeller. Later he recounted how he came down through the cloud, getting into clear visibility at about 1000ft. However the Dragonfly continued to lose altitude, despite full power from the port engine, and briefly stabilised height at about 400ft. The situation was serious and the aircraft continued to descend. Baines quickly ascertained that his passengers could not swim, directed them to open the emergency hatches, main door and windows, and got McBride to move to the rear of the cabin to make the tail heavier and for him to be nearer the door.

Continuing to lose altitude Baines was forced to ditch the biplane into the sea at 9.50am. The touch-down was made tail-down but the fixed undercarriage dug into the water making for a sudden nose-over and swamping. The occupants survived the water impact and all, except Johnson, got out of the cabin, and stood on the trailing edge of the upper wing as the Dragonfly floated in an increasingly tail-up position. Fortunately the S.S. *Kakapo* which had just left Westport bound for Auckland was alerted to the disaster and made haste toward the ditching site. The aircraft was spotted tail up with the hapless swimmers but it was too late for Johnson, Walters and McBride. Only Baines and Hearty were picked up by a lifeboat but Hearty was unconscious and despite resuscitation efforts was later pronounced dead at the Westport wharf. The *Kakapo* reported the position of the mishap as off Westport Breakwater bearing 206 degrees, distant 6¾ miles and in 20 fathoms of water.

The accident led to a Court of Inquiry, convened at Hokitika on 26 January 1943 and then adjourned to Wellington. Efforts were made to try and locate the submerged Dragonfly by trawling but all were unsuccessful. However, the starboard propeller was eventually found in early March washed up on the beach at Patea in the North Island and the Inquiry recommenced. After examination it was considered that either the bolts securing the propeller had sheared, or the nuts had come off, but it was a mystery how this could have happened, especially as the aircraft had only flown five hours and five minutes since a 50-hour check. Mercer reported to the Inquiry he personally had checked the Dragonfly on the Sunday evening and on the Monday morning had started the engines and taxied the aircraft ready for departure. He had considered it safe for flying. Openshaw also gave evidence of inspecting and signing out the aircraft on the morning of the accident and said there was nothing visible that indicated any possible fault or trouble developing.

In May 1943 the Board of Enquiry made its report to the Minister in Charge of Civil Aviation. Loss of height from 400ft was attributed to extra drag caused by

AT FOOT: *An artist's impression of the sinking of ZK-AGP off the coast near Westport on 21 December 1942. The accident lead to the death of the four passengers by drowning. Despite persistent salvage attempts the Dragonfly remained on the sea bed* (Peter Scaife)

BELOW: *Tucked away in an Air Department file at National Archives are these small pieces of fabric from Dragonfly ZK-AGP, trawled up from a depth of 24 fathoms by the fishing boat* Mahutu, *nine months after the tragic accident. Their discovery spurred Openshaw into a concerted but unsuccessful attempt to recover the aircraft so that the cause of the accident could be determined.* (Graeme McConnell)

Arthur Baines flew for Air Travel (NZ) Ltd in the late 1930s and then again during his RNZAF service from early in 1942. He was the pilot of Dragonfly ZK-AGP which was forced to ditch in the sea near Westport on 21 December 1942 and did all he could to rescue the passengers.
(Whites Aviation via MOTAT)

the open hatch, open door and windows, and McBride moving to the rear of the cabin – all necessitating tail angle adjustments which likely accentuated the drag in the final stages of the flight. The Board considered the slackening of the hub bolts was progressive over a period of time and had extended beyond the period of five hours and five minutes since the final check. The Board decided uneven and possibly inadequate tightening of the hub bolts was the reason for their failure and they had not been properly checked by Openshaw. As a consequence, Openshaw's ground engineer's licence was cancelled in July 1943.

The accident was a tragedy for all concerned; four lives lost, no specialist support available to Baines, controversial blame on Openshaw, and damage to the airline's reputation. And there were further repercussions. Baines was convicted in the Hokitika court in April 1943 of assaulting Mercer, after being notified, without warning, of transfer back to the air force. On 7 September 1943 the fishing launch *Mahutu*, skippered by Geoff Brunell, while about five miles off the coast, just north of Denniston, recovered some aeroplane fabric in their trawl at a depth of 24 fathoms. This further spurred Openshaw into action and he obtained the rights to the sunken Dragonfly from the underwriters and in late 1943

RIGHT: *The wreckage of Fox Moth ZK-AEK at about 5000ft on the Franz Josef Glacier, just below the Almer Hut. The port wing took much of the impact and the passengers were fortunate the engine broke away to one side so that they just tumbled out onto the glacier.* (via Des Nolan Collection)

Taking a rest on the ice of Franz Josef Glacier are the four WAAF women (at centre) and 'Ozzie' Openshaw (bandage on head), the morning after the accident of Fox Moth ZK-AEK. The long cold night of 29 October 1943 had been cheered by the company, blankets and hot drinks supplied by the rescue party, seen here with the pilot and passengers.
(A. C. Graham Collection via Dorothy Fletcher)

and early 1944, in a determined effort to recover the wreckage and clear his name, undertook further trawling work. In one letter to Civil Aviation on 4 February 1944, he reported, "The aircraft broke surface but owing to the sea being most unsuitable, there being a heavy swell at the time, we had to abandon it. The aircraft acts as a sea anchor and whilst being hauled in towards the boat with winches very nearly overturned the boat twice, this being due to the heavy swell. The wire ropes were cut to save the situation." For many years a range of conspiracy theories continued to circulate, including very heavy freight in the rear locker and even deliberate sabotage. To add to the sorrow, Arthur Baines died prematurely in Tauranga in September 1947, aged 33 years, leaving his wife and infant daughter.

Notwithstanding wartime restrictions, usual services continued but one noteworthy incident occurred on 8 February 1943. Dragonfly ZK-AFB had the port engine fail while on a Nelson to Westport service, flown by Flight Lieutenant Colin Lewis, with four passengers. This happened about five miles south of Kahaurangi Point just after 1pm. Lewis turned the aircraft about, and by taking advantage of the uplift of wind currents from the hills was able to gain altitude, making 2000ft, and returned to Nelson via Westhaven, Collingwood, Takaka and Motueka, landing at Nelson at 1.53pm. It was a feat of good airmanship and the Dragonfly's ability to stay aloft was in marked contrast to the tragic Westport incident. Openshaw flew to Nelson in ZK-AEK and discovered the port magneto shaft had broken and upset the ignition timing. Soon after, veteran Fox Moth ZK-ADI was impressed into RNZAF service, leaving a reduced Air Travel fleet.

Later in 1943 another mishap occurred which attracted national attention. On 29 October Openshaw was doing scenic flying at Franz Josef. Four young women, all members of the WAAF, were keen for an early morning flight over the glacier before heading north. Margaret Cornwall, Molly Wilson, Clare McQuitty and Nell Ward crammed into the small passenger cabin of Fox Moth ZK-AEK. A fifteen minute flight was expected, but instead the women found themselves tumbling out onto the snow after the Fox Moth crashed high on the glacier. The passengers were unhurt with only Openshaw suffering a facial abrasion. A

Using a specially built skid arrangement, the Fox Moth fuselage is manhandled down the glacier by a team of fourteen men; six locals and eight climbers on loan from the Army and Air Force. November 1943.
(M.C. Lysons via A.C. Graham Collection via Dorothy Fletcher)

Carrying the fuselage of ZK-AEK up the moraine at the end of the lake, near the terminal face of the Franz Josef Glacier.
(M.C. Lysons via A.C. Graham Collection via Dorothy Fletcher)

Salvage complete, the Fox Moth fuselage loaded on the truck ready for the drive back to Hokitika and a long rebuild.
(M.C. Lysons via A.C. Graham Collection via Dorothy Fletcher)

Fox Moth ZK-ADI prominent over typical South Westland lowland forest and slow moving river. This 1997 view of the aircraft is reminiscent of similar flying in the 1930s and 1940s. (John King)

contemporary of Openshaw, and fellow engineer, Spencer Barnard, reminisced in 2007 about the wartime accident. He said, "What happened was a very controlled forced landing. He was forced down by a downdraft, stronger than usual, and came to a fully stalled condition with only 50 yards to go to a drop of 500ft or so off the glacier. His actions were; switch off the motor, so there would be less chance of fire, tell the girls to 'hang on', and drift strongly to port to wipe off the undercarriage. It was due to the skill of 'Ozzie' as a pilot that there were no injuries at all to his passengers."

While Openshaw said the crash was caused by a down-draught, the evidence more likely suggested inexperience and disorientation in white-out type conditions with loss of horizon. No formal inquiry was held but the officers investigating the accident instead recommended the issue of a notice to airmen drawing the attention of pilots to the necessity of maintaining continuous observation of air speed when flying in the immediate vicinity of high mountains. Also the need to recover flying speed in the event of such action becoming necessary and the avoidance of flying in close proximity to high hills on their lee side.

It was reported in late 1943 that the loss of the Fox Moth on the Franz Josef Glacier was indirectly responsible for bringing the whitebait fishing season in the far south of Westland to a premature end! With only one aircraft available for southern services there was no other means of transporting whitebait to Hokitika. More seriously, Mercer lost confidence in Openshaw and refused to allow him to work which made for an awkward stand-off until Openshaw eventually left and went to Australia.

By early 1944 with only one Dragonfly, and one Fox Moth airworthy, there was an urgent need for an additional larger capacity aircraft. Wartime constraints meant a new aircraft was out of the question, so Air Travel (NZ) Ltd negotiated with the de Havilland factory in Wellington to purchase the former East Coast Airways DH84 Dragon ZK-ADR/AER. As NZ551 with the RNZAF, it had suffered a landing accident at Rongotai and was considered surplus to air force requirements. Completely refurbished it was compatible with the other Air Travel aircraft using the same Gipsy Major engines. After flight testing at Wellington John Neave delivered the aircraft, now re-registered ZK-AHT, to Hokitika on 23 March 1944 in a flight time of three hours and fifteen minutes. Even though the Dragon was older and not very elegant it was quickly put to use on the northern routes and made a number of flights south.

Two months later Neave delivered Fox Moth ZK-AEK to Hokitika, following its major rebuild after the spectacular glacier accident. He also brought down in the Fox Moth a couple of officials for the opening of the new Air Travel (NZ) Ltd administration offices at Southside. On 22 May 1944 a festive occasion marked the opening of the new offices and waiting rooms. A contemporary newspaper described the building. "The new premises are of a compact nature, and should prove eminently suitable for their purpose. Entrance by the front door leads into a passage from which branch off the main office, chief clerk's office, a lounge, a pilot's room, director's room, additions to stores department and conveniences. The whole are well lighted, and attractively finished off and furnished."

Air Travel's DH89 Rapide ZK-AHS, formerly Cook Strait Airways ZK-AGT, was purchased in December 1944. The Rapide was mainly used on the northern services but also did flights, like this one, to South Westland. (Suttie Collection)

Fox Moth ZK-AGM, flown by 'Ozzie' Openshaw, on a flight to Nelson, about 1943.
(Openshaw Collection)

Captain James Cuthbert 'Bert' Mercer, 1886-1944.

With the opening of the offices the airline celebrated the 10th anniversary of the company's operations. The Hon James O'Brien, Minister of Transport and MP for Westland, declared the new building open and the airline's Chairman of Directors, Mr Chapman, gave a brief overview of the local expansion of air services and took the opportunity to announce an order for a Rapide aircraft which it was hoped would be shipped from England later in the year. He remarked, "Although Britain is totally at war she can still deliver the goods." Mr Aldridge, Chief Postmaster at Greymouth, commented the South Westland postal air postal service was still unique in the world, because the fees charged were the same as those for the ordinary postal rates.

Many of the speeches at the opening of the new offices paid tribute to the pioneering work done by Bert Mercer. When replying, his comments were carefully noted by a local reporter and printed a day or so later. As it turned out, Mercer's words were to be his last public comment on aviation and have a prophetic tone. "Captain Mercer who was especially well received, said the day was a specially notable one for the opening of the new offices, and he thanked the builder (Mr F. Williamson) for the fine job he had made. He also must mention the great service rendered by Mr Paul Renton, Snr, who had given every assistance, including the strip of land on which the aerodrome stood. He thanked them all for their kind words in regard to his services, but he assured them that had it not been for the fine help he received he could not have made a success. He specially mentioned Wing-Commander Hewett, and said without the help of the others he could not have carried on in the early days. He had also to thank his ground staff and the pilots who had carried on the good work. In the early days they could land almost anywhere, but now regulations must be complied with and they were doing their utmost to comply with them. He thanked the heads of the Civil Aviation and Public Works Department, and Post and Telegraph Department, and the Radio Service for all their kind help. He had never yet found them to fail. He wished to thank the press for much free publicity which he had not to pay for. He had also a wonderful wife and family, who had given him great support. The future of aviation was in its infancy. He predicted great strides in the Air Services of New

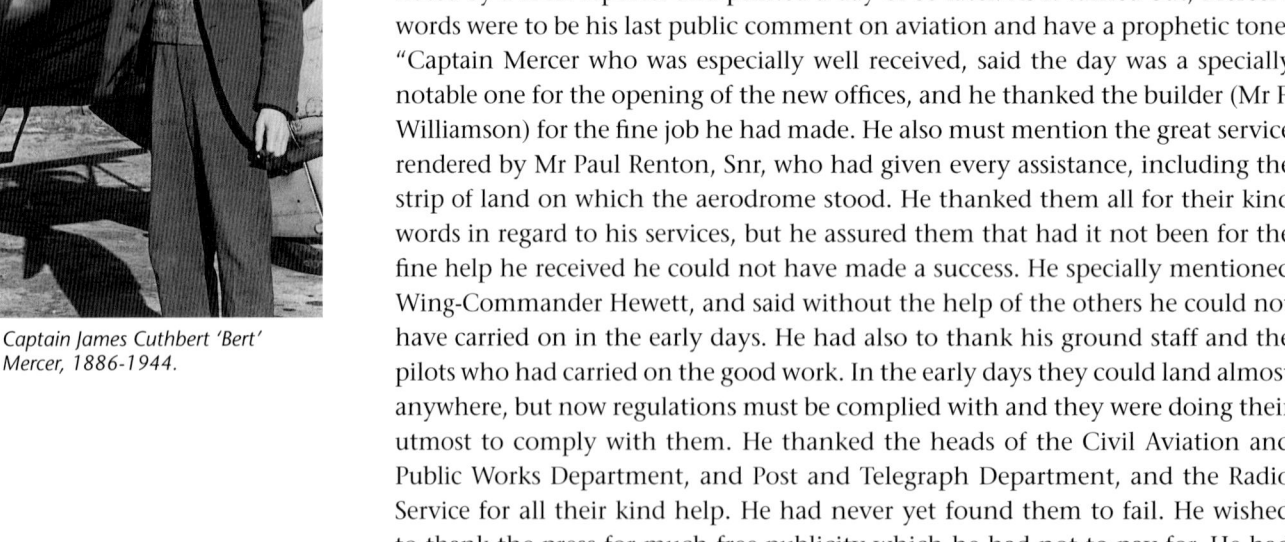

CONTINUED ON PAGE 69

DRAGON CRASH NEAR KAWATIRI JUNCTION

IT ALL HAPPENED in a few seconds. The small Dragon airliner with pilot and six passengers was flying low over the hills to the north east of Murchison. Next moment, the aircraft was caught in unexpected turbulence, banked steeply, suddenly dropped a wing, clipped a large beech tree, and plunged its way through the dense forest canopy. Still strapped to their seats, pilot and passengers were catapulted out of the disintegrating fuselage and thrown down the hillside.

The crash of Air Travel (NZ) Ltd's DH84 Dragon ZK-AHT on a lower slope of Mount Hope, near Kawatiri Junction, on Friday 30 June 1944 was a major national incident, even in wartime.

That afternoon the weather at Nelson had been cold and fine as Flight Lieutenant Colin Lewis prepared for the scheduled service to Westport and Hokitika. Onboard was Bert Mercer and Maurice Dawe, Air Travel's company secretary, both returning from a business trip to Wellington. Passengers George Stratmore and Bruce Perry were senior managers with Macduff's, Wellington, on their way to the West Coast for business. Eva Russell was going home to Granity and Matron Nell Paterson was returning to work at Westport's Buller Hospital.

The Dragon, without any radio equipment, departed Nelson at 1.10pm and headed south. When the aircraft approached Glenhope, on a course slightly to the left of the main road, Lewis observed the edge of a squall in the vicinity of Kawatiri Junction and also the low cloud cover. He altered course a few degrees to starboard to pass over the saddle of a spur, running down the eastern slope of Mount Hope towards Kawatiri Junction, to come out near Gowan Bridge on the South West side of the spur. At 1.48pm the Dragon crossed the saddle at a height of about 200ft and immediately encountered a violent up-draught. Lewis lost control as the aircraft veered up and very quickly developed a steep right-hand turn in a nose-down stalled attitude, continuing through a swing of 160 degrees. The starboard wing hit the forest cover below the northern slope of the saddle at an altitude of about 1760ft above sea level. As a part of the fuselage impaled in the upper branches of a large beech tree, the nose section and wings broke off throwing its occupants to the ground.

Lewis was thrown out through the smashed cockpit and although very dazed was on his feet almost immediately. In the front passenger seats Maurice Dawe was killed instantly and Bert Mercer was severely injured. Nell Paterson found herself sitting on the ground still strapped to her seat but with a broken pelvis. Eva Russell's legs were broken. Perry had been hit in the chest and was ill but conscious. Stratmore was eventually heard moving about in the wrecked fuselage suspended in the trees but soon fell out and rolled down the hill near to where Eva Russell lay.

The first aid kit had fortunately fallen near Nell Paterson, and with Lewis's help, she was able to give Mercer and herself an injection of morphine to deaden the pain. Lewis and Mercer conferred about their position in relation to the main Nelson-West Coast Road. Lewis, Perry and Stratmore then decided to walk out and raise the alarm. They left the crash-site at 5pm as the winter temperature continued to drop and it was getting dark. Stratmore was soon forced back, and the conditions of rain, sleet and cold were very unpleasant for Lewis

ZK-AHT soon after its rebuild by the de Havilland factory at Rongotai, Wellington, ready for Air Travel (NZ) Ltd service. This was the first civil aircraft supplied to a private airline by the de Havilland Aircraft Company of New Zealand. March 1944. (via Don Noble)

and Perry, who were still nursing their injuries. Lewis collapsed after several hours, not far from the road, but Perry was able to make it out to the deserted highway near Woodhen Bend. He had been walking for only about ten minutes when along came a Nelson bound Transport (Nelson) Ltd truck, driven by Arthur Hughes. Taken to the Gowan Bridge store, Perry was attended to by the Diserens family and the police were notified. Percy Diserens and Hughes quickly returned to Woodhen Bend, entered the bush and were soon able to locate Lewis and bring him out to the road.

Westport Aeradio had reported the Dragon half an hour overdue at 3.10pm and Civil Aviation and other authorities were notified by 3.45pm. The Police pursued various reports of sightings but with failing mid-winter darkness it was a tense evening for all concerned, especially family of those on the missing aircraft. Finally at 10pm Murchison Police sent word about Perry and confirmed the aircraft had crashed near Kawatiri Junction. After midnight the news came through of the passenger situation as the local rescue teams, including police and doctor, reached the isolated crash site. Conditions were very serious in the freezing cold. Bert Mercer had sadly succumbed to his injuries and died not long before rescuers arrived. The other passengers were carried out in the early hours of the morning in a four hour rescue exercise and taken to Nelson Hospital for a long convalescent time. A relief party of Public Works employees brought down the two bodies and also collected luggage and other property.

It quickly became apparent the crash-site could not be identified from the air, so the heroic efforts of Perry to struggle out to the road undoubtedly saved lives. The efficient help of rescuers, especially teams of local Murchison, Owen River and Glenhope volunteers, as well as police and doctors who made the arduous tramp to the crash site, all contributed to helping the serious situation.

Extensive media attention was given to the crash and rescue efforts. The death of Mercer was lamented on the West Coast and throughout New Zealand. He was the country's best known pilot with over 11,000 flying hours during the previous 27 years. The Minister of Civil Aviation, the Hon Fred Jones, said Captain Mercer had contributed more than any other single individual to the successful establishment of commercial aviation in New Zealand.

A combined funeral was held for Mercer and 36-year-old Dawe, a public accountant and member of the Hokitika firm of Wild, Wilkinson and Dawe. Their bodies lay in the new administration offices from Sunday 2 July and on Tuesday 4 July an open-air service was led by the local Anglican minister, Reverend H.A. Childs and Presbyterian minister, Reverend K.A. Hadfield. A long cortege of hearses, family and friends, trucks laden with wreaths, mourners in cars and on foot, then made its way from the aerodrome to the Hokitika Cemetery. The cemetery services, amongst the largest seen in Hokitika, were conducted for Mercer by Reverend Hadfield and for Dawe by Reverend Childs. At the conclusion of the service a Fox Moth, flown by Jim Kennedy and draped with black streamers, circled the cemetery three times.

A Board of Inquiry later found the accident arose through the Dragon flying into rough air conditions and getting into an uncontrolled position from which it was not recoverable. It was determined this situation arose because the aircraft was flown in rough air conditions at low altitude over hilly country. The situation could have been avoided, suggested the Inquiry, if the aircraft had maintained more altitude consistent with keeping below the cloud base while crossing the low saddle. The crash served as a timely warning to all commercial operators of the dangers of New Zealand's turbulence when flying low over rugged terrain.

A week after the crash of Dragon ZK-AHT the RNZAF took a special photograph of the crash area. Survivors came down the gully leading to Woodhen Bend (out of sight) on the main Nelson-West Coast road. (RNZAF Official)

KIWI NEWS

NEWSPAPER OF NEW ZEALAND EXPEDITIONARY FORCE IN PACIFIC

VOLUME 2, No 30   TUESDAY, JULY 4, 1944

AIR CRASH ON WEST COAST
Two Killed, Five Injured When Plane Descends in Bush

While on a flight from Nelson to Hokitika on Friday an aeroplane belonging to Air Travel (NZ) Ltd Westport. on Mt Hope in thick bush country between the pilot. The machine was carrying Hokitika, was killed out... One of the passen... also of Hokitika w... Capt...

£2 Million Fund For Care Of Soldiers   **AFTER THE WAR** Plans for an... returned...

Zealand. After the war they could look for Auckland to be reached from Hokitika in 3 ½ to 4 hours, and to Christchurch in 45 minutes. There was nothing to stop anyone leaving Hokitika every hour for the East Coast, with a frequent service to Australia. One would be able to charter a plane to see the Melbourne Cup and to come back the same evening, if desired. He wanted a shingle runway on our aviation ground, as of the 19 days lost last year a few of them were due to the wet conditions of the aerodrome. He wished to thank the de Havilland company for their work on the aircraft and engines, and to thank all present for their presence, support and attention."

After Mercer's death, his wife Jane moved to Christchurch to be closer to relatives. The South Westland air service continued with its usual versatility and the northern routes were re-instituted with Dragonfly ZK-AFB. Bill Dini was appointed Acting Manager and the only pilot was young Jim Kennedy, on loan from the air force. Kennedy was initially only licensed to fly the Fox Moths but eventually gained licences to fly the Dragonfly and later Rapide ZK-AHS. This new aircraft was a former Cook Strait Airways aircraft, ZK-AGT, which had survived extensive wartime use and was only the second RNZAF aircraft to be converted back to civil use.

In late November 1944 John Neave flight tested Rapide ZK-AHS at Rongotai and Flight Lieutenant Suttie delivered it to Hokitika on 3 December 1944. Kennedy later wrote of his admiration of the type and especially one flight in ZK-AHS on the Hokitika to Nelson route. "I consider the Rapide to be the best bad weather

In the days following the accident Air Travel engineers and helpers recover the engines and other salvageable items from the wreckage of Dragon ZK-AHT. (via Ian Woolhouse)

The smashed remains of part of the fuselage among the trees and dense bush on the lower slopes of Mount Hope near Kawatiri Junction. (via Don Perry)

On a Saturday morning in 1945 a Westland Transport Ltd truck delivers mail and freight at Southside for flights to South Westland. Pilot Jim Kennedy recalled, "A lot of the mail was cartons of beer – the cheapest way to send it!" (Jim Kennedy)

Air Travel (NZ) Ltd administration staff Jean Stoop (left) and Margaret Penman on the steps, beside Rapide ZK-AHS, at Southside Aerodrome, 1946. (Margaret McKenzie)

At Westport, Air Travel's Rapide ZK-AHS (right) and Dragonfly ZK-AFB meet up during scheduled flights from Nelson and Hokitika. (Suttie Collection)

aircraft I ever flew. It had particularly good visibility with the two triangular windows opening on either side of the cockpit windscreen. With the cockpit door shut there was little draft, even with both these small windows open. You could go down to 300-400ft no trouble. It was flying by the seat of your pants. I had one memorable flight on the Westport-Nelson route flying AHS with six passengers around Golden Bay, the long way round, with weather very bad and closing in. I was flying low to see the way ahead with windows open. Very low cloud. All of a sudden I saw a headland ahead near the Golden Bay Cement works. I made an evasive turn to port to avoid the headland. I have not forgotten that flight."

In early 1945 the sad news reached Hokitika of the death of 'Ozzie' Openshaw in Australia. On 31 January Openshaw had been flying as co-pilot for Australian National Airways in Stinson Model A VH-UYY on a scheduled flight from Essendon Airport to Broken Hill, via Kerang and Mildura, with eight passengers. While near the farming community of Spring Plains, the Stinson's port outer wing and tail assembly detached, the aircraft quickly broke up and plunged to the ground, killing all on board. Later investigations discovered the wing failure was due to one of the first identified cases of metal fatigue.

With pilot shortages continuing because of the war, John Neave did a number of relieving stints at Hokitika during 1945. Harry Worrall took over the role of Managing Director of Air Travel (NZ) Ltd and his business experience and wide contacts proved useful as the Government took steps to implement recent legislation to compulsorily acquire all private airlines and combine them into the new New Zealand National Airways Corporation (NAC).

Fortuitously Worrall was appointed in August 1946 as one of the foundation directors of NAC and this ensured good communications in the process of Air Travel (NZ) Ltd being absorbed into the new network. Maurice Clarke, NAC's General Manager, and other senior NAC management worked with Worrall to ensure a smooth take-over of the West Coast based operation. The Air Travel directors accepted a £20,000 offer for the share value of the airline. Throughout 1947 there was increasingly close liaison between NAC and Air Travel with the Corporation's Dominie aircraft being utilised for northern route flying. It was planned that Air Travel (NZ) Ltd would be absorbed on 1 April 1947 but this was delayed through the complexity of other challenges facing NAC, until 1 October. The private enterprise efforts of Air Travel (NZ) Ltd had been a considerable success, largely due to the efforts of Bert Mercer and those who took a shareholding in the pioneering airline.

DH90A DRAGONFLY ZK-AFB

DRAGONFLY WITH constructor number 7560 was built in 1937 by the de Havilland Aircraft Co Ltd, at Hatfield, England, and shipped to New Zealand. Assembled at Wigram and registered ZK-AFB, it was flown across the Southern Alps by Bert Mercer, arriving in Hokitika on 29 October 1937.

With fleet "No.3" painted on its nose, it made regular beach landings in South Westland during the late 1930s and early 1940s as part of its versatile use by Air Travel (NZ) Ltd. It was a favourite aircraft of Mercer and flown extensively by him until his death in 1944. With the outbreak of World War II in September 1939 ZK-AFB and Air Travel's other Dragonfly ZK-AGP were used on the Hokitika-Greymouth-Westport-Nelson service, previously operated by Cook Strait Airways Ltd.

During the war years Mercer used ZK-AFB for many reconnaissance patrols from Nelson in the North to Stewart Island in the South. Considering its modest power and capacity and reputation for ground-looping, the Dragonfly did remarkably well on West Coast operations, except for several incidents. The aircraft's undercarriage collapsed at Bruce Bay on 18 January 1942, it ran into a fence after landing at Greymouth on 24 September 1942 damaging the port lower wing and breaking the port propeller and, at Franz Josef, on 19 July 1945, the port lower wing was again damaged when it ran off the runway.

With the prospect of NAC taking over Air Travel, and following the loss of ZK-AGP, Dragonfly ZK-AFB, as last of type, was sold in late 1946 to the Canterbury Aero Club. However it soon after returned to Hokitika for a one month charter to NAC. The aero club made extensive use of the Dragonfly for charter work and advanced training. It continued to be used for ambulance flights and was also utilised for "whooping cough" charter flights to high altitude to help relieve the coughing symptoms of young children.

The Dragonfly design was, because of the small vertical fin and rudder area, prone to directional instability once on the ground during the landing run. Despite careful training and supervision by Chief Instructor John Neave, formerly of Air Travel, several pilots ground-looped ZK-AFB during the late 1940s and early 1950s.

Sold in August 1956 to Aircraft Engineering Ltd of Wellington, it was based in Masterton and used for a variety of charter type roles, including having a hatch fitted for aerial photography work. In late 1959 it was stored for a time before being sold to veteran Nelson pilot Arthur Bradshaw. A major refurbishment was completed during 1960 with the Dragonfly taking to the air again in October wearing new dark blue and white livery and named *Kiwi Rover*. Bradshaw used the Dragonfly for pleasure flying and then sold it to Brian Chadwick of Christchurch in May 1961. ZK-AFB was purchased to expand Chadwick's business which traded under the title "Air Charter", and once again the aircraft was used for a variety of roles. On 12 February 1962, Chadwick, with four passengers, including a honeymoon couple, took off from Christchurch International Airport on a scenic flight to Milford Sound. The aircraft did not arrive and even with the largest aerial search ever undertaken in New Zealand, *Kiwi Rover* and all onboard were never found. Without question Dragonfly ZK-AFB continues to be New Zealand's most-searched-for aircraft.

Flown by Bert Mercer, ZK-AFB takes off from Greymouth in 1939.
(Whites Aviation)

DH90A DRAGONFLY ZK-AGP

THE LAST DRAGONFLY built by de Havilland, with constructor number 7566, came to New Zealand. It was assembled at Rongotai, Wellington, in November 1938 and registered ZK-AGP. Carrying fleet "No.5" it was quickly put to use on South Westland routes and from the following year was busy on the northern route to Greymouth, Westport and Nelson.

At Franz Josef on 13 February 1939 a PWD tractor was started in reverse gear and ran backwards into the Dragonfly, which was parked in the hangar, ramming it and badly damaging the starboard lower wing. While flying ZK-AGP in November 1941 Bert Mercer secured his 10,000th flying hour – a milestone event for a New Zealand pilot.

The fate of ZK-AGP was sealed on 21 December 1942 when it was being flown by Flight Lieutenant Arthur Baines on the northern route through to Nelson. After leaving Westport, and while over the sea, the starboard propeller came off and the aircraft was unable to return to the aerodrome. Although the pilot made a successful ditching the four passengers could not swim and drowned with only Baines surviving. Many attempts were made to trawl and locate the sunken Dragonfly, including extensive charters of Greymouth trawler *Silver Fern* by both Air Travel (NZ) Ltd and the Air Department. In spite of systematic trawling efforts, the search was eventually abandoned. So this Dragonfly also disappeared – except for scraps of fabric retrieved from the sea near Westport and the starboard propeller which eventually washed up on a North Island beach.

Soon after assembly at Wellington ZK-AGP is ready for the delivery flight to Hokitika, November 1938. (Waugh Collection)

WHAT TO SEE TODAY

Hokitika Cemetery

On the hill near the airport is the historic Hokitika Cemetery. A number of graves of people with links to the pioneering aviation era are located here including Jack Renton, Bert Mercer, Maurice Dawe, Tom Harris, Geoffrey Houston, Frank Molloy and Des Wright. Mercer's grave is especially prominent.

Kawatiri Junction Plaque

At Kawatiri Junction, near the old railway station, is a bronze memorial plaque, faced with local river stones, commemorating the 30 June 1944 accident of Air Travel (NZ) Ltd Dragon ZK-AHT. Bert Mercer and company secretary Maurice Dawe died in this accident. Designed by Graeme McConnell this memorial was unveiled by Bert Mercer's daughter, Marie, at a special dedication service attended by about 120 people on 16 December 1994, as part of the 60th anniversary celebrations of the South Westland air service.

Westport Airport Plaque

Situated in the carpark near the Westport Airport Terminal building is a bronze aviation plaque memorial, designed by Graeme McConnell, and dedicated by Rev Richard Waugh on 17 December 2005. It marks the accident of Air Travel (NZ) Ltd's Dragonfly ZK-AGP which crashed into the sea off Westport on 21 December 1942 with the loss of four lives. This was only the second fatal accident involving passengers on a scheduled air service in New Zealand.

NORMAN ALEXANDER SUTTIE
Senior Pilot

Suttie became Air Travel's senior pilot after Mercer's death. He was born on 1 September 1911 at Spreydon, Christchurch, to Alexander and Jemima Suttie and attended Addington School and Christchurch Technical College.

After leaving school at the age of 17 years he worked on Pitt Island, part of the Chatham Islands group, doing farm work, including mustering. He later returned to Christchurch to work for the P & D Duncan Foundry in St Asaph Street. While working there he had a milk and paper round to help pay for flying lessons. He later worked for John Burns & Co Ltd, until he joined the RNZAF.

Suttie learnt to fly under Mr Sidney Gibbons, of the Canterbury Aero Club at Wigram Aerodrome and gained his 'A' licence in July 1936 and his 'B' licence in March 1939. He was commissioned as a pilot officer in the RNZAF on 16 September 1939 and was posted to Taieri as an instructor on Tiger Moths with No.1 EFTS. On 19 June 1940 he was involved in the crash of Tiger Moth NZ712, which resulted in serious injury and he spent nine months in hospital. He later took up navigational instruction. In April 1942 he was promoted to flight lieutenant, lectured at Rotorua and was later engaged in anti-aircraft training at Hobsonville.

From September 1943 to May 1944 Suttie was seconded to Air Travel (NZ) Ltd at Hokitika and flew extensively on the airline's South Westland and northern routes. During this time he flew 791 hours on Fox Moth, Dragon and Dragonfly aircraft. He then returned to the RNZAF and served as a member of No.42 Squadron at Rongotai.

Suttie began employment again with Air Travel (NZ) Ltd in early 1945, and in turn became a New Zealand National Airways Corporation pilot when NAC took over the airline in late 1947. He continued flying until he resigned in 1950 to take up employment as chief flying instructor with the Waikato Aero Club. At this time he had about 6500 flying hours. On 14 July 1951, while engaged in dual flying instruction to student Albert Christoffels in Tiger Moth ZK-ARY, the aircraft went into a spin, struck high-tension power lines and crashed on a farm at Kaipaki. The student survived and recovered from his injuries but Suttie died at the scene, leaving his wife Nancy and children Jill and John.

Flight Lieutenant Norm Suttie at Franz Josef.
(Suttie Collection)

The Dragon memorial plaque at Kawatiri Junction.
(Graeme McConnell)

The memorial plaque for Dragonfly ZK-AGP unveiled at Westport Airport on 17 December 2005.
(Alison Morgan)

COMMEMORATION SERVICE & DEDICATION OF AVIATION MEMORIAL PLAQUE

In memory of: Mr Michael Hearty, Mr Albert Johnson, Mr Geoffrey McBride and Mr Albert Walters, who died in the accident of the Air Travel (NZ) Ltd DH 90A Dragonfly ZK-AGP on 21 December 1942 and in tribute to the pilot, Flt. Lt. Arthur Baines

2pm Saturday 17 December 2005

Westport Airport

Rapide ZK-AHS drying out after major flooding at the Southside Aerodrome, 30 September 1947. Note the high water line on the fuselage. From left: Ross King, Harry Howard, Dick Ferguson and Frank Molloy. (via Jim Jamieson)

(Civil Aviation Branch of Air Department, November 1945)

Betty Eggeling and son Clifford at Haast in 1947. (via Roger Eggeling)

4
Nationalisation
NAC 1947-1956

CHANGE AT AIR TRAVEL (NZ) Ltd had been anticipated for a number of years. The Government had clearly indicated during World War II that the post-war airline scene would be very different and under Government control. The passing of the *New Zealand National Airways Act* into law on 7 December 1945 set the stage for a new era of nationalised airline expansion. From about the time of Mercer's death in June 1944 the management of Air Travel was aware of this impending change and in the early post-war period another Government decision had also confirmed the construction of the new Seaview Aerodrome at Hokitika.

Amid these political decisions the South Westland air service continued as it had done for many years. The pending NAC take-over meant there was a lengthy period of consultation between the new NAC management and Air Travel management about all aspects of the Hokitika based operations. NAC Dominies flew from the Southside Aerodrome for the first time in early 1947 and Frank Molloy did familiarisation flights in ZK-AKT on 14 February.

For the final Air Travel flights in late September 1947 some privately prepared souvenir airmail covers were flown to South Westland. The take-over date had been delayed six months until 1 October 1947, as NAC staff found themselves very busy with the huge task of setting up a national airline network and it was easier to leave the self-contained West Coast operation to carry on by itself for a while longer. On the first day of official NAC operations, Commander Frank Molloy (with his new NAC title) flew Fox Moth ZK-AGM south to the Mussel Point airstrip with mail for Okuru, Upper Okuru and Jackson Bay. On the northern route, Commander J.F. 'Jimmy' Cane, also with long-time West Coast links, flew Rapide ZK-AHS to Westport but encountered engine trouble and was not able to go on to Nelson. On 2 October Dominie ZK-AKS, again flown by 'Jimmy' Cane, took the mail north to Westport where it was transferred to Dominie ZK-AKY, flown by Commander R.E. 'Rocky' Overell, for the flight to Nelson.

The change-over was not without incident. Ross King remembers, "After NAC had taken over, the stopbank gave way toward the tip end of the drome one night about 9pm. Frank Molloy, myself and Harry Howard were on the railway bridge watching the flood and actually saw the water starting to flood the drome. We quickly ran down and Frank and Harry put the tail of ZK-AGM up on a trestle while I ran into the storeroom and quickly grabbed everything up off the floor as the water rose. I put a lot on top of a table which was at least four foot six from ground level but the water went three inches over the table! The oil which we drained from the planes during checks went into drums

Norm Suttie nursing a sore right hand after being whacked by a Fox Moth propellor. Margaret Penman at left with engineer Bert Allard's daughter. (via Margaret McKenzie)

but unfortunately the tops were not on so everything became covered in black oil. It took some time to clean up ZK-AHS and dry her out. ZK-AGM had floated off the trestle but luckily did not get damaged. It was funny to see the water squirting though the gaps in the hangar doors!"

Commander Norm Suttie flew the first official NAC Rapide/Dominie service to Haast on 1 June 1948. While there had been DH89 charters to the glaciers from the late 1930s and ZK-AHS had been used occasionally in South Westland from early 1945 this flight was the first regular service using the type. However it was to be short lived, as from 9 August 1948 Civil Aviation revoked the licence for NAC to operate DH89 aircraft from the Southside Aerodrome, due to continuing surface issues. NAC was therefore forced to reintroduce Fox Moths on all services south and also north to Greymouth and Westport. Commander Bill Miles flew the last NAC Dominie out of Southside.

One of the few incidents during the NAC years occurred on 30 October 1948 when Fox Moth ZK-ASP, flown by relieving pilot Graeme Barnett, was leaving from Haast. Large pools of water on the runway affected the take-off, but with brakes waterlogged and take-off aborted, the Fox Moth continued on through a fence.

NAC Dominie ZK-AKY Tui at Seaview Aerodrome, Hokitika, on the morning of the first charter flight to Milford Sound, 25 July 1956. In front of aircraft from left are Max Dowell, Phillip Dowell, Malcolm Dowell, Kaye Marshall and Murray Marshall.
(Alf Marshall via Kaye McNabb)

FRANK MOLLOY – Senior Route Pilot

SECOND ONLY TO BERT MERCER in Fox Moth flying experience on the West Coast, Frank Molloy was born at Taylorville, near Greymouth, on 22 July 1910, the second of two sons to Emma and James Molloy. He attended Greymouth High School and after leaving school worked in a cycle shop and as a volunteer fireman. Showing good mechanical aptitude he became interested in flying and began lessons at Greymouth in late 1933. By December he was undergoing dual instruction on Robinson Redwing ZK-ADD.

From March 1934 he continued training with the West Coast United Aero Club at Hokitika, achieving his "A" Licence in September 1935 and "B" Licence in January 1939. During this time he did extensive aero club flying on the West Coast and cross-country flights to Canterbury.

Molloy joined the RNZAF in April 1941, and started initial flying at Taieri the following month, with further extensive training in Canada flying Cessna Cranes with No.4 SFTS at Saskatoon. By late 1941 he was with No.3 School of General Reconnaissance at Squire's Gate, Blackpool, England, then posted to Northern Ireland. From December 1942 he gained further experience with RAF Coastal Command's No.5 OTU at Megaberry, near Belfast, on Airspeed Oxford and Handley Page Hampden aircraft. In April 1943 he was posted for metrological duties to No.1407 Flight (later No.251 Squadron) in Iceland flying on Lockheed Hudsons and Venturas and Avro Ansons. This flying involved extensive meteorological reconnaissance flights and air-sea rescue duties over the North Atlantic.

By June 1944 Molloy was back in England and following a posting to No.1525 BAT Flight at Docking, he returned to New Zealand in December. By this time his total flying hours were 736 hours solo and 96 hours dual.

After leaving the air force he worked for Shell Oil at Greymouth, before joining the flying staff of Air Travel (NZ) Ltd. His first flight was in Fox Moth ZK-AGM on 15 November 1945 and his first scheduled service was in the same aircraft on 13 December. Molloy's pre-war West Coast flying, combined with his wartime meteorological flying experience from Iceland, made him especially competent as a West Coast pilot. In May 1946 he undertook instruction on Dragonfly ZK-AFB with Norm Suttie and the following month on Rapide ZK-AHS. He flew all the West Coast based NAC Dominies until the DH89s were withdrawn from use at Southside in late 1948.

Molloy attended an instrument flying course on the NAC Link Trainer at Palmerston North from June to August 1949 and then a short training/familiarisation course in August-September on DC-3, Lodestar and Electra aircraft.

Appointed NAC Senior Route Pilot for South Westland from 1 October 1949, he continued with extensive Fox Moth flying until Rapide ZK-AHS was returned to the new Hokitika Airport in March 1952. From this time Molloy flew the Rapide and a range of Dominies (ZK-AKT, ZK-AKU, ZK-AKY and ZK-ALB) more extensively than the Fox Moths. His last Fox Moth flights were: ZK-AEK on 23 March 1953, ZK-ASP (formerly ZK-ADI) on 30 November 1953 and ZK-AGM on 14 July 1955.

With the sale of the NAC South Westland air service, Molloy declined a transfer from the West Coast and retired from the corporation with his last flight in Dominie ZK-AKY on 29 September 1956. His total flying hours were 7580 with the large majority of these, 6975 hours, flown on Air Travel and NAC routes between 1945 and 1956. This placed him second only to Bert Mercer in South Westland de Havilland biplane flying experience.

Molloy and his family stayed on in Hokitika, unlike most other South Westland air service pilots. He worked for Winter Brothers and Brown Walters garages and then for twelve years as caretaker at the Hokitika Primary School. He died on 3 November 1973, survived by his wife June and four sons, Philip, Richard, Keith and Gavin. ∎

Frank Molloy in a Fox Moth cockpit, July 1947. (Whites Aviation via MOTAT)

Doug Lister commenced a permanent flying appointment at Hokitika in January 1949 with the Fox Moths and later the Dominies. He later reminisced about his first flights being delayed due to bad weather and when he did land at Franz Josef, and step down from the Fox Moth, he was ankle deep in water. He also commented about the ease of flying the Dominie and recalled how he flew most of the way back to Hokitika one day with the aircraft so well trimmed he just put his hand out the cockpit window to slightly change direction!

Noel Finch worked at Hokitika Aeradio in 1949 and 1950 and later wrote, "The receiving station was located a couple of miles south of the old airfield, near the beach. When the NAC Fox Moth was heading for Haast in the mornings, the pilot, often Frank Molloy or Doug Lister, would throw us our copy of *The Press* from the cockpit. They could usually get it pretty close to the doorstep!"

The South Westland air service carried a wide range of people. Thora McDougall was a Plunket nurse from 1949 to 1951 and recently recalled, "Every eight weeks I would fly to Haast in the Fox Moth on the Monday. The mothers at Haast would congregate at one house and I would examine and weigh the babies in the afternoon. Most of the Haast women had husbands who worked on the road being formed to Wanaka. The next day I would go to Okuru and check the babies there and fly back to Hokitika on Wednesday morning. In 1950 I was able to attend the annual Whitebaiters' Ball which was held in the

Captain Frank Molloy in his new NAC uniform. He was appointed Senior Route Pilot in October 1949. (via Ian Woolhouse)

In the Southside hangar, engineer Dick Ferguson does maintenance work on NAC Rapide ZK-AHS Mokai. (via Dick Ferguson)

At Christmas time 1948, Fox Moth ZK-AEK is ready for passengers at Westport's Kawatiri Airport and a flight south. (D.A.Walker Collection)

This Miles Gemini ZK-AQO Mokai *was the first new aircraft purchased by New Zealand National Airways Corporation (NAC). It was briefly put into service on the South Westland route in March 1948 but found to be unsuitable and withdrawn. Engineer Tom Harris (at left) has a smoke while watching Ross King refuelling.* (Suttie Collection)

Okuru Hall, at the end of the whitebait season. The hall was decorated and all the families from Haast and Okuru were in attendance and the festivities didn't end until daylight."

In 1948 Colin Lewis was transferred to clerical staff duties at Paraparaumu and Norm Suttie moved in early 1950 to become Chief Flying Instructor for the Waikato Aero Club. An NAC Internal Services report in February 1950 commented with regard to the South Westland services, "A suitable twin engined type of aircraft is not yet in view and therefore the service must continue to be operated by Fox Moth aircraft." At the same time the idea of a Hokitika to Christchurch service was also noted. "The extension of the present West Coast service to Hokitika and introduction of a service between Hokitika and Christchurch might not be possible in 1950. The latter section cannot be implemented until essential radio and navigational aids are installed." In fact the trans-alpine

Norm Suttie was one of a number of pilots who enjoyed occasional flights in the Miles Gemini while stored at Hokitika from April 1948 to January 1949. (Suttie Collection)

At Haast Aerodrome Fox Moth ZK-AEK is unloaded after arriving from Hokitika, flown by Captain Doug Lister, August 1949. Myrtle Cron is in front of the aircraft. (via D.A.Walker Collection)

Dr JEAN McLEAN – *South Westland's Flying Doctor*

Dr Jean McLean (82) at Hokitika Airport ready for a South Westland flight in October 2005, 50 years after her pioneering flying doctor work in the Fox Moths and Dominies of NAC. (The Press)

HOKITIKA DOCTOR Dr Jean McLean and her husband Dr Donald 'Mac' McLean began in general practice at Hokitika in 1948. During much of the South Westland NAC flying era Dr Jean made regular monthly trips to Haast to hold medical clinics for local residents, including the many Haast Pass road project workers employed by the Ministry of Works.

Fox Moths and Dominies were used to fly Dr Jean south, usually flown by Frank Molloy. Sometimes she was the only passenger, but accompanied in the cabin by an array of supplies for settlers, and on the return flight - tins of whitebait. Often her trips south were made when the weather was bad, so locals joked about "Dr Jean's weather".

Trish McCormack Ross interviewed Dr Jean in 1994 and recorded some of her flying reminiscences, "It was lovely to fly – there was the dull drone in the background and you could go into a state of limbo. No matter what the weather was the pilots would go. It was marvellous the way they could find their way down. I had some great times down there. They were independent people, who were used to the isolation, and well able to make their own fun."

Dr Jean recalls the time in a Dominie when they hit a "gorger" – a very strong wind blowing down a gorge. The engineer's tool kit went up and down with a loud crash, while Dr Jean's medical bag, complete with a number of urine samples, also took to the air. Someone hastily checked the lid of a bottle of hydrochloric acid, while another passenger hit the roof! While staying in Haast she joined in with many of the local family events whether it was birthday parties, baptisms or other parties. There were times when she had to extract teeth, which was a difficult procedure but many local Haast residents preferred her attempts, using anaesthetic, to those of locals. Later Dr Jean helped appoint Rosalie Buchanan as district nurse for the area and this greatly assisted with the ongoing medical demands in the isolated Haast region. Her final flights as pioneer flying doctor were made in the late 1950s but Dr Jean continued in general practice at Hokitika until retirement in 1993. She was pleased to share reminiscences of the South Westland air service at the 60th anniversary celebrations in 1994.

connection was many years away, introduced by NAC in December 1968.

From 1947 the Public Works Department made good progress with the construction of the new Seaview Aerodrome on the terrace above Hokitika. The ground was very rough and swampy and soon became crossed by countless drains and large earthworks. Supervision was given by the PWD engineer in Hokitika, Mr F. Millar. Built at a cost of about £144,000 the new airport was opened on 17 December 1951 – almost 17 years to the day since Mercer had pioneered the air service. Opened by Mr James Kent, MP for Westland, it was an airport not only for Hokitika but a regional airport for the whole of Westland. Unofficial first landings and take-offs had been made by Des Nolan of Haast and in December 1950 by Frank Molloy flying a Dominie on the annual "airlift" of men employed on the Haast Pass road project. The new airport was reported as having runway lengths of 4750 ft and 4300 ft. The inaugural South bound NAC flight from Wellington, via Nelson and Westport, was on opening day with Lockheed Lodestar ZK-AKW *Kopara*, flown by Captain H.C. 'Johnny' Walker and Captain Don Ayson.

The opening of the new Hokitika Airport meant a return of the DH89 Dominies, which had been barred from Southside since 1948. In early 1952 the Dominies inaugurated regular services to Haast. Little scenic flying was

An unexpected visitor at Southside Aerodrome on 25 November 1950 was RNZAF Mosquito NZ2324, low on fuel. Only 90 octane fuel was available and many locals gathered to watch the refuelling. The take-off was exciting as the wooden bomber just cleared the stopbank.
(via Ian Woolhouse)

NAC staff at Hokitika's Southside Aerodrome on a sunny day in 1950. From left: Jean Stoop (Clerk), Bob Nossiter (Traffic), Tom Harris (Engineer), Dick Ferguson (Engineer), Margaret Penman (Clerk), Ross King (Stores) and Harry Howard (Aircraft hand).
(via Margaret McKenzie)

– 81 –

Frank Molloy describes South Westland Flying

Many and varied have been the requests by the settlers in isolated South Westland of the pilots on this unique air service:

Would you try and procure a bottle of whisky for me and send down by the plane this afternoon?
Would you please collect my false teeth which I left behind on the dressing table of a local hotel?
Would you please collect a prescription from the chemist?
Would you please get me two dozen New Year cards?
Would you get me a baby's bottle?
Would you please get me a petrol tank cap for my motor truck?
Would you please phone the Shipping Co., and enquire when the local coastal boat will be leaving for south?
Would you please call at the Post Office and collect a parcel for me, I am expecting a pair of shoes which I want to wear to the Whitebaiters' Ball tomorrow night?
Will you please put this £1 on so and so for a win with the local bookie?

Hundreds of mercy missions have been flown to the South since aircraft became available to the district.

I have been the pilot on numbers of these flights, as have other pilots who have been based in Hokitika. The complaints or injuries of patients have been very varied, ranging from severe scalding, axe cuts to feet and legs, fractured arms caused through cranking engines, fish hooks firmly embedded in hands and facial injuries after a fight, to appendicitis and many other complaints too numerous to mention.

Maternity patients who have left their departure a little late have always been our biggest concern. A doctor and nurse have always been carried and, through the peephole in the Fox Moth, I have seen some very worried expressions on the doctor's face to say nothing of the poor patient.

Many mercy flights have been carried out in very poor weather, when normally the aircraft would be in the hangar.

The mercy flight which I most vividly recall came after a serious fire at Franz Josef Hotel in which four people lost their lives, and others were badly burnt. I received a phone call from the manager of the Hostel in the early hours of the morning, asking for the "Dominie" aircraft to take the injured to hospital. The flight was carried out at daybreak, and the three badly injured patients were back in the Hokitika Hospital 75 minutes later. The operation reflected great credit on the engineering staff, as the aircraft was in the middle of an inspection and had to be hurriedly made airworthy.

A recent flight which I had to perform was to locate a disabled fishing boat somewhere off Greymouth in bad weather. We were lucky in sighting it 17 minutes after take-off from Hokitika. A tug from Westport was able to take it in tow later during the night and Westport was safely reached early on the following morning.

(Captain Frank Molloy, *NAC News*, April 1953)

On the opening day of Hokitika's new Seaview Airport on 17 December 1951, NAC Lockheed Lodestar ZK-AKW Kopara, *inaugurates the first service from Paraparaumu via Nelson and Westport.* (Ian Woolhouse)

done at Franz Josef during this time as Southern Scenic Air Services took most of these flights.

NAC formed Hokitika into a full branch in August 1953 with Frank Molloy as both Manager and Senior Route Pilot. At the same time, Phil Carmine from Christchurch was appointed Traffic Supervisor and given wide responsibilities by Molloy. Carmine later wrote of his experiences, "Similar to many small towns in New Zealand, Hokitika and adjacent settlements, had more than their share of well known locals, who on the coast were known as 'characters'. During my time there, I maintained close interest in the activities of these people together with tales from yesteryear. With the infrequent shipping to Jackson Bay, the death of a settler in the Haast area could present a costly problem for the relatives if the body was to be interred at other than the local cemetery. A Dominie cost £30 to charter for the trip north to Hokitika, a large amount in those days. Our Haast agent [Myrtle Cron] usually assessed the situation and on one occasion knowing the relatives could not afford the costs of the charter, issued a passenger ticket for £4 for the deceased. The body was wrapped in blankets and tied over three seats strapped on a cupboard door. Two passengers who had no objection to the arrangement occupied the other seats on the flight."

Whitebait freighting during the season was a memorable part of the South Westland air service. Carmine recalled, "By far the greatest volume of whitebait came north on charter flights and in the main the families with the freezers were the chartering parties. They endeavoured to control the price of whitebait on the Christchurch market by varying the quantities forwarded but their freezers would only hold so much and at times they would really press for charters. During the season, we would operate flights to Haast from daylight to twilight, most on a charter basis. With such flights, our Haast agent would send advice through the Hokitika Post Office of the required loads. A typical load on a southbound

Fox Moth ZK-AGM at Greymouth with young admirers. NAC maintained scheduled services to Greymouth until about early 1952 when services transferred to Hokitika. (D.A.Walker Collection)

charter in a Dominie was five dozen bottles of beer in sugar bags, one strapped into each seat and the cabin and freight locker filled with up to 140 empty four gallon tins. Dependent of course on the success of the season, it was not unusual for NAC aircraft to bring up from Haast over 5000 pounds of whitebait a day. The Dominie could carry 25 four gallon tins of bait and the Fox Moth 12 to 13 tins, depending on the weight of the pilot. On arrival at Hokitika, the tins were then transported from the airport by a local carrier and consigned by rail to Christchurch."

Despite a variety of freight as well as passengers the South Westland air service continued to sustain losses: for the year ending 31 March 1950 £3956, 1951 £3044, 1952 £5126 and 1953 £4595. During this time the corporation made overtures about selling the air service and Southern Scenic Air Services Ltd in Queenstown became interested, even making a deposit to purchase the route and all facilities, but negotiations failed and NAC continued operations.

A busy time refuelling Fox Moths ZK-ASP and ZK-AEK at Haast Aerodrome on Wednesday 19 September 1951. Note the tall fuel bowsers behind ZK-AEK.
(via Les McKenzie)

Alf Marshall by Dominie ZK-AKY at Haast, while the charter flight makes a brief refuelling stop before continuing to Milford Sound, July 1956.
(Alf Marshall via Kaye McNabb)

Doug Brown and family about to leave Haast in Dominie ZK-AKU after a teaching appointment, 1952.
(via Roger Eggeling)

On 19 February 1954 Molloy made an air ambulance flight to Haast for a suspected appendicitis case. Despite heavy rain and poor visibility the Dominie took off at 4.40pm and arrived at Haast at 5.55pm after battling its way southward through a heavy rain storm. There was a race against time as darkness was closing in. The patient, Henuri Francisas Geerds, aged 28, a Dutch bushman, was quickly placed in the cabin and the Dominie headed back to Hokitika, arriving at 7.15pm. Geerds was taken by ambulance to the Westland Hospital where he recovered.

A few days later on 23 February NAC resumed an "as required" service to the Franz Josef Airfield with Dominie aircraft. This was the result of the airfield having been recently extended by Ministry of Works employees. It was reported a number of the domestic staff of the hostel were waiting at the airfield to welcome the Dominie, flown by Frank Molloy, when it landed.

This development of Franz Josef Airfield also had the effect of the Fox Moths being finally withdrawn from the South Westland air service. However ZK-AGM was retained as a back-up aircraft and stayed on at Hokitika and was flown regularly on the southern route until about July 1955 and then sold in early 1956. It was the end of an era with the DH83 type having flown on the South Westland air service since Mercer began services in late 1934.

– 84 –

DH89B DOMINIE ZK-AKY and DH89B DOMINIE ZK-AKU

DH89B DOMINIE ZK-AKY

WITH CONSTRUCTOR NUMBER 6653, this RAF Dominie, serial HG654, was shipped to New Zealand with two others, HG655 (ZK-BAU) and HG656 (ZK-ALB), on board the *Port Chalmers*, and was Brought on Charge into RNZAF service as NZ525 in October 1943. One of nine such aircraft purchased by the air force it served with Northern Group Communications Flight and the Anti-Aircraft Flight at Mangere before going to No.42 (Communications) Squadron in 1944. One of the six Dominies discharged from military service in 1946 and sold to New Zealand National Airways Corporation (NAC), it was registered ZK-AKY and named *Tui*.

It served all over New Zealand on NAC routes, including time based at Hokitika in the late 1940s and mid 1950s for use on the northern route to Westport and Nelson and on the southern route to the Glaciers and Haast. It was the final Dominie used on the South Westland air service by NAC when flown by Frank Molloy. Along with ZK-AKU it was the last Dominie in NAC service and sold in 1964 to Ritchie Air Services of Te Anau. This began the aircraft's long association with the Southern area of the South Island. ZK-AKY was used for scenic flying and versatile freight work and this continued through changes of ownership to Tourist Air Travel and Mount Cook Airline and change of base to Queenstown. By the mid 1970s the Dominie was only occasionally used and last charter flights were to Big Bay.

In 1978 Tom Williams of *Te Parae*, near Masterton, purchased the Dominie and put it on the line with the Sport and Vintage Aviation Society at Masterton. In early 1983 a full restoration by Ted Ashwell and team commenced at Masterton and first flights were made in December 1985, in time for the aircraft to re-enact the 50th anniversary of the inauguration of main trunk services by Union Airways on 16 January 1986. It operated for a time from Rotorua but since 1991 has been based at the Old Mandeville Airfield near Gore, Southland. Over recent years it has been prominently used for other re-enactment flights – notably the 60th anniversary of Bert Mercer's pioneering South Westland flight on 18 December 1994, the 60th anniversary of Cook Strait Airways on 30 December 1995 and the 60th anniversary of NAC in March 2007. Ownership is now with the Croydon Aviation Heritage Trust. In 2009 ZK-AKY continues for charter hire and is in pristine condition.

Dominie ZK-AKY over the Marlborough landscape, Easter 2009. Restored and painted in NAC livery since December 1985 the Dominie is the best known DH89 in New Zealand. (Gavin Conroy)

Dominie ZK-AKU at Tauranga's Classic Flyers Museum in August 2007. Now based at the museum it is available for local flights. (Glenn Johnston)

DH89B DOMINIE ZK-AKU

THIS AIRCRAFT, with constructor number 6672, was despatched by No. 76 Maintenance Unit of the RAF as HG663 and shipped to New Zealand aboard the *Glenbeg*. It was one of nine Dominies acquired by the RNZAF for training purposes during World War II and was Brought on Charge at Hobsonville on 2 November 1943 and allocated the serial NZ528. It was first used by the Northern Group Communications Flight at Mangere but about October 1944 was transferred to No.42 (Communications) Squadron at Rongotai. One of six Dominies transferred to the newly forming New Zealand National Airways Corporation (NAC) in 1946 to become part of their foundation aircraft fleet, it was registered ZK-AKU and named *Tawaka*.

When NAC took over the operations of Air Travel (NZ) Ltd ZK-AKU was used on their northern route in the late 1940s and on their southern route in the 1950s. From the late 1950s ZK-AKU, with ZK-AKY, was deployed to operate the Northland service from Auckland northwards. The aircraft was sold in June 1963 to the Nelson Aero Club. Patchett Tours of Christchurch purchased the Dominie in 1965 and used it on southern charters for a period before selling it to the Rotorua Aero Club who used it briefly on scheduled services. David Gray purchased ZK-AKU in July 1968 and a year later it became the only New Zealand Dominie to return to Great Britain when it entered in the London-Sydney Air Race. It left New Zealand on 21 November 1969 and arrived back on 14 January 1970 – the first vintage aircraft to fly from New Zealand to England and return.

In 1972 a complete restoration of the aircraft was commenced and it took to the air again in January 1977. For many years it was based at either Ardmore Aerodrome or North Shore Airfield wearing its former air force livery. From 1992 until late 1994 it was out of the air but further restoration work was done in time for it to fly to Hokitika in December 1994 for the 60th anniversary of the South Westland air service. As part of this celebration it also flew overhead during the service at Kawatiri Junction when the plaque commemorating the crash of Dragon ZK-AHT was unveiled on 16 December 1994. A year later it was involved with the 60th anniversary of Cook Strait Airways but suffered an engine failure while crossing Cook Strait. The aircraft, flown by David Gray, with a full load of passengers, made a safe landing at Nelson Airport. After a long ownership Gray sold ZK-AKU in September 2004 to the N.Z. Historic Aircraft Trust. It is maintained in airworthy condition and since 2008 has been based at the Classic Flyers Museum, Tauranga Airport.

Firecrew at Hokitika Airport included the NAC staff. From left: Bill O'Brien, Jean Anderson, Joan Win and Jean Lister, 1952. (via Jean Wells)

In June 1954 the surface of the Hokitika airport grass runways had become dangerously slippery for larger passenger aircraft as moss was growing through the thin grass. DC-3 operations were suspended and Dominie aircraft began to once again operate the northern link to Westport. Local politicians and others urgently raised the issue of having the runways sealed as in the original plan for the new airport.

For a four week period in March-April 1955 capacity on the South Westland route was severely restricted. There was a lack of shipping available to Jackson Bay and consequently no fuel was able to be delivered to the Haast Airfield. This meant the Dominies from Hokitika had to fly south with sufficient fuel for the return trip and this necessitated a smaller payload being carried. On 21 September 1955 the Dominie was forced to turn back when it reached Paringa because of restricted visibility and on the same day a special demonstration flight over Hokitika by a visiting RAF Valiant jet bomber had to be cancelled due to the bad weather.

The whitebait season of 1955 proved especially lucrative. It was reported on 1 November that over 100,000lbs of whitebait had been flown out of South Westland during October by the NAC Dominie. This was on the usual scheduled services as well as on 38 special charter flights.

On 2 March 1956 there was an urgent maternity case in Haast. At midnight Dr Jean McLean was rung at Hokitika about the situation and immediately arrangements were made for her to fly down at first light with Miss E. Hanlon, Matron of the Maternity Hospital. The Dominie, flown by Frank Molloy, was slightly delayed for a short time by overcast weather but took off at 5.40am and landed at Haast at 6.50am. Dr McLean and Miss Hanlon found baby Phillip Wells, new born son of Ashley and Pat Wells, had arrived safely with mother and baby both well. All returned on the Dominie to Hokitika at 8.45am where Pat and her son spent a short time in hospital. Philip was reputed to be the youngest passenger to have flown on an NAC flight and even received a Godwit Club flight badge!

NAC services in South Westland were coming to an end in 1956 as Southern Scenic Air Services successfully entered into an agreement with NAC to purchase the service and operate in accordance with Air Services Licensing approval. The last important NAC South Westland development was on Tuesday 10 July 1956 when a proving flight was made to the newly licensed airfield at Milford Sound. Dominie ZK-AKY, flown by Frank Molloy, carried three passengers: Mr C. McDonald, Aerodrome Inspector; Mr F. Groom, Communications Officer and Mr F. Borthwick, Meteorological Office Representative, all of the Civil Aviation Administration. The route taken was via Haast for refuelling, then after another fifty minutes flying, the Dominie landed at Milford Sound Airfield. The flying time from Hokitika to Milford Sound was two hours.

A couple of weeks later the first charter flight from Hokitika to Milford was made on 25 July. The charter party had to wait several days until the weather was suitable. On this inaugural flight were Malcolm Dowell and his brother Max, Norma Provis, Alf and Dot Marshall and Peter Whiley. Conditions were perfect for the memorable flight.

On Monday 19 November 1956 West Coast Airways Ltd, a subsidiary company of Southern Scenic Air Services, took over and once again a private enterprise operator was flying the historic South Westland air service.

Captain Des Holden with Fox Moth ZK-AGM Matuhi, *at the time of the type's official retirement from the South Westland air service in March 1954. However the veteran aircraft was retained for occasional use until sold in early 1956.* (NAC Official)

Mail and boxed fruit and vegetables at Hokitika ready for a flight to Haast in May 1956. NAC Captain Jack Franklyn at right. (via Jean Wells)

LEFT: *On the last day of NAC operations at Hokitika, before the take-over by West Coast Airways, 18 November 1956. From left: Phil Carmine, Jean Anderson, Joy Staines, Frank Molloy, Peter Whiley and Bill O'Brien.* (via Jean Wells)

WHAT TO SEE TODAY

Dragonfly/Dominie Hangar

At Hokitika Airport is the double-bay hangar originally built at Southside Aerodrome for the two Dragonfly aircraft in late 1938. It was relocated to the new airport in 1951 as the NAC West Coast engineering base. Taken over by West Coast Airways it continued to be used to house the Dominies until the South Westland air service closed in March 1967. In the early 1970s Rapide ZK-AHS was stored in the hangar for a time before being flown to the Museum of Transport and Technology in Auckland in June 1974. One of New Zealand's most historic hangars it is now privately owned.

DH89B Dominie ZK-AKU

One of the last two Dominies operated by NAC in 1963, ZK-AKU was used by NAC on the South Westland air service. Its image was well known as it featured in a large wall-sized photograph displayed for many years in the airways booking office in Weld Street, Hokitika, and from the early 1990s until 2009 at the Hokitika Airport terminal. It is planned to again display this feature photograph in a new building at Franz Josef. ZK-AKU is currently based at the Classic Flyers Museum at Tauranga Airport, owned by the N.Z. Historic Aircraft Trust, and is available for charter flights.

Milford Sound's Bowen Falls makes for an impressive sight from the window of a low flying Dominie.
(Richard Williams)

At Milford Sound on 25 July 1956 NAC Dominie ZK-AKY Tui, flown by Captain Frank Molloy, after the first charter flight from Hokitika. Passengers were Malcolm and Max Dowell, Norma Provis, Alf and Dot Marshall and Peter Whiley. (Max Dowell)

DH89B Dominie ZK-AKY

This Dominie was used on the West Coast by NAC. Restored in the mid 1980s ZK-AKY is owned and operated by the Croydon Aviation Heritage Trust, based at the Old Mandeville Airfield, near Gore in Southland. Over the years it has been used for many re-enactment and historic flights throughout New Zealand and is available for charter.

In January 1962 the Rapide banks tightly to starboard to get a good view of the Franz Josef Motor Camp, operated from 1952 to 1965 by the Worthington family. In recent years the site has been cleared of buildings because of the risk of flooding and river erosion. (N.Z. Herald) BELOW: *With a beautiful day for scenic flights, Captain Geoff Houston (with tie) organises passengers at Franz Josef in January 1962 with Rapide ZK-AHS. The passengers leaving the Rapide seem happy.* (N.Z. Herald)

5

Versatility Returns
West Coast Airways 1956 -1967

THE SALE OF THE SOUTH WESTLAND AIR SERVICE had been mooted by NAC for a number of years. Compared to the corporation's other routes it was a unique and different "bush airline" route and considered more appropriately run by local independent interests. The retirement of the Fox Moth aircraft, concentration on scheduled services and lack of scenic and other charter work made for an increasingly uneconomic NAC operation.

Southern Scenic Air Services Ltd of Queenstown saw the opportunity to extend their business in a complementary way to what they were doing in Otago and Fiordland and in 1953 entered into an agreement to purchase the South Westland air service from NAC. But this deal was unsuccessful and it was three years before another agreement was finally reached, with Air Services Licensing Authority approval, for a subsidiary company, West Coast Airways Ltd, to be formed to run the air service. For it to be economic, a more versatile service was envisaged. In essence, it meant a return to a diverse range of activities like that of Air Travel (NZ) Ltd.

The foundation directors of West Coast Airways Ltd were: John Kilian, Fred 'Popeye' Lucas, Barry Topliss (all Southern Scenic directors) and Tom Harris of Hokitika. Harris was appointed manager and engineer and was the only person to be employed by all three operators of the South Westland air service. Bryan McCook became pilot/operations manager and former NAC staff Jean Anderson and Joy Staines undertook the administration work. Phil Carmine, the NAC traffic manager continued in a brief transitional role.

Services commenced on Monday 19 November 1956 with Hokitika to Haast and return flights flown by Rapide ZK-AHS. In addition to the veteran Rapide, Dominie ZK-AKT was based at Hokitika along with available Southern Scenic Cessnas and sometimes a Proctor and an Anson. Two weeks later on 3 December, McCook, when departing Hokitika for Haast on scheduled flight No. 692, in ZK-AKT, struck and killed a young calf during the take-off run. Damage to the propeller was only slight and after a check the flight proceeded south.

McCook left West Coast Airways after a short time and Jack Humphries

– 91 –

Des Wright's Auster ZK-AUO at Hokitika in 1960. This aircraft was used extensively by West Coast Airways on the Hokitika-Greymouth-Hokitika route. During one flight on 21 March 1960, Brian Waugh was picking up Lew Tuck for a flight to Haast, and had two engine failures making successful forced landings on the Blaketown Beach and South Beach. (via Raeoni Wright)

BELOW: At Haast in July 1964 Rapide ZK-AHS is ready for a return West Coast Airways flight to Hokitika with pilot Dave McDonald. Myrtle Cron talks to a passenger, and behind them fuel drums are scattered around the fuel bowser. In the near distance the seaward end of the bush covered Mark Range runs down from the cloud obscured 5899ft Mt Mark, and on the Browning Range, separating the Okuru and Turnbull Rivers, above the nose of the Rapide, the snow capped peak of Mt Warren (5850ft) is clearly visible. Towards the right are the snow covered tops of the Selbourne Range rising to over 6000ft. (Dave McDonald)

replaced him in February 1957. Humphries had learned to fly in 1943 with the RNZAF and served in the Pacific during the closing period of the war. He helped introduce a variety of aerial work for West Coast Airways, including topdressing. On 30 June 1957 Humphries flew a Dominie to Whataroa to pick up the District Nurse, Sister King, along with Mrs Nolan, who was a stretcher patient requiring immediate hospital attention. In the opinion of Dr Hogg it was a "life or death" situation necessitating an air-ambulance flight.

Ken Eden joined Humphries in July 1957. He had learned to fly in 1945 and had considerable topdressing experience. West Coast Airways' operations continued to expand, including an unscheduled but regular Auster air service from Greymouth to Hokitika to link up with the Dominie flight to Haast. Sadly Tom Harris, the manager and engineer, was killed on 29 October 1957 in the crash of Auster ZK-AYB, near Maruia Springs, while checking out a potential topdressing job. Harris was born at Kaniere and had worked for the local airline since pre-war days. He was a member and past President of the Hokitika Aero Club and also an active member of the Lake Kaniere Yacht and Power Boat Club and had raced several speedboats over the years.

Longtime resident Nora Cron cuts the ribbon for the Haast Pass road opening on 12 November 1960. At right, wearing a striped sweater, is veteran pilot Arthur Bradshaw who had flown to Haast in his newly refurbished Dragonfly ZK-AFB. (via Raeoni Wright)

The official opening of the Haast to Wanaka road over the Haast Pass was celebrated on a sunny warm day on 12 November 1960. West Coast Airways Dominie ZK-AKT and Rapide ZK-AHS, flown by pilots Brian Waugh and Paul Legg, flew special guests to the nearby aerodrome. (Paul Beauchamp Legg)

Haast district nurse Joy Lawler photographs fellow passengers Haast Post Office and Aeradio Station staff Eric Robson (at left) & Allan Brown together with West Coast Airways pilot Brian Waugh and Joy's daughter Karen, after a magnificent scenic flight from Haast to Milford Sound and return in early February 1960. (via June Hodgkinson)

Humphries made his last West Coast Airways flight on 16 December 1957 and went to James Aviation and single pilot DC-3 topdressing flying. Later he joined TEAL/Air New Zealand and eventually retired from flying the DC-10. He remarked in a 1996 interview that his West Coast Airways flying was one of the highlights of his career. "Life on the Coast was one long adventure punctuated by the conflicts of the locals in Haast. There was some tremendous rivalry and fights when passions ran high. Some of the South Westland women could knit barbed wire!" In a further 2009 interview he commented, "I fell in love with flying the Dominie as it was an aircraft that just wanted to fly, not overly powerful, and so called for your input as pilot."

Paul Beauchamp Legg began a three year flying stint for West Coast Airways from February 1958. 'Popeye' Lucas from Queenstown did Legg's brief training on the Dominie and his first flights were with freight and mail before carrying passengers to Haast. As well as the scheduled flying and other charter work Legg worked hard to develop the scenic flying potential. In a 2009 interview he recalled, "When I was based at Franz Josef Glacier I would start scenic flying at daybreak. This would be about 5am when the only way I can describe the beauty of the November to January flights is to liken them to the beauty of a young bride on her wedding day. She has a special glow as did the ice and snow high up. Towards the middle of February and onwards the delicate colours were replaced by a harsher scene of black rocks and the hard contrast of the white ice and snow. This was because of the summer warmth melting the extra little frosty bits of ice."

Legg described two main scenic flights. "From memory I think the first one was about two pounds and ten shillings and then we had

Cessna ZK-BJY, seen here with contrasting transportation, ready to collect whitebait from the Paringa riverbed in 1960.
(Paul Beauchamp Legg)

Cessna 180 ZK-BJY

This Cessna was the only one painted in West Coast Airways livery, but several other Southern Scenic Air Service Cessnas were also used by the airline. Their main use was top dressing, venison recovery, freight work and some scenic flying. In many respects the Cessna 180 was the successor to the versatility and reliability of the DH83 Fox Moth but was rarely used for scheduled services.

ZK-BJY was imported new into New Zealand in April 1955 with the American test registration of N4522B for Rural Aviation Ltd. It was severely damaged in an accident at Palmerston North in July 1957 and subsequently rebuilt. Bought by West Coast Airways it commenced flying from Hokitika in January 1958 and was used until the early 1960s when it reverted to Southern Scenic livery and spent time as a Queenstown based floatplane until 1968. After several changes of ownership it was back at Hokitika from 1990 to 2004, and operated for most of that time by Wilderness Wings. In 2009 it continues to fly with Brian Doig in Ashburton.

one for about five pounds which went along Mount Cook. The cheaper flight was the most popular. I took off from Franz Josef and turned left toward the Fox Glacier settlement, then climbed the Fox Glacier in a series of turns until we were on the relatively flat area at the top of the Glacier. Then I crossed between some spectacular dark peaks that divided the Fox from the Franz Josef Glacier. There was a very large area at the head of the Franz Josef above which we flew at possibly five hundred to one thousand feet gradually descending close enough to the ice for the passengers to be able to look down the crevasses. For a brief period, when the glacier drops very steeply, and we descended sharply, I became more skilled and did a turn at the narrowest point. The passengers often screamed at this stage and when we landed they were very enthusiastic and their talking did all the selling of more scenic flights for me!"

On 17 August 1959 Ken Eden flew a memorable air ambulance flight in Cessna ZK-BJY from Hokitika to Dunedin with four month old Philip Judge, from Westport, who needed emergency surgery. Unable to land at Taieri because of heavy rain a landing was made on Forbury Park Racecourse. Eden later described the weather as

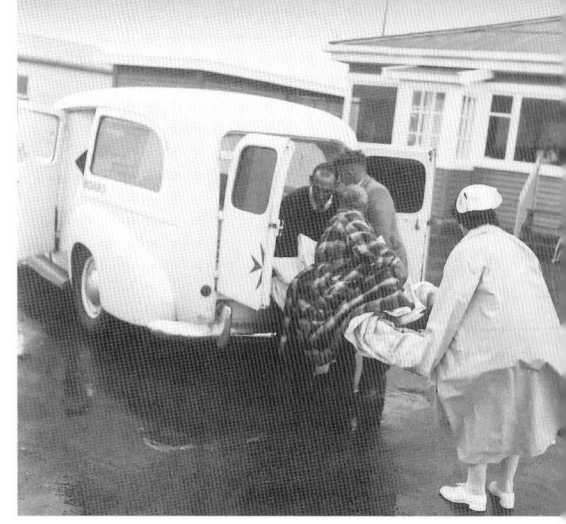

West Coast Airways, like its predecessors Air Travel (NZ) Ltd and NAC, did frequent air-ambulance flights from South Westland. Here a patient has just been lifted from the Dominie and is being placed in a Humber Ambulance. The ambulance driver is Laurie Wickes, helped by Des Wright, 1960. (Paul Beauchamp Legg)

RIGHT: *Haast from a West Coast Airways Dominie, after a scenic flight by several Haast residents to Milford Sound and return, in February 1960. This area is now known as Haast Beach.* (Eric Robson)

BELOW: *Outside the Haast Post Office and Aeradio Station, Haast postmaster Eric Robson changes the record card in the pole-top sunshine recorder, about March 1961. This communications station transmitted daily Met reports, provided ground-to-air flight information, and at scheduled times a public point-to-point radio-telephone link with Hokitika. This building had also been in use at Jackson Bay when the PWD settlement was established in the 1930s and was later relocated to Haast in the early 1950s.* (Eric Robson)

marginal on the way from Hokitika but it had been a surprise to find he could not land at Taieri so he chose in the circumstances to put down for the sake of the baby. "All the other bits of green seemed to have goalposts and things sticking up, so I just landed where I could." While the landing was successful, the ambulance got stuck in the mud and Eden, soaked to the skin in the rain, together with children from St Clair School, got the ambulance and baby on their way to hospital. Eden left the airline five months later to return to topdressing work, based in Amberley, North Canterbury.

Brian Waugh commenced duties with West Coast Airways as Chief Pilot and Chief Engineer from late 1959. He later wrote of his first impressions of flying from Hokitika. "Looking south from the Hokitika Airfield, the view was magnificent. The Southern Alps, gleaming white, stretched as far as the eye could see, with Cook and Tasman standing majestically head and shoulders above their neighbours. To the right, the Tasman Sea pounded the beach, the white surf-line brilliant against the shingle. It's a sight I shall always remember. That's my new territory, I thought: the winding rugged coastline; Okarito Lagoon; Lakes Ianthe, Wahapo, Mapourika and Paringa and many smaller lakes unknown except to the flier. The Coast – like a beautiful woman, must be wooed with patience. And like any beautiful woman, she can be savage and terrible. That's the Coast!"

A well prepared passenger ready to board Dominie ZK-AKT at Hokitika in 1960. The West Coast Airways steps had recently been made by engineer Basil de Jong.
(Paul Beachamp Legg)

TOP: *On a charter flight to Timaru. From left, Mick Taylor, Neil Roberts, Malcolm Duggan and Roy King with Brian Waugh busy in the cockpit. Note the lifebelt sign (different to the circumstances of the 1942 Dragonfly ditching tragedy) and the speaker in the ceiling which enabled Waugh to describe the scenery.*
(via Jim Jamieson)

RIGHT: *Captain Paul Legg, with Rapide ZK-AHS, at Franz Josef after a scenic flight in February 1961. Legg left the airline that same month after three years on the South Westland air service.*
(Paul Beauchamp Legg)

DH89A RAPIDE ZK-AHS *and* DH89B DOMINIE ZK-AKT

DH89A RAPIDE ZK-AHS

MANUFACTURED BY DE HAVILLAND at Hatfield in England, Constructor Number 6423 flew from Hokitika for each of the airlines which operated the South Westland air service - Air Travel (NZ) Ltd, NAC, and West Coast Airways Ltd. The aircraft was imported as the fifth and final DH89 Rapide for Cook Strait Airways Ltd of Nelson. Shipped to New Zealand on the *Rangitata* it arrived in Wellington on 16 November 1938 and soon went to Nelson, still in its large packing case, as deck cargo on the *Arahura*. It was partly assembled at Nelson's new airport at Tahunanui, but because of problems with wind-blown sand from the new airfield surface the fuselage was towed to the old Stoke Aerodrome site. Final assembly was completed at Stoke before the Rapide was test flown on 30 November. The Rapide, registered ZK-AGT, and named *Neptune,* flew the Cook Strait routes and also the service to the West Coast, including inaugural services to the new Westport aerodrome at Carters Beach on 15 March 1939.

Impressed into RNZAF service in October 1939 as NZ558 it was used as both a flying classroom and a VIP Communications aircraft with No.42 Squadron. During this time it was frequently flown by former Air Travel pilot Jim Hewett. With the arrival of newer Dominies for the RNZAF the Rapide was overhauled by de Havillands and sold to Air Travel (NZ) Ltd and registered ZK-AHS on 30 November 1944 as a replacement for Dragon ZK-AHT. It was the second RNZAF aircraft to be released for civil use and in Air Travel colours of silver and orange was primarily used on the Hokitika-Westport-Nelson service. Despite it being a pre-war Rapide, rather than a war-time Dominie trainer, over subsequent years it was usually referred to as a 'Dominie'.

With Air Travel's absorption into NAC from 1 October 1947 ZK-AHS flew in the red and silver NAC livery, as *Mokai*, and continued on West Coast routes. On 1 June 1948 it flew the first DH89 scheduled flight from Hokitika to Haast. Soon afterwards, with the closure of the Southside Aerodrome to DH89 aircraft, it was deployed to other NAC routes around New Zealand.

As part of the West Coast Airways take-over of the South Westland air service from November 1956, ZK-AHS along with Dominie ZK-AKT, was sold by NAC and painted in Southern Scenic and West Coast Airways livery. ZK-AHS flew the Haast service with regular overhauls at Queenstown. During the late 1950s and early 1960s West Coast Airways was one of only four small airlines, apart from NAC, authorised to operate scheduled services in New Zealand and ZK-AHS became synonymous with the regular South Westland air service.

By the mid 1960s the pre-war Rapide was one of the most extensively flown DH89 aircraft and probably the last to operate scheduled services in the world. It continued a versatile range of flying including scheduled services, airmail and freight, charters, supply dropping, air-ambulance and aerial photography work. As early as 1966 inquiries had been made about ZK-AHS eventually going to the expanding historic aircraft collection at Auckland's Museum of Transport and Technology (MOTAT). In March 1967 the Rapide made the final West Coast Airways flights to South Westland and was then transferred to New Zealand Tourist Air Travel's Queenstown base from where it continued to fly scenic and other charter flights.

Retired by Mount Cook Airline in 1972 it was stored in the former West Coast Airways hangar at Hokitika, and also outside, until being flown to Queenstown in May 1974 and prepared

ZK-AHS at Franz Josef in 1960 with both engines running.
(Paul Beauchamp Legg)

for the ferry flight to Auckland and donation to MOTAT. On 5 June 1974 it made its final landing at Auckland's Ardmore Airport and by the early 1980s was displayed at the museum's Western Springs hangar as an example of a pioneering New Zealand airliner. During 1998-1999 ZK-AHS underwent a major refurbishment at MOTAT and this involved stripping off the old fuselage fabric, repairs to some wood structure, cleaning of the engines, and re-painting in NAC colours. This most historic airliner is displayed as the oldest continuously based twin engine passenger aircraft in New Zealand.

DH89B DOMINIE ZK-AKT

WITH CONSTRUCTOR NUMBER 6673, this RAF Dominie, serial HG674, was shipped to New Zealand with one other, HG669 (later ZK-BBP), on board the *Port Huon*, and was brought on charge into RNZAF Service as NZ530 in January 1944. One of nine such aircraft purchased by the air force it served with No.42 Squadron at Rongotai, until sold to New Zealand National Airways Corporation (NAC) in 1946. As *Tareke* it operated the first flights for the newly forming corporation on 2 September on the Cook Strait service. The Dominie flew on NAC routes all over New Zealand, including the South Westland air service, for the next ten years until sold to West Coast Airways Ltd in late 1956.

Repainted in West Coast Airways and Southern Scenic livery and based at Hokitika it was used for scheduled services, charters, scenic flying, air-ambulance and supply dropping work. Returned to Queenstown in 1965 it was in service with Tourist Air Travel (TAT) when it force landed in the Shotover River near Queenstown Airport on 15 April 1967. In the type's long history in New Zealand it was (and still is) the only DH89 crash caused by mechanical failure and the only time a DH89 pilot and passenger were injured. Pilot Brian Waugh suffered severe ankle injuries and passenger Dr Sage, from Indianapolis, U.S.A, broke his nose. The cockpit and front fuselage of the Dominie were badly smashed and after the engines and other salvageable parts were removed the remains were burnt and buried in the riverbed. ∎

ZK-AKT at Fox Glacier in September 1959. Pilot Paul Legg in the cockpit.
(Whites Aviation)

Waugh further recalled, "On my first day in the office at the back of the hangar, Mervyn Rumsey, the airline manager, ex RAF Hurricane pilot and DFC type, said to me, 'You'll carry dentists, farmers, doctors, deerstalkers, sight-seeing types, trampers, alcoholics, dead bodies, bobby calves, crates of butter, bicycles, bread – anything that will go through the Dominie door.' And that's what we did carry, and often in atrocious weather conditions too. Barry Topliss had never mentioned the weather when he gave me the Hokitika job. Nine o'clock every night very soon became a sacred moment – the weather forecast. What would it be like tomorrow? Would we be able to get the workmen back from their grog sprees in town? In the morning we would often be delayed: 'Haast closed due to fog;' 'Bruce Bay visibility nil.' I would haunt the Met people. Meteorologists Frank Collyer and Jim

Dominie ZK-BAU in early Southern Scenic livery at Haast in September 1960. The ticket office, at left, was built in the late 1940s and the Cron homestead, at right, was a regular stopping off place for pilots and passengers. The ticket office was restored in 2009 as part of the 75th air service celebrations.
(Paul Beauchamp Legg)

BELOW: *West Coast Airways agent Myrtle Cron working in the Haast ticket office. The Renton Hardware calendar says November 1960 and the NAC notice reminds passengers not to be late – even from Haast!*
(Paul Beauchamp Legg)

Harper would shake their heads: 'It'll never clear today, Brian. Ring the bakery and tell them to take the bread back.'"

The volatile weather in South Westland was always a challenge for the de Havilland biplane pilots. As Waugh wrote, "With experience, all West Coast pilots eventually learn to judge weather conditions pretty well. They need to know when not to fly. One day a frustrated passenger spoke to Billy O'Brien, the local fire officer who had lived in the town all his life and had worked at the aerodrome for twenty years; 'That's right, ain't it, Bill? Old Bert Mercer often used to go in this weather, didn't he?' Quick as a flash came the caustic reply: 'Sure he did – and he returned a lot oftener too. Besides, he didn't have the thousand and one regulations to comply with like Brian here has today – just to protect the necks of ignorant buggers like you.'"

BELOW: *At Haast in November 1960 Dominie ZK-AKT and Rapide ZK-AHS. On occasions the two DH89s were together at Haast on busy days. A woman is picking up boxes, with suitcases carefully placed near the aircraft tail. At right is Robbie Nolan's 1957 Chevrolet.*
(Paul Beauchamp Legg)

Taken from a West Coast Airways Dominie in the early 1960s, the new highway and Haast bridge are nearing completion. Note the centre bridge span being worked on. At 2417ft the bridge, single-lane with two passing bays, is the longest bridge in South Westland. It was designed with a clearance of 10ft above the level of the Haast's highest recorded flood. (Bruce Bertram)

A *New Zealand Forest Service* supply dropping flight being prepared outside the West Coast Airways hangar at Hokitika. Merv O'Reilly (left) and unidentified man. The large 44 gallon drums are filled with building materials for hut construction. Note parachutes attached to sacks and timber. (via Jim Jamieson)

West Coast Airways did regular supply dropping work for the New Zealand Forest Service. Brian Waugh later wrote in his aviation memoirs, "I often used to quip that dropping bombs from Lancasters over Germany was nowhere near as dangerous as supply dropping with the Dominie." (John Willems)

On 12 November 1960 the Haast Pass road was finally opened, linking South Westland to Otago. This is the lowest main-divide crossing in the whole length of the Southern Alps, at only 1847 ft. Work had begun about 1929 on the Otago side, on a road from Wanaka and Hawea toward Haast Pass, but the 1930s depression halted progress at Makarora. In the late 1930s a road had also been developed from Jackson Bay to Haast and was completed in 1945. Work had recommenced on the road between Haast and Makarora soon after the war had ended. The road opening was marked by a large gathering at Haast with Waugh and Legg flying in guests in Dominie ZK-AKT and Rapide ZK-AHS.

From 1959 to 1962 Alan Mayne worked as a junior accounts clerk for the Ministry of Works at Greymouth. A large portion of time each month, just before pay day, was spent manually preparing the workers pay in cash. He recently recalled, "Haast was part of the Greymouth Residency and at that time there was no road access. Workers were paid four weekly and the pay clerk had to fly to Haast from Hokitika with a small suitcase full of cash. The pay clerk was escorted to the plane at Hokitika and then flew to Haast in the Dominie. He had to keep the pay suitcase with him at all times. He was met by someone from the Haast office when the plane landed there. The flight from Hokitika to Haast was my first flight in an aeroplane and I eventually flew this trip in the Dominie many times. On one occasion I arrived at Haast but there was no one to meet me. The aircraft returned to Hokitika and I was left sitting on a bag of cash waiting and hoping the right person from the office would pick me up! I remember one pilot flying low out to sea so that we could have a closer look at a flock of mollyhawks that were feeding and another time to have a closer look at a fishing boat. I also remember having to fly low over the Haast Aerodrome to chase stock off before we could land. On one pay trip to Haast the weather deteriorated after the Dominie returned to Hokitika and we were unable to get out for about five days."

Six months after Paul Legg's departure, Geoff Houston was appointed assistant pilot to Brian Waugh.

Four pilots with extensive West Coast flying experience. From left; Ken Eden, Fred 'Popeye' Lucas (a founding West Coast Airways director), Russell Troon and Tex Smith while attending a topdressing conference about 1959. Eden flew the Dominies on the South Westland air service from July 1957 to December 1959 and also did topdressing flying. (via Joyce Eden)

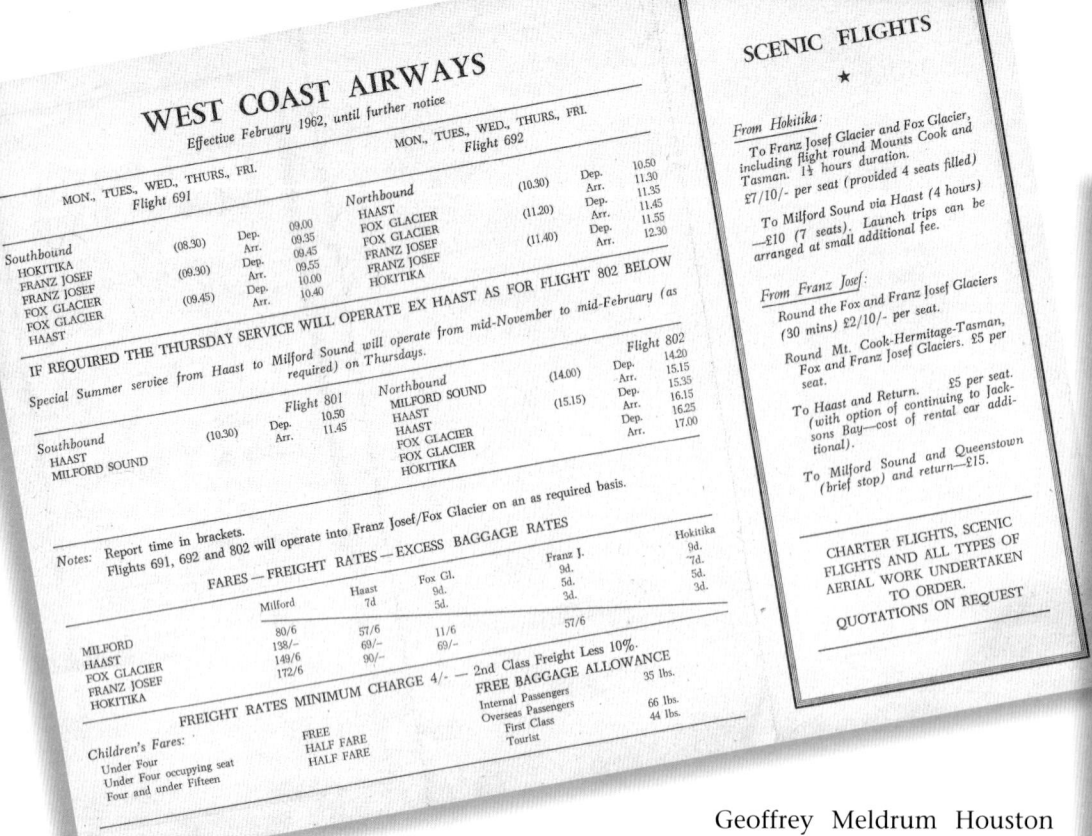

WEST COAST AIRWAYS
Effective February 1962, until further notice

	MON., TUES., WED., THURS., FRI. Flight 691			MON., TUES., WED., THURS., FRI. Flight 692		
Southbound			Northbound			
HOKITIKA	(08.30)	Dep. 09.00	HAAST	(10.30)	Dep.	10.50
FRANZ JOSEF		Arr. 09.35	FOX GLACIER	(11.20)	Arr.	11.30
FRANZ JOSEF	(09.30)	Dep. 09.45	FOX GLACIER		Dep.	11.35
FOX GLACIER		Arr. 09.55	FRANZ JOSEF		Arr.	11.45
FOX GLACIER	(09.45)	Dep. 10.00	FRANZ JOSEF	(11.40)	Dep.	11.55
HAAST		Arr. 10.40	HOKITIKA		Arr.	12.30

IF REQUIRED THE THURSDAY SERVICE WILL OPERATE EX HAAST AS FOR FLIGHT 802 BELOW

Special Summer service from Haast to Milford Sound will operate from mid-November to mid-February (as required) on Thursdays.

	Flight 801			Flight 802	
Southbound			Northbound		
HAAST	(10.30)	Dep. 10.50	MILFORD SOUND	(14.00)	Dep. 14.20
MILFORD SOUND		Arr. 11.45	HAAST	(15.15)	Arr. 15.15
			HAAST		Dep. 15.35
			FOX GLACIER		Arr. 16.15
			FOX GLACIER		Dep. 16.25
			HOKITIKA		Arr. 17.00

Notes: Report time in brackets.
Flights 691, 692 and 802 will operate into Franz Josef/Fox Glacier on an as required basis.

FARES — FREIGHT RATES — EXCESS BAGGAGE RATES

	Milford	Haast	Fox Gl.	Franz J.	Hokitika
		7d	9d.	9d.	9d.
		5d.	5d.	5d.	7d.
			3d.	3d.	5d.
					3d.
MILFORD		80/6	57/6	11/6	57/6
HAAST	138/-		69/-	69/-	
FOX GLACIER	149/6	90/-			
FRANZ JOSEF	172/6				
HOKITIKA					

FREIGHT RATES MINIMUM CHARGE 4/- — 2nd Class Freight Less 10%.

FREE BAGGAGE ALLOWANCE
Internal Passengers 35 lbs.
Overseas Passengers
  First Class 66 lbs.
  Tourist 44 lbs.

Children's Fares:
Under Four FREE
Under Four occupying seat HALF FARE
Four and under Fifteen HALF FARE

SCENIC FLIGHTS
★

From Hokitika:

To Franz Josef Glacier and Fox Glacier, including flight round Mounts Cook and Tasman. 1½ hours duration.
—£7/10/- per seat (provided 4 seats filled)

To Milford Sound via Haast (4 hours) —£10 (7 seats). Launch trips can be arranged at small additional fee.

From Franz Josef:

Round the Fox and Franz Josef Glaciers (30 mins) £2/10/- per seat.

Round Mt. Cook-Hermitage-Tasman, Fox and Franz Josef Glaciers. £5 per seat.

To Haast and Return. £5 per seat. (with option of continuing to Jacksons Bay—cost of rental car additional).

To Milford Sound and Queenstown (brief stop) and return—£15.

CHARTER FLIGHTS, SCENIC FLIGHTS AND ALL TYPES OF AERIAL WORK UNDERTAKEN TO ORDER. QUOTATIONS ON REQUEST

WEST COAST AIRWAYS
SEAVIEW AIRPORT
— HOKITIKA —

D.H.-89B and AUSTER AIRCRAFT

★

Scheduled Service Timetable

★

FARES AND FREIGHT RATES

P.O. BOX 106, HOKITIKA
NEW ZEALAND
Telephone 134

One dead Dominie engine! Paul Legg snaps the stationary starboard propeller on a return flight from Haast, fortunately with only freight and mail aboard. While the Gipsy Queen engines were usually very reliable both Legg and Waugh encountered several engine failures while flying the South Westland air service. (Paul Beauchamp Legg)

Geoffrey Meldrum Houston was born at Queenstown in 1935. He had learned to fly with the Greymouth Aero Club and did much whitebait and other freight flying with Fox Moth ZK-APT and Apache ZK-BLP on South Westland routes. This was not without incident as in 1960 he was involved in an aircraft accident where a passenger drowned.

Houston's first scheduled Dominie flight to Haast was on 23 August 1961. The following month he married Noeline Gibson in Gore. Noeline remembers, "Geoff was always interested in the country around him and enjoyed remote places and the hunting opportunities that much of the West Coast offered. He spotted a likely strip of open ground in the Copeland Valley and successfully put the Cessna down at Welcome Flat. This was the first of three airstrips that Geoff and Des Wright organised to be formed, with the hope that they would be able to be licensed. The airstrip at Castle Flat in the Karangaroa was licensed, but the Douglas Neve and Welcome Flat ones did not reach the required specifications, although they were still used by some. One weekend Geoff and I spent a weekend at Welcome Flat lounging around in the natural hot pools and hoping the weather would stay right to facilitate take-off again!"

The versatility of West Coast Airways continued with topdressing, venison recovery, air-ambulance work, scenic flying and supply dropping as well as the usual busy scheduled flights while the major road building project continued between Paringa and Haast. Scenic flying was continually promoted by West Coast Airways, especially at Franz Josef but also with more extensive flights to Milford Sound. The scenic flights proved popular all year round, depending on weather conditions, but the summer always brought more tourists to see the delights of South Westland. From Boxing Day 1961 Waugh spent seven consecutive days scenic flying from Franz Josef due to the busy demand and clear weather. West Coast Airways statistics for 1961 showed total flying hours were 1234, of which 122 hours were on charter flights and 78 hours on scenic flights.

Haast Aerodrome in September 1958 with the broad Haast River winding its way down from the Southern Alps. Mosquito Hill is prominent at left. (Whites Aviation via MOTAT)

Hokitika Airport in June 1958. The airport had opened in December 1951 and had excellent proximity to the nearby town (out of the photograph at lower right). In the foreground, (at left) are the Wio, Iringatau and Te Marie villas of Seaview Hospital and (at right) the Hokitika cemetery where Mercer's grave is located (Whites Aviation via MOTAT)

BRIAN KYNASTON WAUGH – Last Pioneer Pilot

Captain Brian Waugh at Haast in October 1965. (Jack Moore)

BORN IN SHREWSBURY, Shropshire, England, on 26 September 1922, the younger of two sons to Walter and Helen (née Kynaston), Waugh was the most experienced DH89 Rapide/Dominie pilot to fly the South Westland air service. He joined the Royal Air Force (RAF) in August 1938 as an engineering apprentice and trained at Halton and Cosford. Sailing to South Africa in 1941, he then worked on aircraft at No.27 Air School before being remustered for pilot training with the South African Air Force on de Havilland Tiger Moth and Airspeed Oxford aircraft. He gained his RAF wings on 24 September 1943.

Returning to England in 1944 he was posted to No.1653 Heavy Conversion Unit and trained on Avro Lancaster bombers with their four Merlin engines. Posted to No.75 (NZ) Squadron and based at Mepal in Cambridgeshire, he saw active service in the last six months of the war with a combined British and New Zealand crew. Bombing raids included Bremen, the Leuna Oil Refinery at Merseburg, the Howaldt Works and the inner dockyard at Kiel where the German pocket battleship *Admiral Scheer* was capsized. From early May to late July 1945 bombing was replaced by Lancaster flights that included dropping food to the starving Dutch at The Hague, ferrying prisoners of war home to the U.K, and long survey (Baedeker) flights over Germany, Belgium and Denmark.

Waugh continued in the RAF after the war with a number of transport squadrons, flying Oxford and Douglas Dakota aircraft all over England and Europe. This included brief Airspeed Horsa glider flying and glider towing with Dakotas. From April 1947 he was posted to No.48 Squadron based at Changi, Singapore, flying Dakotas throughout South East Asia.

In 1948 he left the RAF and obtained civil aircraft engineer and pilot licences. His first flying jobs were with Spalding Airways and Air Navigation & Trading Company, and from late 1951 with Oldstead Aircraft at Newcastle-upon-Tyne, on Fairchild Argus, Auster, Miles Magister and de Havilland Rapide aircraft. This flying involved charters around the north of England, to the Isle of Man, Ireland and the continent. He was badly injured in the crash of Rapide G-AFMF on 19 February 1954, when the aircraft became severely iced-up while on a charter flight to Dublin and crashed near Hexham, Northumberland.

Immigrating to New Zealand with his wife and two children he began flying DH89 Dominies with South Island Airways from September 1954, helping pioneer South Canterbury services with his friend Brian Chadwick and on the northern route to Nelson, until operations ceased in February 1956. His first Dominie scenic flight to South Westland was in November 1954.

Waugh then flew scheduled services with Christchurch based Trans Island Airways on Dominie, Beechcraft D18S, and Lockheed 10A Electra aircraft from April 1956 until April 1959. This included charters and scenic flying to Mt Cook, Hokitika, the glaciers, Queenstown and Milford Sound. In late 1959 he was employed by Southern Scenic Air Services and appointed Chief Pilot and Chief Engineer for West Coast Airways flying Dominies, Cessnas and Auster ZK-AUO. In January 1960 he took leave from Hokitika flying duties to ferry Beechcraft D18S ZK-BQE from Christchurch to Sydney via Norfolk Island.

On the West Coast, Waugh was involved in many community organisations including the Methodist Church, representative and selector for the West Coast Table Tennis Association, and news reporter for 3ZA. In 1965 he polled second highest in the Hokitika Borough Council elections and served on the airport and library committees.

By the time West Coast Airways closed in March 1967 Waugh had over 6000 flying hours on DH89 Rapide/Dominie aircraft, more than any other pilot in New Zealand. Ironically, just two weeks after leaving Hokitika he experienced two engine failures in Dominie ZK-AKT on 15 April 1967 and forced-landed in the Shotover River near Queenstown. His injuries prevented him flying again, and he re-trained in Meteorology and returned to serve at Hokitika Airport from 1968 to 1971. He subsequently transferred to Gisborne and then moved to Nelson to own and operate a motel business.

Waugh was one of only a few pilots to write his memoirs of small airline flying in New Zealand during the 1950s and 1960s. He died on 7 October 1984, and seven years later his aviation autobiography *Turbulent Years – A Commercial Pilot's Story* was published. He was survived by his wife Jean and children Lesley, Alec, Richard, Kathryn and Michael. ■

Dominie ZK-AKT in the Shotover River at Queenstown after its engine failures and forced-landing by Brian Waugh, 15 April 1967. (Jim Dimoff)

At the end of the May school holidays in 1962, (from left) Gloria Buchanan, Margaret Eggeling and Heather Buchanan prepare to leave Haast on the afternoon flight. Gloria and Heather going to board at Greymouth Technical High School and Margaret to board at St Marys School at Hokitika. The mailbags and freight are stacked up inside the rear cabin windows of Rapide ZK-AHS. (Roger Eggeling)

In 1963 Captain Brian Waugh flies Rapide ZK-AHS on a scenic flight near the head of the Franz Josef Glacier, toward the Minarets. (Kevin Worthington)

On 12 February 1962 Waugh's pilot friend Brian Chadwick, well known to many West Coasters, went missing on a Christchurch to Milford Sound scenic flight in Dragonfly ZK-AFB – Mercer's original Dragonfly. There were a myriad of reports both from the West Coast side of the main divide and from the eastern side. Waugh was the first to take-off in the search and spent ten hours of fruitless searching for the Dragonfly. Houston also joined in the search and the two Dominies covered a good part of the West Coast in what became the largest aerial search conducted in New Zealand. Still missing, the Dragonfly has become the most-searched-for aircraft in New Zealand aviation history.

Helen Hutchison started work in the West Coast Airways office in 1962. She recalls, "From the first day I loved the airport atmosphere. Merv Rumsey was our manager, an English gentleman and good teacher of airport procedures." Like many of the airline staff through the years Helen got to know the regular passengers and some became friends. "I remember a woman I'd befriended as she often flew up from Haast. One trip she went to hospital and I visited her there and did some messages for her. This was just part of a love of having contact with the isolated people of South Westland. One time when the woman was weather-bound at Hokitika, and knew no-one local, I took her home to my parents for a meal and bed for the night. Later she returned the hospitality and I stayed with her at Haast."

The weather was a constant challenge on the South Westland air service and each of the pilots became experienced reading the conditions. Waugh's logbook for July 1963 records: 17 July "Returned due strong wind"; 21 July "Returned due weather"; 22 July "Returned due fog". Getting to Haast was sometimes a challenge. Conversely, getting out of Haast had its moments too. Just prior to one scheduled flight a local woman phoned the Haast ticket office and said, "I'm still in the bath. Can the Dominie please wait until I'm dressed and get my suitcase together? I'll be about ten minutes."

During most of 1963 and into 1964 Geoff Houston concentrated on the venison recovery, supply dropping, topdressing, poison drops and freight work, leaving Waugh to do the scheduled services and scenic flights. In February 1964 the weather was a key factor in a tragic accident for West Coast Airways. On 7 February while on a return flight from Haast and Fox Glacier the weather deteriorated and Waugh was forced to land Rapide ZK-AHS at Franz Josef and stay the afternoon and the night with the Worthington family who owned the motor camp. The same afternoon Houston in Cessna 180 ZK-BJW was returning to Hokitika after venison recovery work at Haast. The weather continued to deteriorate while the Cessna flight was in progress, including an unusually thick fog which rolled in from the sea. Houston's non arrival that afternoon did not cause immediate concern as he often landed in all sorts of remote strips and just the year before had made a forced landing near the mouth of the Paringa River when his Cessna's engine had failed. The following day conditions remained the same and the Cessna was posted missing. Waugh attempted an aerial search from Franz Josef but conditions were so bad he was compelled to return.

Sunday 9 February brought perfect weather and at first light Des Wright took off from Hokitika in Auster ZK-AUO and Brian Waugh in Rapide ZK-AHS from

Merv Rumsey, West Coast Airways manager, outside the newly opened airline office at No.12 Weld Street, Hokitika, August 1965.
(Whites Aviation via MOTAT)

Franz Josef both searching for Houston. Wright spotted the wreckage on Green's Beach, near the base of Opuku Cliff, but with no radio it was Waugh who first sent a radio report of the accident. A Rudnick Helicopters Ltd Bell 47 brought out Houston's body. Later investigations indicated the Cessna had crashed while in a steep diving turn to starboard, likely caused by pilot disorientation and loss of control in the thick fog. The air accident report attributed no blame to Houston stating there was unavoidable entry into cloud and fog in the deteriorating conditions. At the age of 28 his death was tragic for his wife Noeline and young sons David and Kelvin. His funeral was held at Hokitika on 11 February 1964 attended by a large crowd. Brian Waugh's wife Jean gave birth the same day to their fifth child, Michael Geoffrey, named in Houston's honour.

Veteran DH89A Rapide ZK-AHS fog bound at Haast and fenced in to stop cattle eating the fabric. The heavy 44 gallon fuel drums were manhandled for regular refuelling.
(Clarrie O'Brien)

West Coast Airways Rapide ZK-AHS gathers speed ready to lift off from Hokitika Airport about 1964, flown by Brian Waugh. The veteran airliner flew reliably on the coast for many years and is now displayed at Auckland's Museum of Transport and Technology. (Bill Cropp)

WEST COAST AIRWAYS LTD.
SUBSIDIARY OF NEW ZEALAND TOURIST AIR TRAVEL LTD. AUCKLAND

Principal Agents—N.A.C.
District Master Agents—S.P.A.N.Z.
Booking Agents—Mt. Cook Airlines Ltd.
Golden Coast Airlines Ltd

SCHEDULED SERVICES
CHARTER FLIGHTS
SCENIC FLIGHTS
AIR AMBULANCE
AERIAL WORK
TOP DRESSING
SUPPLY DROPPING
SEED SOWING
PHOTOGRAPHY

P.O. BOX 106,
TELEPHONE 134.
HOKITIKA.

The wreckage of Geoff Houston's Cessna ZK-BJW (circled), near the base of Opuku Cliff, Green's Beach, from the port side of Rapide ZK-AHS. Brian Waugh reported sighting the wreckage early on Sunday morning 9 February 1964, two days after the tragic accident - due to deteriorating South Westland weather, including fog. (via Noeline Watson)

Early in 1965 Brian Waugh taxies Dominie ZK-AKS for a flight south from Hokitika. Note the small script on the fuselage which reads, "Southern Scenic Air Services Ltd and West Coast Airways Ltd". (Don Noble)

Dominie ZK-AKS crash landed on the northern slopes of Mount Soho (5750ft) on 15 June 1965, after being returned to Queenstown from service at Hokitika. It was doing low level cattle spotting. Fortunately the pilot and four passengers escaped unhurt. In the late 1990s the aircraft remains were salvaged with a long term plan toward restoration. (John Muir)

The following month Waugh entered Dominie ZK-AKS in the Rothmans Air Race from Masterton to Christchurch. With passengers Bill Cropp and Alec Waugh the Dominie went to Christchurch on 7 March and the next day flew four hours Christchurch-Masterton-Christchurch, being placed sixth in the race, and then back to Hokitika. From late June for about six weeks Waugh was off flying duties due to a serious back injury which he attributed to manhandling the heavy fuel drums at Haast. Relief flying on the scheduled service was done by veteran pilot Arthur Bradshaw and young pilot Dave McDonald. Bradshaw was 58 years old and had pioneering pre-war flying experience with his Southland Airways and had known Bert Mercer personally.

The new highway between Paringa and Haast was being worked on with increasing resources. The air service in the meantime continued its versatile operation with Waugh in January 1965 recording 25 scenic flights from Franz

FARES

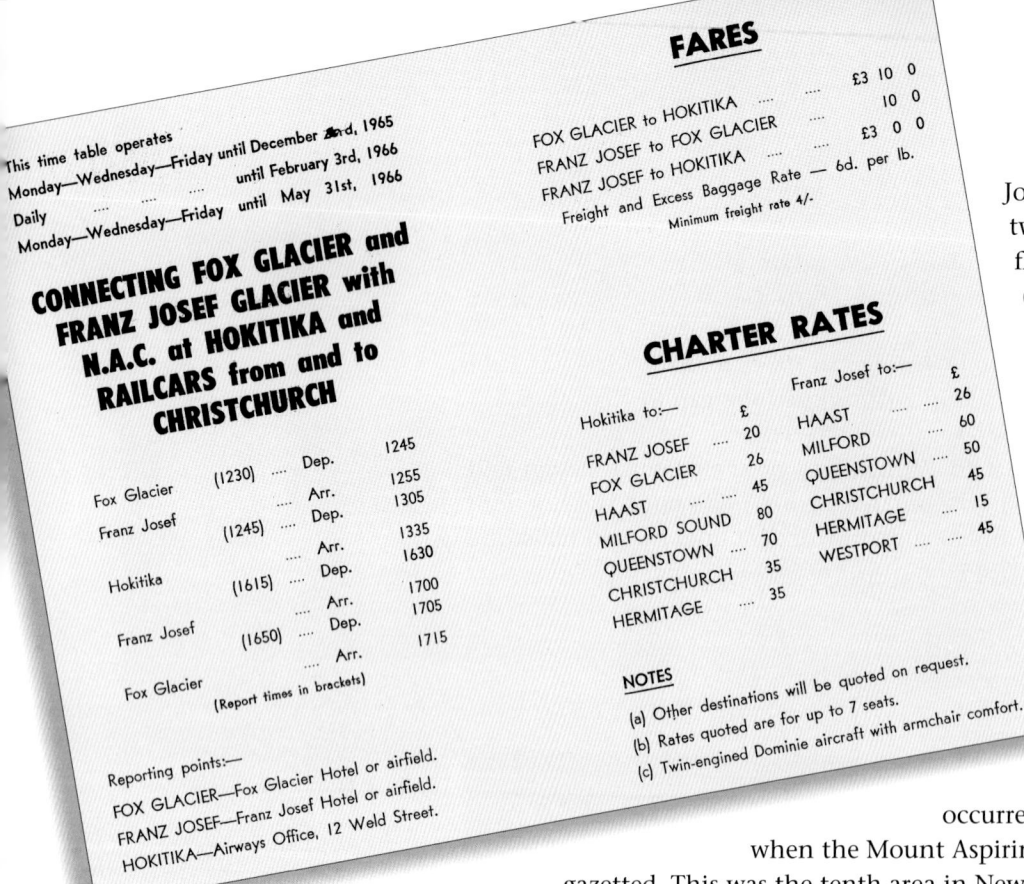

FOX GLACIER to HOKITIKA		£3 10 0
FRANZ JOSEF to FOX GLACIER		10 0
FRANZ JOSEF to HOKITIKA		£3 0 0

Freight and Excess Baggage Rate — 6d. per lb.
Minimum freight rate 4/-

This time table operates
Monday—Wednesday—Friday until December 3rd, 1965
Daily ... ... until February 3rd, 1966
Monday—Wednesday—Friday until May 31st, 1966

CONNECTING FOX GLACIER and FRANZ JOSEF GLACIER with N.A.C. at HOKITIKA and RAILCARS from and to CHRISTCHURCH

Fox Glacier	(1230)	Dep.	1245
		Arr.	1255
Franz Josef	(1245)	Dep.	1305
		Arr.	1335
Hokitika	(1615)	Dep.	1630
		Arr.	1700
Franz Josef	(1650)	Dep.	1705
		Arr.	1715
Fox Glacier			

(Report times in brackets)

Reporting points:—
FOX GLACIER—Fox Glacier Hotel or airfield.
FRANZ JOSEF—Franz Josef Hotel or airfield.
HOKITIKA—Airways Office, 12 Weld Street.

CHARTER RATES

Hokitika to:—	£	Franz Josef to:—	£
FRANZ JOSEF	20	HAAST	26
FOX GLACIER	26	MILFORD	60
HAAST	45	QUEENSTOWN	50
MILFORD SOUND	80	CHRISTCHURCH	45
QUEENSTOWN	70	HERMITAGE	15
CHRISTCHURCH	35	WESTPORT	45
HERMITAGE	35		

NOTES
(a) Other destinations will be quoted on request.
(b) Rates quoted are for up to 7 seats.
(c) Twin-engined Dominie aircraft with armchair comfort.

Josef, two ambulance flights, two Milford Sound scenic flights, three special charters (including two supply dropping flights) and all the usual weekday scheduled services, of which two flights had to return due to poor weather and severe turbulence. Whitebait in season continued as prominent freight with Waugh flying out the biggest single recorded load of 1523lb on 13 October 1964. A milestone recognition of the scenic splendours of South Westland occurred on 10 December 1964 when the Mount Aspiring National Park was formally gazetted. This was the tenth area in New Zealand to be given National Park status and the third largest with an area of 199,205 hectares. Of this, 121,000 hectares were in Otago and 78,205 hectares in Westland. Only the Fiordland and Urewera National Parks were larger in area.

Occasional air-ambulance flights to South Westland continued. On 8 February 1965 Waugh flew to Haast in bad weather and brought out a child for an emergency eye operation in Christchurch. On 12 May he landed Rapide ZK-AHS at Whataroa to pick up a maternity case, probably the last de Havilland airliner to land at Whataroa. For the year ending 31 March 1965 it was reported West Coast Airways had carried 1309 scheduled passengers and flown 456 scheduled hours. 1205 passengers were to and from Haast as were all the 43,956lb of freight and 36,399lb of mail.

In May 1965 New Zealand Tourist Air Travel (TAT) took over Southern Scenic Air Services and in turn West Coast Airways. This meant belonging to a larger airline which had interests throughout the country. A new airways office was opened on the corner of Weld and Tancred Streets in the centre of Hokitika. Despite the impending Haast road opening, optimism was high that the air service would continue in a viable way, helped by the NAC agency. Helen Hutchison remembers, "The new office was Merv Rumsey's pride and joy – especially the wall-sized photograph of an NAC Dominie on the airfield at Franz Josef. We had a cocktail party to celebrate the opening and it was a special occasion. There was a freight room at the back and we handled a lot more freight for Westport, Nelson and Wellington, after moving to town. Previously it was handled by the Gold Band taxi office. We also did more bookings off the street. At aircraft arrival and departure times we closed and headed up to the airport."

A memorable air-ambulance rescue occurred on 23 October 1965 when Mount Cook Air Services Cessna 185 ZK-CEW crashed on the Albert Glacier, a tributary of the Fox Glacier, at about 9,000ft, injuring the five occupants. A

West Indian air hostess, Unice King, on a skiing holiday, was injured along with three male skiers, George Pinckney, Peter Wilding and Simon Chaffey and pilot Harry James. West Coast Airways staff and many locals flare-lit the Hokitika runway for three rescue Cessnas to land at 8.15pm that evening, bringing the injured to Westland Hospital.

The long awaited and important Paringa to Haast road opening was held on 6 November 1965 at Knight's Point. This closed the gap in New Zealand's network of national highways and meant all of Westland was linked to Otago. The 35 mile section from Haast to Paringa had presented huge design and construction challenges. Work had begun in the early 1930s but it was not until the mid 1950s that with Government support work got underway in full swing on what was probably the most difficult road project ever undertaken in New Zealand. The route traversed a mass of towering bush-clad ridges intersected by deep valleys with swift-flowing rivers. Ironically aerial photography from the West Coast Airways Domines was very helpful during the road planning stage. The challenge was not only the extremely rugged terrain but heavy rainfall with

Just south of the Epitaph Rift in 1964 men and heavy machinery work to complete the last section of the new Paringa to Haast highway.
(Les McKenzie)

At Franz Josef on 6 January 1966 Rapide ZK-AHS parked in front of Bert Mercer's 1930s hangar and extension. Brian Waugh flew the veteran aircraft on four scenic flights over the glacier that day and nine more flights the next day.
(Don Noble)

Construction work in the Grave Creek – Breccia Creek area in February 1965. The earthworks were massive – good on a fine day, but making for atrocious conditions when wet! (Les McKenzie)

Prime Minister Keith Holyoake admiring the plaque after its unveiling on a wet day at Knight's Point on 6 November 1965. No planes flew that day but the road opening was ominous for the historic South Westland air service.
(Otago Daily Times)

– 112 –

240 inches being recorded in the region in 1964. In the four-mile stretch from Whakapohai River to Breccia Creek, one million cubic yards of earth and rock were moved, and in this length there were nearly sixty culverts, ranging from two that were 25 feet wide down to pipes 2 feet in diameter. The new direct 269 mile route from Hokitika to Wanaka completed State Highway 6. The day before the official road opening Waugh flew two trips to Haast but on 6 November 1965 it was very wet and miserable with no flying. The following day Waugh flew to Haast but had to stay the night as the weather again deteriorated.

The weeks following the road opening proved challenging for West Coast Airways and the air service. A new timetable was introduced and a variety of charter work undertaken, including Waugh doing an extensive air ambulance flight in Rapide ZK-AHS on 21 November for the Greymouth Hospital Board from Hokitika to Auckland, via Wanganui and return, in a total flying time of nine hours. But demand for the air service to Haast virtually disappeared as the new bus service eliminated the bulk of the airline's freight and passenger work. Waugh flew a flight to Haast on 29 November but then only occasionally during the next thirteen months. On one flight, 28 January 1966, fog prevented ZK-AHS leaving Haast and Waugh stayed the night – like old times! Probably the last Dominie charter flight to Haast was on 4 December of that same year. During 1966 the airline made some changes with Merv Rumsey leaving and staff being cut to a minimum. Working as pilot and manager Waugh sought to further diversify operations with scenic, air-ambulance, supply dropping and charter flying, including innovative educational flights for school children. However the aging Rapide was increasingly obsolete compared to the versatility of what helicopters and ski-equipped aircraft could offer.

Less than eighteen months after the excitement of the road opening, another transport milestone occurred with the closure of the South Westland air service. The new road brought many advantages to the people of Haast but the regular air service was now uneconomic. Waugh operated final scenic flights at Franz Josef over Easter weekend 1967. On 1 April Rapide ZK-AHS, with the Waugh

At the Franz Josef Airfield, not long before the final South Westland air service flights in March 1967, Brian Waugh stands by Rapide ZK-AHS. Waugh was New Zealand's "Mr Rapide" with over 6,000 flying hours on the type over the period 1951 to 1967. (Lyall Hood)

COMMEMORATING THE 75th ANNIVERSARY OF NEW ZEALAND'S FIRST LICENSED SCHEDULED AIR SERVICE

On 18 December 1934, pioneer airline Air Travel (N.Z.) Ltd, founded by Captain J.C. (Bert) Mercer, commenced air services from Hokitika to South Westland with de Havilland DH.83 Fox Moth ZK-ADI.

Places on the early scheduled service were, at various times, Whataroa, Waiho (Franz Josef), Weheka (Fox Glacier), Bruce Bay, Haast, Upper Okuru, Okuru (Mussel Point) and Jackson Bay.

The air service was taken over by New Zealand National Airways Corporation (NAC) in 1947 and by West Coast Airways Ltd (WCA) in 1956.

Nearby Haast Aerodrome was the main southern terminus for the passenger, airmail, freight and air-ambulance services provided by Air Travel, NAC and WCA.

The air service greatly reduced the isolation of all who lived in South Westland, before any road access was completed.

The world's longest running de Havilland biplane air service ended in March 1967, due to the effects of the new Haast Highway.

Dedicated on 19 December 2009.

family aboard, left Hokitika to be based at Queenstown. The veteran pre-war Rapide, which had flown for Cook Strait Airways Ltd, Air Travel (NZ) Ltd, NAC and West Coast Airways Ltd, made a couple of low passes over Hokitika and also at Haast as Waugh flew over familiar territory for the last time. Gordon Bowman, Hokitika Airport Superintendent, who had long associations with the air service remarked, "Today sees the end of an era on the West Coast, as West Coast Airways ceases to exist. So this is really the end of the effort which was started by Bert Mercer."

WHAT TO SEE TODAY

DH89A Rapide ZK-AHS

Displayed at Auckland's Museum of Transport and Technology (MOTAT) in the colours of NAC, this historic pre-war airliner flew for all three operators of the South Westland air service as well as Cook Strait Airways Ltd in the late 1930s..

Dominie aircraft steps

At the Hokitika Airport Terminal are displayed the restored aircraft steps made about 1960 for the West Coast Airways Dominies.

Haast Aviation Plaque

Situated near the entrance to the Department of Conservation (DoC) Visitor Centre at Haast Junction, this aviation plaque, designed by Graeme McConnell, commemorates the historic air service. It was dedicated by Rev Richard Waugh on 19 December 2009 as part of the 75th air service anniversary celebrations (see above).

Teichelmann's Bed and Breakfast

This historic house at 20 Hamilton Street Hokitika was built about 1910 for Dr Ebenezer Teichelmann, Surgeon Superintendent of the Westland Hospital. From this home he undertook many mountaineering expeditions and the first aerial flight to South Westland. Later Dr Teichelmann was an early supporter of Captain Bert Mercer's airline. Captain Brian Waugh, Chief Pilot for West Coast Airways, and family, owned the house from 1960 to 1972.

Haast Aerodrome and Ticket Office

The site of the Cron's landing ground for some of Mercer's early flights, the aerodrome was later constructed during World War II as an emergency landing ground and served as the main southern terminus of the South Westland air service. The aerodrome is now privately owned. The small ticket office survives from the South Westland air service era and was recently renovated.

6

Gone, but not Forgotten
Remembering the air service

THE LATE 1960s were a time of significant change for West Coast aviation. In early 1967 the historic South Westland air service finished with little media attention and no special event to mark its passing. For more than 30 years the reliable air service had served South Westland becoming the world's longest running de Havilland biplane air service. In late 1968 NAC introduced jet-prop Fokker F27 Friendship aircraft to the West Coast with its new trans-alpine service and soon after a pure jet airliner visited Hokitika for the first time to park on the tarmac recently occupied by the Dominies. The old de Havillands were quickly relegated to the past and fading memories.

One small but immediate legacy from the past was the return of an honoured name with the start of a new Hokitika company. Air Travel (Hokitika) Ltd was formed by Des Wright as the new principal agents for NAC/Air New Zealand, Mount Cook Airlines and Golden Coast Airlines. The Air Travel name was again to be prominent in Hokitika for the next two decades. Helen Hutchison recalls, "At the time Des Wright offered me work at Air Travel I had just been assigned the family whitebait trench. I told Des and he said, 'Just work when you can and fish the tides.' I could not believe my luck so that's what I did for the next ten

The last DH89 Dominie to be based in South Westland was ZK-BCP, seen here in the old Air Travel (NZ) Ltd hangar at Franz Josef on 11 February 1971. At right in the dark background of the hangar, near where the people are standing, can be seen the upright posts of Mercer's original 1935 hangar. (Jim Sullivan)

– 115 –

Flying from Hokitika to South Westland on the 60th anniversary day of Captain Bert Mercer's pioneering flight, 18 December 1994, Dominie ZK-AKY and Fox Moth ZK-AEK ride comfortably in the smooth conditions. (John King)

Fox Moth ZK-ASP (formerly ZK-ADI) on the beach at Pukutuaro, South Westland, in July 1972 during its re-enactment flight tour down the West Coast with owner David Lilico and passengers Alister Barry and John King. (John King)

years. In fact Des and I both fished the tides. If the airport was busy we worked to suit. Between us we fed most airports in New Zealand with whitebait!"

In 1968 the long-time dream of Mercer and many other West Coast pilots for a permanent trans-alpine scheduled air service came to fruition. NAC had landed a Fokker Friendship at Hokitika on a charter flight on 4 November 1967, and then followed with a number of other flights, including a proving flight on 3 September 1968. Scheduled services commenced on 20 December that year, with Friendship ZK-NAF *Korimako,* flown by Captain Dick Patterson, First Officer Rod Trowsdale and Hostess Miss J.Gilbert. A special passenger on the flight was Mr Bill Harrington who had accompanied Captain Maurice Buckley on the first trans-alpine flight on 4 June 1924. The Friendship was the first turbo-prop aircraft to operate on the West Coast and the trans-alpine was the last new route to be inaugurated by NAC, before the airline was amalgamated with Air New Zealand in 1978. Big crowds gathered at Hokitika to welcome the Friendship aircraft on these important flights.

Modern turbine aircraft, new tourism opportunities, continuing social change and a new 1970s decade beckoning, made people look to the future. But one prominent guest on the Friendship proving flight drew attention to the past. He was 84 year-old Mr T. E. Y. Seddon, son of 1890s Prime Minister Richard John Seddon, and himself the MP for Westland from 1906 to 1920 and again from 1925 to 1928. Seddon recalled how he had travelled to the West Coast by coach in his infant days and then rode in a cattle truck on the first train from Greymouth to Hokitika in the early 1890s. He had been present in 1908 when the first shot had been fired for the Otira Tunnel construction and was among the first to travel through it at the opening some years later. And he was at

Following its retirement in the early 1970s by Mount Cook Airlines ZK-AHS was stored in its old West Coast Airways hangar at Hokitika and eventually parked outside. It is seen here in April 1974 shortly before it made its final flight to Auckland for delivery to the Museum of Transport and Technology. (Don Noble)

BELOW: *During the airshow to mark the opening of the new Hokitika Airport Terminal on 18 March 1979, Brian Waugh stands by the old Dominie steps of West Coast Airways. The steps were later discarded to a dump area behind the hangars and in 1985 were restored by Jim Jamieson and are currently on display in the Hokitika terminal.* (Richard Waugh)

TUESDAY, MARCH 20, 1979.

Met Many Old Friends

Captain Brian Waugh Pays Visit To Hokitika

A former resident and Borough Councillor of Hokitika, and West Coast Airways pilot, returned to the town last Saturday after an absence of eight years. He was Captain Brian Waugh, who finished a twenty-six year pilot career at the bottom of the Shotover River in Queenstown, in 1967.

"The only pilot to go panning for gold · in an aeroplane," he says with a smile. "Yes it was rather an inglorious end to a long flying career but that's life. u can't do anyth...

South Westland pilots to follow. "Of course" he mused "my old friend Myrtle Cron...

Southside on 31 December 1934 when Mercer flew the first airmail flights. Looking back at all this transportation advance Seddon paid tribute to the aviation pioneers and remarked, "Two days then – 40 minutes now by NAC!"

Soon afterwards, on 1 March 1969, Fokker F28 Fellowship airliner PH-MOL landed at Hokitika Airport while on a demonstration flight around New Zealand. Commanded by Fokker's Chief Test Pilot, Captain A.P. Moll, it was the first pure jet aircraft to use unpaved airfields in New Zealand. To have a modern jet airliner at Hokitika was a far cry from the NAC DC-3 and West Coast Airways Dominies. Time was marching on and the old aircraft, including the DC-3, withdrawn from the West Coast in June 1970, were quickly forgotten in the face of rapid aviation change.

At the same time that the new trans-alpine service was introduced in December 1968, Mount Cook Airlines began a new service from the glaciers to Hokitika with Cessna aircraft and this included the last commercial Dominie flying. DH89B Dominie ZK-BCP was based at Franz Josef and was occasionally used on the service to Hokitika, until it was withdrawn in 1971.

In 1972 Aerial Sowing Ltd bought the former West Coast Airways hangar, which had originally been built by Air Travel (NZ) Ltd at Southside before the war, and moved to the new airport in 1951. As well as loaders and other equipment a couple of aircraft were housed in the old hangar. The hangar became the centre for their topdressing activities until Aerial Sowing became Rowley Aviation in 1978.

A turning point of historical recognition for the South Westland air service came five years after its demise. In July 1972, the 25th anniversary year of NAC, Fox Moth ZK-ASP (originally ZK-ADI) returned to the West Coast for a nostalgic visit. Owned and flown by David Lilico, the veteran aircraft retraced the Air Travel (NZ) Ltd and NAC routes. At Wellington former NAC Fox Moth pilots Doug Lister and Des Holden

– 118 –

LEFT: *On 30 November 1991 many people with connections to West Coast aviation gathered at the Hokitika Airport Terminal for the book launch of Brian Waugh's* Turbulent Years – A Commercial Pilot's Story. *Seated from left: Jack Renton, Jim Jamieson, Norm Bishop, Des Nolan, Paul Hutchison, Gavin Molloy and Dorothy Fletcher (nee Graham).*
(West Coast Times/Hokitika Guardian)

CENTRE: *The airshow at Hokitika Airport on Saturday 17 December 1994 to celebrate the 60th anniversary of the South Westland air service. Sir Tim Wallis's Spitfire ZK-XVI is ready for display with Dominies ZK-AKY and ZK-AKU and Proctor V ZK-AQZ in the background.* (John King)

BELOW: *Former NAC Fox Moth pilots from the late 1940s and the early 1950s at Hokitika during the December 1994 60th anniversary. From left: Doug Lister, Shem Dowd, Jock McLernon and Des Holden with Simon Spencer-Bower in the cockpit of Fox Moth ZK-AEK.*
(John King)

(Mike Keenan)

viewed their old aircraft and Holden took it for a quick flight quipping it was very different from his current Vickers Viscount aircraft. After over-nighting in Nelson, the Fox Moth, carrying passengers Alister Barry and John King, flew through heavy rain to Westport. At Greymouth a crowd of several hundred people welcomed the aircraft's return. Then on to Hokitika where the spectators included many with direct links to the historic air service including Frank Molloy, Jean Wells and Dr Jean McLean. A brief stop was made at Franz Josef and an overnight at Fox Glacier. The following day a South Westland beach landing was made and then on to Haast and Mussel Point. Many school children came to view the old Fox Moth and the visit did much to stir interest in local aviation history. John King's photographs and published account of the Fox Moth's return to South Westland helped people remember the stories of the South Westland air service.

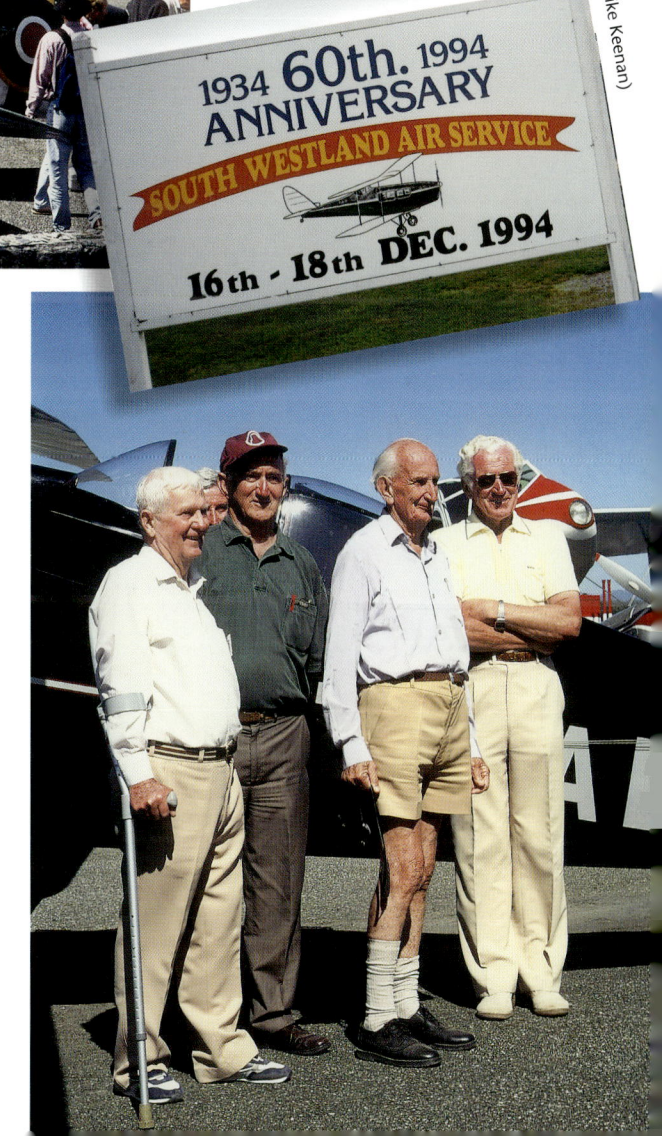

On Saturday 17 December 1994, Fox Moth ZK-ADI flies again! The replica in Air Travel (NZ) Ltd livery is lifted by crane before a large airshow crowd. At left, Marie Lindsay (nee Mercer) looks on after unveiling the commemorative plaque and at right Rev Richard Waugh leads the dedication ceremony. (Jane St George Waugh)

In August 1994 Max Dowell helps build the replica of Fox Moth ZK-ADI in the Westland District Council's Kaniere depot for the 60th anniversary. (Mike Keenan)

This mannequin of Captain Mercer stands beside the Fox Moth replica in the specially built display buidling at Hokitika Airport. The building was opened in September 1996 with many guests present, including the two daughters of Bert Mercer. (Waugh Collection)

At much the same time as the Fox Moth visit, veteran Rapide ZK-AHS, the only aircraft used by all three operators of the South Westland air service, was flown to Hokitika for storage, pending sale. The Rapide was in need of major overhaul and this was uneconomic. Interest in historic aircraft was at a low point and the attitude was either "scrap it or put it in a museum". The pioneering airliner was for sale for $8000 but there no takers. Stored in its old West Coast Airways hangar it was soon moved outside and parked forlornly for some time. Des Wright regularly started the engines and even taxied it about. In early 1974 ZK-AHS was donated by the owners, Mount Cook Airlines, to the Museum of Transport and Technology in Auckland and after some work at Queenstown the airliner made a long ferry flight north. Its last flights over South Westland were nearly 40 years after Mercer's first de Havilland air service flights.

Hokitika's new airport terminal was opened in March 1979 with much fanfare, including a well attended airshow. Dominie ZK-AKY gave joy-rides, still painted in its silver and light blue Mount Cook livery, despite being sold by

Restored Fox Moth ZK-AEK soon after landing at the former Southside Aerodrome site on Sunday 18 December 1994, the first landing there by a Fox Moth since 1952. The "HOKITIKA" letters at the old aerodrome were placed there in the late 1930s but covered up during World War II for security reasons. For the 60th anniversary they were uncovered and painted. (John King)

Mount Cook Airlines the previous year. The old West Coast Airways steps were rolled out and used by eager passengers keen for an experience of vintage Dominie flying. Local aviation historian Bill Cropp had a large photographic display in the old hangar and a framed colour photograph of Rapide ZK-AHS was donated to the Airport Committee for display in the new terminal lounge.

On 29 December 1984 the Waiho River burst its banks and completely engulfed the Franz Josef Airfield. Half buried and destroyed by water and rubble was the historic 1930s Air Travel (NZ) Ltd hangar. It was two years later before a replacement airfield was ready at a different site. Named in memory of Bert Mercer it was opened on 20 December 1986 by special guest Marie Lindsay (nee Mercer). Although repaired, the original airfield site was not suitable for fixed wing aircraft use but has continued as a landing site for helicopter operations.

The 50th anniversary of the pioneering of the South Westland air service had passed unnoticed but for the 60th anniversary, in December 1994, aviation historian Rev Richard Waugh and Michael Keenan, from the Westland District Council, took the initiative to mark the air service's historical contribution to the region. Keen interest developed on the West Coast and from

80 year-old Marie Lindsay, daughter of Bert Mercer, at the 60th anniversary dinner at Hokitika, 17 December 1994. The flying scale model of Fox Moth ZK-AEK was donated by David Hope-Cross for display at the West Coast Historical Museum. (Martin Erasmussen)

The Hokitika celebration dinner for 425 people at the Hokitika Boys Brigade Hall, 17 December 1994, was a key event of the 60th air service anniversary with excellent West Coast hospitality. The Royal New Zealand Air Force Band provided musical entertainment. (Martin Erasmussen)

FROM LEFT: *'Gar' Graham reminisces about early flying from Franz Josef at the celebration dinner.*
(Martin Erasmussen)

June Molloy, wife of Air Travel and NAC pilot Frank Molloy, speaks of the NAC flying era.
(Martin Erasmussen)

Paul Beauchamp Legg, West Coast Airways Dominie pilot from 1958 to 1961 shares stories about his time flying in South Westland.
(Martin Erasmussen)

Jean Waugh, wife of pilot Brian Waugh, recalls the West Coast Airways era. (Martin Erasmussen)

people throughout New Zealand and from overseas who were captivated by the nostalgia of de Havilland biplane flying amid some of the most beautiful and dramatic scenery in the world.

Aviation journalist and photographer John King later wrote, "When an airline operation serves a remote and roadless region for more than 30 years, it has a major social significance, and so a celebration marking 60 years since its founding is a major social occasion. And when that airline operation has used almost exclusively de Havilland biplanes during three separate phases in those 30 years, the celebration tends to take on a 'DH' flavour. Add to all such jollity and nostalgia a spell of perfect weather in a region renowned for its spectacular scenery and rainfall, and the scene in Hokitika, on the West Coast of New Zealand's South Island was almost too much for mere mortals to cope with. Flying displays, celebration dinner for hundreds of people, memorial unveilings, open-air church service at the airline founder's graveside, re-enactment flights into a long-disused aerodrome and down the full length of South Westland – so much was packed into a single weekend that Christmas a week later was something of an anticlimax."

Excellent public attendance at the variety of events for the South Westland air service celebrations demonstrated the increasing interest in West Coast aviation history and social history. The first event was the unveiling on 16 December 1994 of a memorial plaque at Kawatiri Junction, close to the crash site of Dragon ZK-AHT where Bert Mercer and Maurice Dawe had died in June 1944. The following day, many

SOUTH WESTLAND AIR SERVICE CELEBRATIONS
HOKITIKA 17 – 18 DECEMBER 1994
Newsletter No 4 — January 1995

OUTSTANDING SUCCESS

The Fox Moth replica memorial in the air for its first and only flight after unveiling on Saturday 17 December 1994. The replica was built by Max Dowell assisted by the Westland District Council.
(Lawrence Acket)

One of the world's great de Havilland air services was celebrated in of the 16-18 December at Hokitika on the scenic West anniversary of **Captain Bert Mercer** attracted thousands of Fox Mo

60th Anniversary of the of the First Licensed Sche Air-Service in New Zealan

Air Travel (N.Z.) Ltd 1934 –
National Airways Corporation
West Coast Airways 1956 –

▲

PATRON
John Neave
(Air Travel Pilot 1938 –

▲

BOARD OF REFERENCE
Billee Douglas
(Daughter of Bert Mercer)

Jim Jamieson

AT TOP: *Low tide at Big Bay in February 1997, Fox Moth ZK-ADI and Dominie ZK-AKY, along with other aircraft, re-enact the pre-war South Westland beach landings of Bert Mercer's Air Travel (NZ) Ltd. The aircraft are on a flight from Mandeville to the airshow at Westport via Haast and Hokitika.* (John King)

ABOVE: *Reminiscing at Haast Airfield in February 1997 with Fox Moth ZK-ADI, newly arrived back in New Zealand. From left long-time local residents John Nolan and Allan Cron with Colin Smith, founder of the Croydon Aviation Heritage Trust.* (John King)

thousands of people converged on Hokitika Airport for an airshow in perfect weather, with Sir Tim Wallis giving a memorable display in Spitfire ZK-XVI as a tribute to the aviation pioneers. In the evening a celebration dinner at the Boys Brigade Hall at Hokitika was attended by more than 400 people with many reminiscing about South Westland flying. Early on Sunday 18 December a service at Bert Mercer's grave was conducted by Rev Richard Waugh, followed by the unveiling of a commemorative plaque and information panels, funded by the Renton family, near the old Southside Aerodrome site. Recently restored Fox Moth ZK-AEK made a landing on the old aerodrome site. In the afternoon of the 60th anniversary day Dominie ZK-AKY and recently restored Fox Moth ZK-AEK flew south to Franz Josef. With deteriorating weather they did not land at Haast but flew low-level.

The book *When the Coast is Clear* was launched at the celebrations with contributions by John King, Paul Beauchamp Legg and Richard Waugh. This was the first time the whole story of the South Westland air service 1934 to 1967 had been described together. Legg also wrote his own book which complimented the efforts of the late Brian Waugh, whose book had been launched at Hokitika three years earlier. The South Westland air service was finally getting the published attention it deserved.

Amid the anniversary celebrations the "Hokitika Aviation Heritage Trail", the first of its kind in New Zealand, was launched highlighting important sites associated with early aviation and especially that of the South Westland air service. The heritage trail included one of the most tangible aspects of the air service celebrations, the replica Fox Moth ZK-ADI memorial.

The idea of a replica aircraft for display in Hokitika had been mooted in the early 1990s and the idea was taken up by Westland District Council General Manager Jon Olson for the 60th anniversary celebrations. This council decision marked a turning point in the public recognition of the South Westland air service and led to many other local initiatives including songs about the air service, model aircraft being made, paintings, drawings, books, articles and special airmail covers. Construction of the replica Fox Moth started in July 1994 at the Westland District Council's Kaniere Depot with funding from the New Zealand Lotteries Board and Westland District Council. Rob Daniel, Council's Manager of Operations prepared construction plans from original Fox Moth drawings and Max Dowell provided technical expertise from his background in timber construction and boatbuilding. The fullsize replica made of fibreglass coated plywood was a major project involving considerable voluntary assistance from many people. The Fox Moth, in original Air Travel (NZ) Ltd colours, was unveiled at the beginning of the anniversary airshow.

On 28 September 1996 a specially built display building, funded by the Westland District Council, was opened at Hokitika Airport to house the replica Fox Moth. Both of Bert Mercer's daughters, Marie Lindsay and Billee Douglas, attended. Deputy Mayor, Ross Overton, officiated and Haast raconteur Des Nolan spoke of his memories of Captain Mercer. He described events surrounding a flight north with a severe bout of appendicitis and commented, "I'm one of the many people who owe my life to the air service." Colin Smith from the Croydon Aviation Heritage Trust was pleased to report the original Fox Moth ZK-ADI had recently been purchased by Gerald Grocott and was being shipped back to New Zealand for some refurbishment and would soon return to Hokitika for a

On the occasion of the 50th anniversary celebrations of the opening of Hokitika Airport on 15 December 2001, Fox Moth ZK-ADI and Dominie ZK-AKY outside the terminal building with Air New Zealand Link Raytheon/Beech1900D ZK-EAA. At left is the Alpine Fighter Collection's Hawker Hurricane Mark 11A ZK-TPK. (Mike Condon)

Unveiled by Dick Smith 75 years to the day after Guy Menzies' historic flight, this commemorative information display and plaque is at the end of a short unnamed road, off La Fountaine Road, about 12 kilometres from Harihari, and only a short distance from the actual 1931 landing spot, (out of photograph to the right). The well known Australian electronics-business entrepreneur and aviator had, earlier on 7 January 2006, completed a significant solo re-enactment flight direct from Sydney to Harihari in his single-engine Cessna Caravan VH-SHW. (Graeme McConnell)

BELOW: *Dedicated during the Warbirds Over Wanaka airshow in April 2006, this Graeme McConnell designed plaque is the only memorial to the five people missing aboard Dragonfly ZK-AFB. This Dragonfly was Bert Mercer's favourite and has become New Zealand's most-searched-for aircraft.* (Graeme McConnell)

LOWER: *Graeme McConnell (at left), John Rowan (one of passenger Lewis Rowan's brothers) and Rev Richard Waugh (author of LOST... without trace?), soon after the unveiling ceremony.* (Pam McConnell)

visit. Within six months, Smith's prediction was fulfilled when ZK-ADI, along with other vintage de Havillands, called at Hokitika in February 1997 on a flight north to the Westport airshow. It was a nostalgic time, with a crowd gathering and media interest in Bert Mercer's original Fox Moth returning to its former home base.

Sadly, a couple of months earlier, on 4 December 1996, the former Mercer home at the old Southside Aerodrome site was destroyed by fire. Likely caused by an electrical fault, the house, owned by Matthew and Lesley Syron, was gutted and another tangible link to the pioneering aviation days of Bert Mercer was gone.

In the late 1990s at the Museum of Transport and Technology in Auckland progress was made with the displays of historic de Havilland aircraft. Alongside Rapide ZK-AHS was placed a replica of Fox Moth ZK-AEK, resplendent in 1930s Air Travel (NZ) Ltd colours. The Fox Moth had been constructed from an assortment of parts and the finished product was a fine tribute to the operations of the pioneer airline. Soon afterwards ZK-AHS was given its first refurbishment after 25 years with the museum. This included stripping back, repairs, cleaning of the engines and a repaint in the red and white livery of NAC.

During the first decade of the new millennium a number of special flights and aviation commemorations were organised. The 50th anniversary of the opening of the new Hokitika Airport was celebrated in December 2001 with Fox Moth ZK-ADI and Dominie ZK-AKY giving popular joy rides. During the Easter 2006 Warbirds over

DES WRIGHT AND AIR TRAVEL (HOKITIKA) LTD

DESMOND ROBERT WRIGHT was a well known personality in Hokitika and West Coast aviation circles from the 1950s to the 1980s. He was born at Reefton on 17 March 1926. The family lived at Blackball and then moved to Harihari in South Westland. He worked as a bus driver, served in the RNZAF, and after the war worked as a car and truck mechanic with his own garage business at Harihari.

Wright moved to Hokitika in the late 1950s and was employed as a mechanic/engineer with West Coast Airways, assisting the licensed engineer. He maintained a private pilot's licence and owned and operated Auster ZK-AUO for several years. His engineering expertise and skill were widely recognised and he also did much administration work.

When West Coast Airways finished operations in March 1967 Wright took over the NAC and other travel agencies. After consulting with Paul Renton he decided to resurrect Mercer's Air Travel name for the new company, calling it "Air Travel (Hokitika) Ltd." The company became the Principal Agents for NAC and in 1975 opened new offices on the corner of Tancred and Hamilton Streets. Wright continued with his aviation business until his death on 15 February 1987, leaving his wife Raeoni and children Vivien and Robert (Buster). Air Travel (Hokitika) Ltd was sold to the Westland Savings Bank and later evolved into a branch of the House of Travel.

Des Wright with NAC hostess Marilyn Pilgrim on the Friendship steps at Hokitika in 1975. Wright owned and operated Air Travel (Hokitika) Ltd, the principal agents for NAC and Air Zealand from 1967 to 1986. (NAC Official via Murray Whitehead)

Wanaka airshow, a plaque was unveiled at Wanaka Airport commemorating Dragonfly ZK-AFB, Mercer's favourite aircraft, which was lost without trace on a scenic flight from Christchurch to Milford Sound on 12 February 1962. The dedication of the plaque on 15 April 2006 marks the only place where the five names of those onboard the ill-fated Dragonfly are permanently recorded: Captain Brian Chadwick (pilot), and passengers Louis Rowan, honeymooners Elwyn and Valerie Saville, and Darrell Shiels. Occasional searches still continue for ZK-AFB with the hope that the aircraft, its pilot and passengers, will eventually be found and the long-time mystery solved.

In March 2007, for the 60th anniversary of New Zealand National Airways Corporation (NAC), a special DC-3 and Dominie flight was made to the West Coast. Dominie ZK-AKY, wearing its NAC livery, landed at Haast to also mark the 40th anniversary of the end of the South Westland air service. A large crowd of locals gathered and the Dominie flew a number of local joyriding flights. All the children from the Haast School gathered around the de Havilland biplane as pilot Ryan Southam pointed out the zip-up fabric of the fuselage, the wooden and fabric construction, and opened the cowlings to reveal the engines still hot and ticking from their recent running. It was all reminiscent of children's

Restoration of former Air Travel (NZ) Ltd and NAC Fox Moth ZK-AGM progresses at Hungerford in England with the wings temporarily attached, July 2009. (Bruce Broady)

– 127 –

In May 2008 former Haast school boys who went to boarding school in Christchurch in the 1950s, chartered Dominie ZK-AKY to re-live their South Westland flights and again flew Hokitika to Haast. From left: David Glubb, Kerry Eggeling, Roger Eggeling, Peter Eggeling, Cliff Eggeling and John Buchanan ready to board at Hokitika on 10 May. (Roger Eggeling)

A new generation pilot! Noah Waugh, a grandson of Brian Waugh, plays on his Rapide/Dominie model in 2009. (Theresa Waugh)

rapt attention and delight in the early 1930s when the first aircraft appeared in South Westland. Later that day Dominie ZK-AKY and DC-3 ZK-DAK made a formation flight up the coast to Hokitika where an appreciative crowd watched them land.

Typical of the continuing interest in the restored de Havilland biplanes on the West Coast, was the 2008 charter of Dominie ZK-AKY by several men who as schoolboys in the late 1950s, had flown from Haast on the air service. Brothers Kerry, Roger, Peter and Cliff Eggeling, with John Buchanan and David Glubb, chartered the Dominie in May for a nostalgic flight back to South Westland. Peter Eggeling commented about how amazing perceptions change over the years. "The plane seemed so big back then, now it looks tiny. I am not sitting in the tail this time. They used to make me sit back there among all the bread and newspapers that were for the Haast shops because I was so little."

With the 75th anniversary of Mercer's pioneering efforts being planned for December 2009, the South Westland community grasped the opportunity to celebrate the occasion. In June 2009 a massive voluntary effort by many locals worked to renovate the historic Haast Aerodrome, thanks to the ready co-operation of land owner Dave Saxton and family. An extensive array of heavy machinery was used to clear more than 20 years of moss and grass growth from the runway as well as gorse and other rubbish. The aircraft parking area was reclaimed from the encroaching swamp and given a fresh layer of gravel. This all-age voluntary effort was a vivid expression of the commitment by the Haast community to both its aviation history and aviation future. Planned for unveiling near the aerodrome on the 75th anniversary weekend is a commemorative plaque which will mark the significance of the unique South Westland air service – New Zealand's pioneering licensed scheduled air service.

Appendix 1

South Westland air service staff
by Richard Waugh

AIR TRAVEL (NZ) LTD 1934-1947
Pilots
Bert Mercer....................1934-1944
Jim Hewett 1936-1940
Cliff Lewis.....................1937-1942
John Neave 1938-1940
 and 1945
Arthur Baines 1938-1939
 and 1942-1943
Orville 'Ozzie' Openshaw 1941-1944
Des Patterson.......................1942
Colin Lewis 1942-1947
Norm Suttie 1943
 and 1945-1947
Jim Kennedy..................1944-1945
Frank Molloy..................1945-1947

Engineers/Stores etc
Bert Mercer....................1934-1944
Owen Templeton 1936-1942
Roy Markland.................1937-1941
Ted Toohey 1938-1941
Jack Carroll....................1938-1942
Tom Harris 1938-1947
Ron Barltrop 1941-1944
Ross Grant 1940-1944
Bill Little........................1940-1942
Ross King......................1941-1947
Alan Salter 1942
Orville 'Ozzie' Openshaw 1941-1944
Dick Ferguson 1942-1947
Emil Rosel 1942-1945
Bill Dini.........................1943-1947
Harry Howard 1945-1947

Administration
Billee Mercer..................1935-1936
Maureen Neale...............1936-1938
 and 1942
Andy Drummond 1938-1942
Marie Mercer 1938-1945
Miss Polbury........................1942
Griff O'Neil 1943
Roy Quinn 1943-1944
Nadine Hunter 1943-1947
Jean Stoop 1945-1947
Margaret Penman............1946-1947

NZ SERIES II: 1 of 4. The four passenger De Havilland Fox Moth was used extensively by Air Travel (NZ) Ltd. This pioneering airline played an important part in servicing isolated areas of the West Coast of New Zealand in the 30's and early 40's.

March 2007 - 40th Anniversary of the close of the historic South Westland Air Service. DH89A Rapide ZK-AHS of West Coast Airways (1956-1967) with long serving Chief Pilot Captain Brian Waugh at Haast Airfield with Mosquito Hill in the background.

NEW ZEALAND NATIONAL AIRWAYS CORPORATION 1947-1956

Pilots
Norm Suttie 1947-1950
Colin Lewis 1947-1948
Frank Molloy....................1947-1956
Jock McLernon 1948-1951
Doug Lister 1949-1953
Des Holden 1953-1955

Relief:
Vincent Moran 1947-1948
Jimmy Cane.....................1947-1948
Blatchford Smith 1947-1948
Shem Dowd 1948
Graeme Barnett 1948
Jack Leech............................. 1949
Doug Lister 1953-1955
Maurice Cronin................1955-1956
Jack Franklyn....................1955-1956

Engineers/Stores etc
Bert Allard.......................1947-1950
Tom Harris 1947-1956
Dick Ferguson 1947-1951
Ross King.........................1947-1949
Harry Howard 1947-1956

Administration
Jean Stoop 1947-1952
Margaret Penman.............1947-1950
Bob Nossiter....................1947-1953
Joan Win 1951-1954
Jean Anderson..................1951-1956
Phil Carmine....................1953-1956
Peter Whiley....................1954-1956
Diane Thompson.................... 1954
Joy Staines 1955-1956

Haast Agent
Myrtle Cron.....................1947-1956

WEST COAST AIRWAYS LTD 1956-1967

Pilots
Bryan McCook 1956-1957
Jack Humphries...................... 1957
Ken Eden.........................1957-1959
Paul Beauchamp Legg........1958-1961
Brian Waugh....................1959-1967
Geoffrey Houston 1961-1964

Relief Pilots
Arthur Bradshaw 1964
Dave McDonald....................... 1964

Numerous Southern Scenic Air Services pilots flew occasionally for West Coast Airways, especially in the earlier years, including Fred Lucas, Tex Smith, Russell Troon, John Killian and Rex Dovey.

Engineers/Stores etc
Tom Harris 1956-1957
Bill Hende.......................1956-1957
Arnold Ingham 1956-1957
Des Wright.......................1957-1967
Brian Waugh....................1959-1967
Basil de Jong......................... 1960

Administration
Phil Carmine....................1956-1957
Jean Anderson (Wells) 1956-1957
Joy Staines 1956-1958
Mervyn Rumsey 1958-1965
Helen Hutchison 1962-1966
Lindy Agnew 1966-1967

Haast Agent
Myrtle Cron.....................1956-1965

This staff list was first published in 1994 for the 60th anniversary. There have been some revisions in the light of further research. However some dates are still best estimates.

Appendix 2

Airlines operating on the West Coast
by Bruce Gavin

INTRODUCTION

In the 75 years since Air Travel (NZ) Ltd commenced scheduled air services to South Westland on 18 December 1934, other airlines have provided regular air links to, from and within the West Coast region. This long narrow strip of land lying between the Tasman Sea and the mountainous spine of the Southern Alps presents considerable geographical, weather-related and operational challenges for aviation operators. Enthusiasm, innovation and hard work, often coupled with a strong independent streak, have been common characteristics among those who have been involved in developing and operating services for the West Coast.

The following is a brief account of the various airlines that have provided regular air links to the communities of the greater West Coast region, from Karamea in northern Buller to Haast and further south.

Note: *Air Travel (NZ) Ltd, West Coast Airways Ltd and the South Westland air service operated by NAC are excluded from this summary as they are dealt with in the main body of the book.*

COOK STRAIT AIRWAYS LIMITED

The second airline to provide the West Coast with scheduled air services was Nelson based Cook Strait Airways, which was established in 1935. On 30 December of that year

Cook Strait Airways Rapides ZK-AGT Neptune (later ZK-AHS) and ZK-AEC Mercury at the opening of Westport's new Carters Beach Aerodrome on 15 March 1939. Cook Strait Airways was the pioneer operator from Nelson to the West Coast, inaugurating services to Greymouth and Hokitika from 24 February 1937. (Whites Aviation)

NAC DC-3 Skyliner ZK-BEU Westport at Hokitika on one of the final DC-3 flights, 1 June 1970. The West Coast was one of the last regions in New Zealand to have scheduled NAC DC-3 services. At left is the former Air Travel, NAC and West Coast Airways hangar. (Brian Whebell)

the new airline began scheduled air services between Wellington, Blenheim and Nelson with two twin-engine de Havilland DH89A Rapides. With the arrival of the company's fourth aircraft, the building of Karoro Aerodrome at Greymouth, and the upgrading of Hokitika's Southside Aerodrome, the airline soon extended services southwards to these two destinations from Wellington and Nelson. The first scheduled flight of the thrice-weekly service was flown from Nelson to the West Coast on 24 February 1937.

Westport was linked into the service on 15 March 1939 and the frequency of flights was doubled to six return services a week, a situation that lasted only six months because of the declaration of World War II on 3 September 1939. The Government quickly impressed Cook Strait Airways' five aircraft and aircrew into RNZAF service and by early November Air Travel (NZ) Ltd had taken over the route from Nelson to the West Coast, which it continued to operate until it in turn was superceded by NAC in October 1947.

NEW ZEALAND NATIONAL AIRWAYS CORPORATION (NAC)

As well as taking over the South Westland air service from Air Travel (NZ) Ltd on 1 October 1947, the New Zealand National Airways Corporation (NAC) took over the routes from Hokitika, Greymouth and Westport to Nelson and Wellington. De Havilland DH83 Fox Moth and de Havilland DH89 Rapide and Dominie aircraft were based at Hokitika to fly the South Westland services. Initially they also flew to Westport and Nelson, although Lockheed 10A Electra aircraft soon flew many of the services from Westport

NAC Friendship ZK-BXC Kerangi at Hokitika Airport, surrounded by many admirers while on an early NAC promotional flight. Inaugural trans-alpine flights began on 20 December 1968 introducing the first jet-prop service on the West Coast. (Ian Woolhouse)

– 132 –

northwards. NAC's flights through Greymouth were operated with smaller de Havilland DH83 Fox Moth aircraft due to runway constraints at Karoro Aerodrome and NAC removed Greymouth from its flight schedule effective from December 1951. The air service to Greymouth was replaced by a road link between Greymouth town centre and Hokitika Airport to connect with scheduled flights. The change was brought about by the opening of Hokitika's new Seaview Aerodrome on 17 December 1951, an event that heralded the introduction of larger and faster Lockheed 18 Lodestar aircraft on flights from Wellington and Nelson to Westport and Hokitika. However NAC's decision to dispose of their Lodestar fleet saw the return of the Dominie feeder service in March 1952. This situation continued until 2 March 1953 when the reliable Douglas DC-3 took over and became the mainstay of the service.

Following the sealing of the Hokitika Airport runway, the West Coast's airline services received a major boost with the introduction of 40-seat Fokker F-27 Friendship jet-prop aircraft from 20 December 1968. The Friendship, with its superior performance and pressurised cabin, made possible the introduction of scheduled trans-alpine flights between Christchurch and Hokitika. Eighteen months later, and after 17 years of faithful service, the Douglas DC-3 was eventually retired from West Coast air routes on 6 June 1970, the last flight being from Westport to Nelson and Wellington. Fokker Friendship flights into Westport's new sealed runway commenced on 1 November 1970 with services linking Wellington, Nelson, Westport, Hokitika and Christchurch.

After operating for over 30 years NAC's service to the West Coast ended on 31 March 1978 following the Government initiated merger of NAC into an enlarged Air New Zealand, which took over operations the following day.

GOLDEN COAST AIRWAYS LIMITED, GOLDEN COAST AIRLINES LIMITED and GOLDEN COAST AIRLINES (1965) LIMITED

Bill Evans formed Golden Coast Airways in early 1960 to provide the isolated settlement of Karamea in northern Buller with a fast link to the outside world. Evans was a flying enthusiast and his airline soon developed a loyal following. As well as passengers and urgent supplies he flew anything that would fit inside his small wood and fabric Auster ZK-AWZ, including whitebait, venison and small animals such as calves. To provide greater financial stability he started flying Nelson newspapers to Karamea, and from December 1960, the route was extended southwards to Westport. The Auster was replaced by a more modern four-seat Cessna 180, which in turn was followed by the six-seat Cessna 185 ZK-CAK, the first of its type to be operated in New Zealand. When the company obtained its first twin-engine aircraft, the six-seat Piper Apache ZK-BYB, the route was extended further south to Greymouth on 11 July 1963.

Shortly after this Bill Evans sold out to a group of investors led by a Masterton aircraft leasing firm Aircraft Hire Ltd and the restructured company was renamed Golden Coast Airlines Ltd. In 1964 the new company took over Greymouth based Phoenix Airways and Merv Dunn, a long time identity in West Coast aviation, joined Golden Coast Airlines and later became their chief pilot.

Further financial restructuring took place in 1965 with another name change to Golden Coast Airlines (1965) Ltd. The airline continued the six times per week service from Nelson to Karamea, Westport and Greymouth using Piper PA-23 Apache ZK-BLP. At the end of 1966 the company purchased a larger aircraft, Aero Commander 500 ZK-CTM, but was unable to operate it into Greymouth for six months until the runway was upgraded to meet Civil Aviation Authority requirements. The Aero Commander flew its first service to Greymouth on 30 June 1967 and it soon became a popular aircraft. Members of Parliament, Hugh 'Paddy' Blanchfield and Wallace 'Bill' Rowling were regular passengers who were transported to Nelson from Greymouth and Westport respectively, en route to Wellington for their Parliamentary duties. In an attempt to increase revenue, the airline extended the service northwards from Nelson to New Plymouth from 23 March 1966. An extension to Hamilton was introduced for a time but services to both centres had been withdrawn by December 1968.

Phoenix Airways' Piper Apache ZK-BLP (leased from Buchanan Enterprises of Haast) at Christchurch in 1961. Long-time Greymouth Catholic parish priest Monsignor James Long, and his housekeeper Miss Sheila Atkinson, had just arrived from Greymouth. Flying was the safer way to travel – on Long's return to Greymouth the car in which he was travelling blew a tyre and the car rolled! Fortunately no one was hurt. (Gerry O'Connor)

PHOENIX AIRWAYS
PHOENIX AIRWAYS
PHOENIX AIRWAYS
PHOENIX AIRWAYS

ANNOUNCES
ANNOUNCES
ANNOUNCES
ANNOUNCES

New Trans Alpine Service.
Depart Greymouth,
8.15 a.m.

Arrive Christchurch,
9.00 a.m.

Depart Christchurch
4.15 p.m.

Arrive Greymouth,
5.00 p.m.

MONDAY — WEDNESDAY
FRIDAY

FARE:
£4/-/- Single.

Freight 6d per lb, minimum 5/-.

PRINCIPAL AGENTS—

NANCARROW & CO
NANCARROW & CO
NANCARROW & CO

PHONE 5005.

Agents—

CHRISTCHURCH: N.Z. National Airways Corp.

HOKITIKA: West Coast Airways Ltd.

In 1969 there was a proposal for Golden Coast Airlines to take over NAC's air service to Westport because of insufficient funds to seal the runway to Fokker Friendship standard. Buller interests applied strong political pressure against this and subsequently funds were found and approval to seal the runway was given. Golden Coast Airlines continued on and provided an interim service to Westport while the upgrading work was being carried out. Eventually the company ran out of funds and was placed in receivership. The final flight of the Greymouth service was made on 17 September 1970.

SOUTH PACIFIC AIRLINES OF NEW ZEALAND LIMITED (SPANZ)

During the late 1950s NAC pilots Rex Daniell and Bob Anderson worked to form SPANZ, with a major shareholding initially being held by the large Australian airline operator Ansett Transport Industries Ltd. From 14 December 1960 the airline flew to provincial centres between Auckland and Invercargill, some of which had previously been without regular air links. For a short period SPANZ became the only other airline, apart from NAC, to operate Douglas DC-3 aircraft on timetabled air services to the West Coast. Each Saturday from October to December 1961 one of the airline's modernised DC-3 Viewmaster aircraft flew a weekly southwards only service from Nelson to Invercargill which included a stop at Hokitika en route.

PHOENIX AIRWAYS

Phoenix Airways flew air charter services from Greymouth in the early 1960s using the six-seat Piper PA.23 Apache registered ZK-BLP, owned by Buchanan Enterprises of Haast. From 18 September 1963 Phoenix launched a thrice-weekly trans-alpine air service between Greymouth and Christchurch. A four-seat Cessna 180 ZK-BVQ later replaced the Apache and in 1964 both the Cessna and the air services licence of Phoenix were sold to Golden Coast Airlines Ltd of Nelson.

Piper Apache ZK-BLP had been part of an earlier attempt to operate an air service in Westland in conjunction with Henry Buchanan and Coast Aviation, which owned de Havilland DH83C Fox Moth ZK-APT. West Coast pilots Malcolm Forsyth and Merv Dunn were also involved in the venture which mainly flew whitebaiters, hunters and supplies southwards from Greymouth and Hokitika to South Westland airstrips and beaches and returned northwards with whitebait and venison for processing and onward sale. Operations of this type did not require an air services licence but during the late 1950s Coast Aviation began to utilise the restricted joy riding air services licence belonging to the Greymouth Aero Club by uplifting fare paying passengers and commercial freight. However West Coast Airways, the licensed operator, complained that it was facing severe financial repercussions from this unlicensed competition. The Air Services Licensing Authority forced the curtailment of the commercial operation, although the whitebait and venison business continued.

NELSON AERO CLUB

When Golden Coast Airlines (1965) Ltd ceased business in September 1970 there was still a need to transport the *Westport News*' newspaper, which was printed in Nelson, to Karamea and Westport. The Nelson Aero Club applied for a non-scheduled air services licence and from 12 October 1970 commenced flying the newspapers as well as any passengers or urgent freight offering, from Nelson to Karamea and Westport with its twin engine Piper PA-23 Apache or single engine Cessna 180 and Cessna 172 aircraft. The service continued until 19 August 1972 when the newspaper contract was taken over by NAC. From that time Karamea lost its regular air link but a number of air charter operators have since linked the isolated district and the popular Heaphy Track with Takaka, Motueka, Nelson and other centres as required.

REX AIR CHARTER

Rex Aviation (NZ) Ltd was a large New Zealand aviation business, a major division of which acted as sales and service agents for Cessna aircraft. With maintenance and sales branches at several New Zealand locations, Rex Aviation also owned or controlled flying schools and air charter operations at several airports. These included Ardmore and Paraparaumu, with well-known pilot Harry Jenkins managing the Paraparaumu base. On 31 January 1972 Rex Air Charter commenced a non-scheduled air service three times a week between Paraparaumu, Westport and Greymouth in association with Westland Air Ltd. Initially calls were also made at Wellington and Hokitika if required, but these were soon deleted and the flights reduced to twice weekly. Four to seven-seat Cessna single engine aircraft were used as well as a twin engine Cessna 337 Skymaster in the latter stages. The operation continued and briefly overlapped the beginning of the service introduced by Capital Air Services Ltd in December 1974 before it petered out.

CAPITAL AIR SERVICES LIMITED

During the 1960s the commercial air charter and air taxi business of the Wellington Aero Club grew and in 1965 they imported an all-weather twin-engine Piper PA-23 Aztec ZK-CEU to support these activities. Other twin-engine aircraft were leased or purchased to develop additional services, including the transport of newspapers across Cook Strait and to support oil exploration companies. The aero club formed Capital Air Services Ltd to provide a structure to expand commercial air services and also give Wellington Aero Club members an element of financial protection. Under the enthusiastic guidance of Murray Turley, the company grew and gained an air service licence to operate passenger and freight services from Wellington to Blenheim and Nelson.

From mid 1973 the company began to introduce Cessna 402 10-seat mini airliners into service and became a busy Cook Strait commuter airline. On 2 December 1974 the airline extended its Wellington to Nelson service southwards to Westport and Greymouth, and from 1 February 1975 it was extended onwards to Christchurch. All services ceased on 29 June 1977 when the company was placed in receivership and its four Cessna 402 aircraft were grounded. Scheduled services resumed on 15 August 1977 and the airline continued to serve the West Coast until 30 June 1978 with James Aviation Ltd acting as manager on behalf of the receiver.

MOUNT COOK AIR SERVICES LIMITED

The Mount Cook and Southern Lakes Tourist Company was a pioneer and innovator in South Island tourism services from early in the 20th century. From the company's base at The Hermitage, Mount Cook during the early 1950s, chief executive Harry Wigley, pioneered the landing of Auster aircraft, equipped with skis and retractable wheels, on Southern Alps snowfields from The Hermitage, Mount Cook. After much trial and error a subsidiary company, Mt Cook Air Services Ltd, started a commercial ski plane scenic flight service also based at The Hermitage. These flights became a popular drawcard for tourists during the 1960s when more powerful Cessna 180 and 185 aircraft replaced the underpowered Austers. Additional ski plane bases were established on the West Coast at Franz Josef and Fox Glacier. To coincide with the introduction of NAC's Fokker Friendship service between Christchurch and Hokitika in December 1968, Mt Cook Air Services operated one of its ski equipped Cessna aircraft from Fox Glacier via Franz Josef to Hokitika to connect

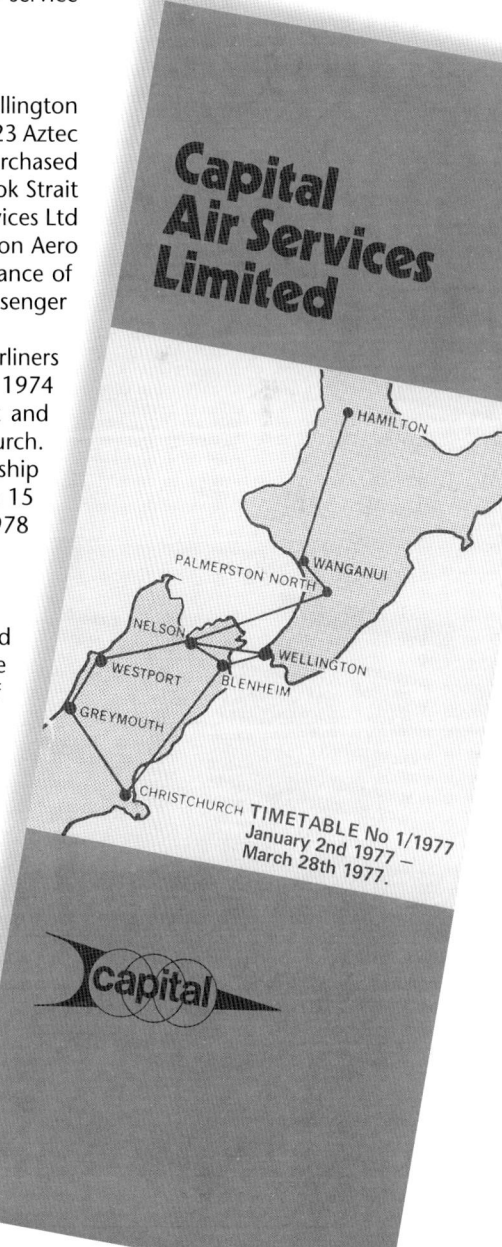

– 135 –

At Franz Josef Airfield in February 1970 Mount Cook Air Services pilot Jerry Savage with Dominie ZK-BCP and Cessna 185 Skiplane ZK-CKP. The Dominie was soon painted in Mount Cook colours and operated on the West Coast until the following year – the last de Havilland biplane airliner flying glacier scenic flights and occasional flights to Hokitika.
(Jerry Savage)

West Coast Service
FOX GLACIER - FRANZ JOSEF - HOKITIKA

NAC CONNECTIONS These services connect at Hokitika with the NAC services from and to Christchurch and with the Northbound and Southbound services from Wellington, Nelson, and Westport.

EFFECTIVE 13 OCT. TO 18 DEC. 1969
MON. TUES. WED. THUR. FRI.

NM101 Northbound		NM102 Southbound
1.20 p.m. dep FOX GLACIER	arr. 3.40 p.m.
1.30 p.m. arr. Franz Josef Glacier	dep. 3.30 p.m.
1.35 p.m. dep. Franz Josef Glacier	arr. 3.25 p.m.
2.10 p.m. arr. HOKITIKA	dep. 2.55 p.m.

SUNDAYS

NM103 Northbound		NM104 Southbound
3.00 p.m. dep FOX GLACIER	arr. 5.05 p.m.
3.10 p.m. arr. Franz Josef Glacier	dep. 4.55 p.m.
3.15 p.m. dep. Franz Josef Glacier	arr. 4.50 p.m.
3.50 p.m. arr. HOKITIKA	dep. 4.20 p.m.

From 19 DEC. to 1 FEB. 1970, this Service will operate DAILY to the following timetable:
DAILY

NM101 Northbound		NM102 Southbound
12.25 p.m. dep. FOX GLACIER	arr. 2.35 p.m.
12.35 p.m. arr. Franz Josef Glacier	dep. 2.25 p.m.
12.40 p.m. dep. Franz Josef Glacier	arr. 2.20 p.m.
1.15 p.m. arr. HOKITIKA	dep. 1.50 p.m.

As the NAC timetable for the period from 2 FEB 1970 had not been confirmed at the time of going to print, it is not possible to give a timetable schedule for this period. However, Mount Cook flights to and from the Glaciers will connect with NAC flights at Hokitika, and agents are requested to contact Mount Cook Airlines or NAC Reservations Offices for further details.

FARES (in New Zealand currency)

	Fox Glacier	Franz Josef
Franz Josef Glacier	$ 3.00	
Hokitika	$11.00	$ 9.00

All Fares per person. Children under 15yrs. half-fare.
Luggage allowance 35lbs for trans-shipping passengers.
REPORT: All airports 20 mins. prior to flight.

---

with the regular NAC flights. Occasionally the veteran de Havilland DH89B Dominie ZK-BCP was also used on the service. After just over two years of operation the service was withdrawn in early 1971.

AIR NEW ZEALAND LIMITED and its subsidiary companies AIR NELSON LIMITED and EAGLE AIRWAYS LIMITED both of which operated as AIR NEW ZEALAND LINK

Air New Zealand took over the operation of all air services previously operated by NAC on 1 April 1978. These included daily Fokker F-27 Friendship air services over the Wellington-Nelson-Westport-Hokitika-Christchurch route. Operated by both NAC and later by Air New Zealand, the Friendships provided the West Coast with almost 20 years of very reliable air services. Despite replacing many of the older and smaller Friendship Series 100 aircraft with new Series 500s, Air New Zealand found their operation increasingly expensive. To cut costs and increase the frequency of services to provincial centres Air New Zealand first acquired part ownership, and later complete control, of three smaller airlines- Air Nelson Ltd, Eagle Airways Ltd and Mt Cook Airline. Although each of these companies retained control of its own day-to-day operations, their flight services were fully integrated into Air New Zealand's reservations system.

In September 1988 Air New Zealand acquired a 50% shareholding in Air Nelson as a precursor to the withdrawal of its Friendship aircraft from provincial air routes including the West Coast. Air Nelson Ltd had expanded from a small Motueka flying school into a fast growing commuter airline based at Nelson under the energetic leadership of Robert Inglis and partner Nikki Smith. Air Nelson took over the running of Air New Zealand's air services on the West Coast from 31 October 1988 but initially had to lease a number of aircraft from other operators (including at times Air New Zealand's recently withdrawn Fokker Friendships) until it built up its own fleet of Fairchild Metro aircraft. Air Nelson linked Westport with Wellington and Hokitika with Christchurch offering a higher frequency service more suited to business people than the daily Friendship service and from the beginning the Hokitika service performed well. A mix of Metros and smaller Piper Chieftains were used on Westport flights, either direct to Wellington or via Nelson. Between 6 August 1990 and 9 February 1991 an attempt was made to once again link Westport to Christchurch via Hokitika but as with the earlier Air

Air New Zealand operated its Friendship aircraft into Hokitika from 1978 to 1988. F27-100 ZK-BXF Karuwai *outside the airport terminal on 18 March 1984.* (Steve Lowe)

Fairchild-Swearingen SA227AC Metroliner III ZK-NSI in original Air Nelson livery at Hokitika on 26 August 1991. Air Nelson had taken over West Coast services from Air New Zealand on 31 October 1988. (Steve Lowe)

BELOW LEFT: *Longtime West Coast aviation enthusiast and Air Nelson employee Jim Jamieson refueling Air New Zealand Link Metroliner ZK-NST at Hokitika in the late 1990s.* (Philip Miles via Jim Jamieson)

New Zealand experience the "round the rocks" service proved uneconomical and was withdrawn.

In 1991 Air Nelson, (which became fully owned by Air New Zealand in 1995), Eagle Airways and Mt Cook Airline began to operate under the Air New Zealand Link brand and all aircraft were painted in Air New Zealand colours. Later, when Air Nelson began to replace the Fairchild Metros with larger SAAB SF340 and Bombardier Q300 aircraft, Eagle Airways based at Hamilton took over the West Coast services on behalf of Air New Zealand Link. Eagle Airways began operating flights between Wellington and Westport and Christchurch and Hokitika in July and August 2002 respectively with their fleet of new Raytheon 1900D aircraft (often known as the Beech 1900) and leased BAe Jetstream 19-seat commuter airliners. In 2009 Eagle Airways continued to operate all scheduled services to both Hokitika and Westport on behalf of Air New Zealand, including from 6 July 2009, direct Westport-Christchurch flights on a six-month trial.

WESTLAND FLYING SERVICES LIMITED

Mr N.G. 'Norm' Bishop of Hokitika, a keen pilot and aircraft owner, started a commercial flying service based at Hokitika with his business partner Pat Pascoe during the latter part of the 1970s. With their first aircraft, Piper PA-32 Cherokee 6 ZK-ECV, they operated scenic flights for tourists over Mount Cook, the glaciers and the Southern Alps. The flights became popular and more aircraft were acquired as the company built up a busy air charter, flying instruction and scenic flight services business.

The partners saw the need for return early morning and late afternoon commuter flights to Christchurch particularly for business people, because at that time Air New Zealand operated only a single daily Fokker Friendship service to Hokitika. To prove the potential of such a service the company gained a non-scheduled air services licence and purchased a 10-seat Cessna 402A aircraft registered ZK-DHW. Flights began on 5 December 1979 from Hokitika to Christchurch via Greymouth and operated twice-daily return three days a week.

However Westland Flying Services found that although the Cessna 402 was fast and stable in turbulence, operating costs were very high. The lack of pressurisation prolonged journey times because of the need for the aircraft to spend long periods climbing and descending. In addition restrictions at Greymouth Airport, which in winter reduced the effective load to six passengers, seriously affected profitability. During 1980 the company entered into negotiations with Air New Zealand to take over most of that airline's uneconomic West Coast Fokker Friendship flights with turbo prop pressurised 19-seat Jetstream aircraft. Very strong local opposition arose, which, despite the possibility of more frequent flights, did not want the West Coast to lose the Friendship service and have it replaced by a private airline using a smaller aircraft type. As a result Westland Flying Services ended its trans-alpine air service on 31 January 1981. The company wound down its services and the Cessna 402 and other aircraft were sold.

BELOW RIGHT: *Westland Flying Services Ltd Cessna 402A ZK-DHW leaving Hokitika, with gear retracting, on a flight to Christchurch in 1980. The Cessna had previously been used on the West Coast by Capital Air Services.* (Norman Bishop)

WESTLAND FLYING SERVICES LTD.

WINTER TIMETABLE

TRANS - ALPINE

FLIGHTS

HOKITIKA - GREYMOUTH - CHRISTCHURCH

TWICE DAILY

MONDAY - WEDNESDAY - FRIDAY

Effective Date:
Monday, April 21st to Monday, September 1st inclusive

At Greymouth in March 1986, Coast Air's DHC-6-300 Twin Otter ZK-OTR ready for a scheduled flight to Christchurch. (Steve Lowe)

COAST AIR CHARTER LIMITED

In the early 1970s Government regulation gave New Zealand Railways a stranglehold on the movement of freight throughout New Zealand, other than for relatively short distances. This caused major frustration for people such as Mr B.L. 'Bert' Waghorn, an earthmoving contractor from Reefton. Replacement parts for broken down machinery often had to be sourced from the North Island and could take over a week to be delivered. To enable him to get parts quickly he learned to fly in a Cessna 150 under the instruction of Nash Taurau at Greymouth. But the small Cessna 150 was unsuitable for transporting machinery parts so the pair bought a Cessna 172 in partnership. Later Bert Waghorn and Frank Hallaran formed Coast Air Charter Ltd and purchased Taurau's share in the aircraft. A new Cessna 177 Cardinal ZK-DIH, with stretcher capability for air ambulance duties was obtained. John Royds was employed as pilot/manager for the air charter work and as business built up, staff numbers increased and three Cessna 172 aircraft and a 7-seat Cessna 207 were added to the fleet. The larger Cessna 207 ZK-EJD could be fitted with two stretchers, giving an improved service for transporting patients from the West Coast to larger hospitals for treatment. As well, a Cessna 152 Aerobat was acquired to give pilots an opportunity to further their flying capabilities.

Operating from bases at Westport, Reefton, and Hokitika as well as Greymouth, this company was to play a significant role in the development of air services on the West Coast for about 15 years. It provided flight training, air charter, scenic flights, aerial photography and air ambulance services to the whole West Coast region. Doctors and medical staff were transferred every Thursday to Westport in the mornings with a late afternoon return flight back to Greymouth Base Hospital. Coast Air Charter also transported operators and equipment for Ferguson Brothers, contractors engaged in investigating the potential of the asbestos deposits in the Red Hills in South Westland. They would fly the workers and their equipment down on Monday mornings, landing on the beach at Big Bay and pick them up again on Friday.

During the early 1980s there was interest from Greymouth business and civic leaders to establish a commuter airline service between Greymouth and Christchurch. A survey revealed a potential load factor of 70% for a 19-seat aircraft. Although initially reluctant, Bert Waghorn was persuaded and in December 1983 the company made an unsuccessful application to the Air Services Licensing Authority to operate twelve return flights a week over the route with a 19-seat turboprop aircraft. Despite a number of hold-ups they persisted and through the efforts of people such as Phil Heaphy, Doug Truman, Hugh and Malcolm McLellan and Bert Waghorn, finance was arranged and an air services licence gained.

Operating as Coast Air, scheduled services between Greymouth and Christchurch began on 17 January 1986, but only after financially crippling delays to meet Civil Aviation Authority requirements. The aircraft used was a de Havilland Canada DHC-6-300 Twin Otter registered ZK-OTR, at that time by far the largest and most sophisticated aircraft ever to have been operated by a West Coast based airline. However the traffic did not reach forecast expectations, so to increase revenue and utilisation the airline briefly added a Christchurch to Timaru link, later replaced by a service between Christchurch and Nelson. Profitability with the Twin Otter was never achieved so in December 1986 it was replaced by an 8-seat Piper PA-31 Navajo, leased from Como Holdings Ltd.

As a result of the 1987 share market crash and financial crisis Coast Air started to sell its smaller aircraft and scale down operations. Scheduled services continued but were halted on 15 April 1988 when the company was placed in receivership. Flights resumed again two weeks later after the receivers, Devlin and Wilding Ltd arranged for the lease of a Piper PA-31 Navajo aircraft from Air Nelson. The final blow to Coast Air came with the announcement that Air Nelson would operate pressurised Fairchild Metro aircraft into Hokitika, flying at similar times to the Coast Air service. After five months in receivership Coast Air made its final flight on 17 October 1988, not long before Air Nelson took over services to Hokitika on behalf of Air New Zealand, on 1 November 1988.

AIR WEST COAST LIMITED

Air West Coast Ltd was a company formed and operated by the Gloriavale Christian Community of Lake Haupiri in the Grey Valley, some members of the community having had strong aviation links for many years. In 2002 they established Air West Coast Limited as an air transport operation offering air charter and scenic flight services from Greymouth Airport. Several aircraft were purchased, including twin-engine Piper PA-34 Seneca ZK-KAE and Piper PA-31-350 Navajo Chieftain ZK-VIP. With these aircraft the airline began to operate scheduled services from Greymouth to Westport and Wellington from 30 October 2002. The airline also ran a trial twice-weekly service from Greymouth to Christchurch via Westport in late 2002 and early 2003.

A significant upgrading to the service came in the form of Dornier Do228-202 ZK-VIR, a 19-passenger turbo prop commuter airliner. The Dornier entered scheduled service between Greymouth, Westport and Wellington on 8 October 2007, but only after a prolonged delay in getting the aircraft certified by the Civil Aviation Authority. Although unpressurised, the aircraft had very good slow flying and short take off and landing characteristics as well as having a fast cruising speed and a comfortable cabin. These characteristics made the aircraft particularly suitable when operating from the short runway at Greymouth Airport, which prevented the use of most other types of similar sized commuter aircraft.

As the airline operated only five return services over the route per week there was insufficient utilisation for the Dornier aircraft, a situation that worsened further in mid 2008 when Air New Zealand Link doubled its weekday flights into Westport. Unable to make the service economic the company ceased all scheduled services on 1 August 2008 when the last Greymouth-Wellington return flights were made. After this date the company continued to offer its air charter and scenic flight service from Greymouth with its smaller aircraft. The Dornier was sold overseas in early 2009.

COASTAIR (Operated by ASHBURTON AIR SERVICES LIMITED)

During 2008 Ashburton Air Services Ltd began flying air charter services, principally from Ashburton and Christchurch with its Cessna 404 Titan ZK-NDY. Under the trading name of Coastair, Ashburton Air Services Ltd commenced flying between Christchurch and Westport, stopping at Greymouth on demand in April 2009. The first flight between Christchurch and Westport took place on 8 April 2009 and initially flights were made morning and afternoon on three days a week and once daily at weekends but only if passengers were offering. On 6 July 2009 Air New Zealand introduced competitive direct Christchurch-Westport flights on a six-month trial. Unable to compete, Coastair immediately withdrew its service to the West Coast to concentrate on air charter services.

AERO CLUBS, AIR CHARTER AND AERIAL WORK OPERATORS ON THE WEST COAST

The wave of interest in flying which occurred in the early 1930s led to the formation of the Hokitika Aero Club in 1932 and the Greymouth Aero Club in 1933 as well as other aero clubs at Westport and smaller centres. The West Coast United Aero Club was formed as an umbrella organisation and provided flying instructors and aircraft to these local aero clubs. Up until it was disbanded in 1953, the West Coast United Aero Club at various times owned five de Havilland DH.82A Tiger Moth aircraft (ZK-AFW, ZK-AFY, ZK-AJQ, ZK-ALP and ZK-AND). The strong co-operative and social structure of the aero club movement did much to promote aviation to the people of the West Coast. In 2009 both the Hokitika and Greymouth aero clubs continued to operate.

Pilot Kevin Anderson of Anderson Helicopters Ltd in Bell 206B Jet Ranger ZK-HSG loading fertilizer into a sowing bucket for pine plantation application, Ahaura, Hochstetter Forest, November 2001. Anderson had flown ZK-HSG from Hokitika since October 1982.

– 141 –

Until the late 1960s most of the West Coast's commercial air charter and scenic flying needs were met by Hokitika based Air Travel (NZ) Ltd, followed later by NAC and West Coast Airways Ltd. From then on a gradual relaxation in the air services licensing regime saw an increase in the number of private organisations such as Westland Air Ltd, Nairn Aviation Ltd, Westland Flying Services Ltd and Coast Air Charter Ltd providing locally based commercial air services and also providing aircraft and flying instructors to the aero clubs.

Most commercial air charter operators which operated in the Buller region after World War II were based outside the district and have included: the Golden Coast Airways and Airlines group of companies, the Nelson Aero Club, Karamea Heaphy Air Charter Ltd, Golden Bay Aviation Ltd, Nairn Aviation Ltd, Coast Air Charter Ltd and Flight Corporation Ltd. The only local operator ever to originate from Westport was Air West, which operated Cessna 207 ZK-DSE and Cessna 172 ZK-DHS on air charter and ambulance services in the early 1990s. In 2009 the Buller District was serviced by outside air charter operators often involved in providing air taxi flights ferrying trampers using the Heaphy Track. Operators included: Abel Tasman Aviation Ltd of Motueka, Remote Adventures Ltd and Golden Bay Air Ltd (previously known as Capital Air) based at Takaka, and Sounds Air Tourism and Travel Ltd which had aircraft based at Nelson, Picton and Wellington.

Up to 2009 there had only ever been one commercial floatplane permanently based on the West Coast. For a number of years from 1997 Westland Air Charter Ltd based Cessna U206F ZK-PCS on Lake Brunner before moving it to Picton.

Greymouth, being the largest residential, business and administrative centre on the West Coast, has had a number of locally based commercial aviation related businesses since the late 1950s. These have included: Coast Aviation Ltd, Phoenix Airways, Westland Air Ltd and its associated operation West Coast Air Charter, Coast Air Charter Ltd and the Greymouth Aero Club Flight Centre. In 2009, Air West Coast Ltd, which had offered fixed-wing air charter services from Greymouth since 2002, was the local operator.

Hokitika, being closer to the West Coast Glaciers and South Westland has also supported a number of air charter and small airline operators, most of which became well established for a time. Air Travel (NZ) Ltd, NAC and West Coast Airways Ltd initially provided Hokitika with locally based air charter services for 33 years up until 31 March 1967. Following a 10-year break, Westland Flying Services Ltd was established in 1977 and operated for about five years. Since that time Hokitika has supported a number of locally based air charter operators including: Westland Transport Ltd, Coast Air Charter Ltd, Wilderness Wings Ltd, Westair Flying Ltd and West Coast Flightseeing. In 2009 the locally based operator was Wilderness Wings Ltd, formed by Murray Bowes in 1993. The company operated Cessna 180 ZK-BJY, a veteran aircraft on the West Coast until 2004.

After World War II scenic flights for tourists over the Franz Josef and Fox Glaciers became a regular feature when Southern Scenic Air Services Ltd of Queenstown would base Percival Proctor, Auster, Cessna 180 or Dominie aircraft there over the busy summer season. West Coast Airways Ltd continued these flights until 1967. From the late 1950s the introduction of ski-plane landings on the snow by Mt Cook Air Services Ltd opened a new dimension for tourists. A boom in scenic flying followed and ski-equipped Cessna 180 and Cessna 185 aircraft were based at airstrips at Franz Josef and Fox Glacier. In late 2002 the ski-plane operation was sold to Aoraki Mount Cook Skiplanes Ltd and in 2009 this company continued to base ski-plane aircraft on the West Coast. The other long-term scenic flight operator based at Franz Josef in 2009 was Air Safaris and Services (NZ) Ltd.

South Westland's isolation began to be broken down by the aircraft of Air Travel (NZ) Ltd from 1934 and beaches, riverbeds and rough strips were often used as landing grounds. Arthur Bradshaw's Southland Airways of Invercargill was also an early flying operator into South Westland from 1936 until the outbreak of World War II. From the late 1940s Southern Scenic Air Services Ltd began to service the area as required and there was a peak of operations each spring when the seasonal run of whitebait in the rivers attracted adventurous people determined to make their fortune by catching and selling the delicacy. Over following years other licensed operators and many private individuals have flown out whitebait and venison and have provided air charter services to the people of South Westland.

As well as air charter and scenic flights, fixed-wing aircraft have been put to use as aerial workhorses in a variety of roles on the West Coast including: aerial topdressing, spraying and poisoning, carrying urgent freight and supply dropping. For many years commercial operators from outside the West Coast used their aircraft to service specific aerial agricultural contracts. Early operators from the 1950s were Southern Scenic Air Services Ltd of Queenstown and its subsidiary West Coast Airways Ltd. Other operators came from Nelson, Canterbury and at times from other regions. From 1972 Aerial Sowing Ltd (later renamed Rowley Aviation Ltd) became the first operator to permanently base an agricultural aircraft on the West Coast at Hokitika using aircraft types, which included Fletcher FU-24, Snow Commander and Piper PA-25 Pawnee. In the early 1990s Darrell Williams, one of Rowley Aviation Ltd's pilots, formed Airsow Westport. Based at Westport this operator continued aerial agricultural operations on the West Coast for about 10 years. In 2009 outside operators provided fixed-wing agricultural aviation services to the West Coast.

The helicopter first appeared on the West Coast in the early 1960s and since then has found a natural niche amongst the rugged terrain of the region. With no need for runways the flexibility of the helicopter has seen it put to many uses including: scenic flights, deer hunting, log lifting, spraying, aerial topdressing, search and rescue, aerial ambulance and ferrying supplies. By the 1970s some operators involved in aerial deer hunting began to permanently base helicopters on the West Coast. These included: Alexander Helicopters Ltd, Winged Hunters Ltd (later renamed Glacier Helicopters Ltd), Alpine Enterprises Ltd, Alpine Helicopters Ltd and South West Helicopters Ltd. The licensed operators among these also engaged in other types of commercial activities. Helicopters also became used increasingly in tourism and in 1980 Mount Cook Airlines based Bell 206A Jet Ranger ZK-HPP at Franz Josef for this purpose. Three years later the operation was taken over by Whirl-Wide Helicopters Ltd. Over the following years there were many other helicopter operators, some of which operated for short periods only. In 2009 the number of helicopter operators on the West Coast outnumbered licensed fixed wing operators three to one and included: Ahaura Helicopters Ltd, Alpine Adventures and Fox and Franz Heli Services, Anderson Helicopters Ltd, Garden City Helicopters Ltd, Air West Helicopters Ltd, Coastwide Helicopters Ltd, Glacier Heliventures, Glacier Southern Lakes Helicopters Ltd, Helicopter Charter Karamea (2006) Ltd, Heliventures Ltd, Kokatahi Helicopters 2000 Ltd, Mountain Helicopters and Scenicland Helicopters.

Bibliography
by Richard Waugh

New Zealand's most memorable air service, the South Westland air service, continues to receive frequent mention in books, magazines and other sources. From a paucity of references until the 1970s, much researched information and a flood of photographs has been more recently published, especially from the early 1990s.

Alexander, Vonnie Clarke
WESTLAND HERITAGE. A Journey of Nostalgia
Christchurch: Alexander Publications, 1994, 201p., illus., map.
Reminiscences and stories of Westland history by a former Whataroa resident, including chapter seven on "Alpine Aviators", mostly compiled from secondary sources.

Bain, Gordon
DE HAVILLAND. A Pictorial Tribute.
Leicester, England: Promotional Reprint Company Ltd, 1995, 148p., illus. First published by Airlife Publishing Ltd.
A photographic history of classic de Havilland aircraft including air-to-air photography of Fox Moth G-ADHA (ZK-ADI), Dominies ZK-AKU & ZK-AKY and Dragonfly G-AEDT (later ZK-AYR).

Beauchamp Legg, Paul
WEST COAST MEMORIES. Volume One.
Picton: Paul Beauchamp Legg, 1994, 161p., illus.
A veteran pilot's reminiscences, including his memorable time as a West Coast Airways pilot from 1958 to 1961. Includes many photographs he took at the time. Later updated and expanded in Volume Two (1996) with other stories from West Coast characters. A valuable West Coast record.

Birtles, Philip
DE HAVILLAND. Planemakers 3.
London, England: Jane's Publishing Company, 1984, 160p., illus.
De Havilland company history by a former employee with a short description about each de Havilland aircraft type, including specifications.

Bradshaw, Arthur
FLYING BY BRADSHAW. Memoirs of a Pioneer Pilot 1933-1975.
Edited by David Phillips and Graeme McConnell.
Nelson: Proctor Publications, 2000, 223p., illus.
Probably the only book by a pre-war New Zealand commercial pilot. Bradshaw operated his own pioneer airline, Southland Airways, with de Havilland Puss Moths during the same time as the early years of Bert Mercer's Air Travel (NZ) Ltd. In the winter of 1964 Bradshaw also did a brief stint flying the Dominie of West Coast Airways on the South Westland air service.

Bradshaw, Julia
THE FAR DOWNERS.
The People and History of Haast and Jackson Bay.
Dunedin: University of Otago Press, 2001, 152p., illus, maps.
Beginning with the early history of the region this book tells the life stories of nine people who grew up "far down" in South Westland, including well known pilot Des Nolan. Frequent mention is made about the air service. For example Henry Buchanan said, "I think the aircraft was the real turning point for the district." Mary Cowell was Bert Mercer's first air ambulance patient and commented, "When the air service went in there, that was an absolute godsend."

Carmine, Phillip F.
ON THE JOB 1936 TO 1975
Christchurch: Unpublished manuscript, 1984, 98p.
Career reminiscences of Carmine (1916-1993), an NAC staff member who served as Traffic Supervisor at Hokitika, August 1953 to January 1957, which included the transition to West Coast Airways. In four chapters he describes many experiences and stories from the South Westland NAC era and writes, "My term in Hokitika abounded in incidents…"

Dodds, Colin N.
THE STORY OF THE DE HAVILLAND DRAGON TYPES.
Kent, England: Air-Britain (Historians) Ltd, 2005, 272p., illus.
A detailed history, complementary to the book by John Hamlin, which covers the history of the de Havilland family of small commercial biplane airliners built between the two world wars. It includes photographs and some written material about the South Westland air service.

Driscoll, Ian H.
FLIGHTPATH SOUTH PACIFIC.
Christchurch: Whitcombe and Tombs, 1972, 303p., illus.
Describes the opening up and development of air routes in the South Pacific. Includes brief mention of Air Travel (NZ) Ltd and the NAC era of the South Westland air service, with a description of Driscoll's flight from Hokitika to Haast in a Fox Moth in a chapter he titles, "Bush Lifeline to Main Trunk Jet 1947-72".

Ewing, Ross & Ross Macpherson
THE HISTORY OF NEW ZEALAND AVIATION.
Auckland: Heinemann, 1986, 287p., illus.
A milestone general aviation history book with some brief references and photographs about the South Westland air service.

Fulton, Myra
OKURU. The place of No Return.
Takaka: Myra Fulton, 2004, 320p., illus.
Fulton, nee Buchanan, moved to Okuru as a child with her family in 1931, just prior to the first landing of an aircraft at nearby Mussel Point. Her detailed story of life in South Westland is an interesting blend of personal experience, opinion and historical narration. The air service and its significance to the South Westland families is mentioned numerous times.

Geelen, Janic
MAGNIFICENT ENTERPRISE. Moths, Majors and Minors. The history of the de Havilland Aircraft Company: Volume Two: 1926-1939.
Waiuku: NZ Aviation Press, 2004, 237p., illus.
An important new history with material and photographs which includes the de Havilland biplane transports. Material collected and 3-view drawings were done by Norman Eastaff, a former de Havilland employee, and subsequently written and taken through to publication by Janic Geelen. Contains some photographs and references to the South Westland air service.

Grimmer, Gavin
TRACED … yet still missing!
Hastings: Grimmer Productions, 2009, 165p., illus.
Resulting from extensive research into the disappearance of Dragonfly ZK-AFB, Grimmer's book was inspired by Waugh's 2005 'LOST … without trace? book on the same subject. He sets out his research theories, google earth work and describes several aerial and ground searches about where the Dragonfly is likely to be, together with theories about missing Corsair NZ5517 and Cessna ZK-BMP.

Hamlin, John F.
THE DE HAVILLAND DRAGON/RAPIDE FAMILY.
Kent, England: Air -Britain (Historians) Ltd, 2003, 240p., illus.
A comprehensive history of the DH84 Dragon, DH86 Express, DH89 Rapide/Dominie and DH90 Dragonfly aircraft types with information on each aircraft produced. Includes histories, photographs and references to each of the aircraft flown on the South Westland air service.

Hayes, Paul & Bernard King
DE HAVILLAND BIPLANE TRANSPORTS.
Surrey, England: Gatwick Aviation Society, 2003, 184p., illus.
A history of the DH83, DH84, DH86, DH89, DH90 and DH92 aircraft types with brief individual histories, including the aircraft flown on the South Westland air service.

Hill, Larry R
AN AVIATION BIBLIOGRAPHY FOR NEW ZEALAND
Auckland: Larry R. Hill, 2009, 256p., illus.
An invaluable record of New Zealand aviation history, including rare and unpublished material.

Hope-Cross, David
"DH Fox Moth" in Aero Modeller magazine, March 1983, p.110-113.
Hope-Cross was a long-time aviation enthusiast and model aircraft builder, with the construction of his free flight/RC 1/8th scale model of Fox Moth ZK-AEK. This article described, to an international audience, the recovery of ZK-AEK from the Franz Josef Glacier in 1943, and some of his model making experience with the Fox Moth.

Hopkins, Jim (Editor)
WORDS ON WINGS.
An Anthology of New Zealanders in Flight.
Auckland: HarperCollins, 2004, 377p.
An interesting compilation of previously published Kiwi aviation reminiscences, including extracts about NAC by Ian Driscoll and West Coast Airways by Paul Beauchamp Legg and Brian Waugh.

Jackson, A.J.
DE HAVILLAND AIRCRAFT SINCE 1909.
London, England: England: Putnam, 1962 & 1978 (new material copyright 1987), 544p., illus.
Revised third edition of an important early reference work on all de Havilland aircraft.

Jarram, A.P.
BRUSH AIRCRAFT. Production at Loughborough.
Leicester, England: Midland Counties Publications (Aerophile) Ltd, 1978, 37p., illus.
Contains a history of the 335 Brush-built DH89 Dominie aircraft from the Brush 'Falcon' works and flown from Loughborough Aerodrome, Derby Road, Leicestershire. A number of these Dominies later flew on the South Westland air service.

Jenks, Cliff & David Phillips
NEW ZEALAND TIGER MOTHS 1938-2000.
Wellington: Aviation Historical Society of New Zealand (Inc), 2000, 158p., illus.
A comprehensive history of the DH82 type in New Zealand. While not operated by any of the airlines which flew the South Westland air service, the type is synonymous with de Havilland operations in New Zealand.

Kay, Rupert A. (Editor)
WESTLAND'S GOLDEN CENTURY 1860-1960. Official Souvenir of Westland's Centenary
Hokitika: Westland Centennial Council, 1960, illus.
Contains a chapter on "Pioneers of Air Transport" by R.W. Nelson (p85-89).

King, John
"A de Havilland Celebration" in *The Moth*, Enterprise No. 91, p.33-35.
A well illustrated account of the 1994 60th anniversary celebrations of the South Westland air service, written for an international audience.

King, John
"Capt J.C. Mercer and his airline" in Aviation Historical Society of New Zealand, Journal Volume 22, No.3 (Spring 1979), p.44-49.
A summary of Mercer's exploits and aircraft flown.

King, John
FAMOUS NEW ZEALAND AVIATORS.
Wellington: Grantham House, 1998, 199p.
The story of 13 of New Zealand's prominent pilots, including Captain Bert Mercer (chapter four) with an overview of his life and significant aviation career.

King, John
NEW ZEALAND TRAGEDIES. Aviation Accidents & Disasters.
Wellington: Grantham House, 1995, 292p., illus.
A useful and well written overview of many air accidents in New Zealand including those involving Air Travel (NZ) Ltd (Dragonfly ZK-AGP, Fox Moth ZK-AEK and Dragon ZK-AHT). Also other associated accidents including that of Brian Chadwick's Dragonfly ZK-AFB, Geoff Houston's Cessna ZK-BJY and Brian Waugh's Dominie ZK-AKT.

King, John
"Whatever happened to ... John Neave?" in *New Zealand Wings*, August 1994, p.14-17.
First hand information from a pre-war Air Travel pilot, interviewed by John King in the early 1990s. Neave also served as the honorary patron of the 60th anniversary celebrations of the South Westland air service in 1994.

King, Ross
AIR TRAVEL (N.Z.) LTD 1941-1949.
Hokitika: Unpublished paper. c1997.
Reminiscences of Ross King who started work at Air Travel (NZ) Ltd at Hokitika in June 1941 as a storeman and who continued employment in the early years of NAC. This first-hand account of the 1940s operations highlights many of the incidents and dramas of the air service, and the personalities involved.

Lucas, F.J.
POPEYE LUCAS QUEENSTOWN.
Wellington: A.H. & A.W. Reed, 1968, 186p., illus.
The popular flying and farming story of Fred 'Popeye' Lucas, well known New Zealand wartime pilot. Includes his years with Southern Scenic Air Services Ltd in Queenstown and his work in the 1950s to help form subsidiary company West Coast Airways Ltd. Lucas retired from commercial flying in 1960.

Martyn, Errol W.
FOR YOUR TOMORROW. A record of New Zealanders who have died while serving with the RNZAF and Allied Air Services since 1915.
Christchurch: Volplane Press, Volume One: Fates 1915-1942, 1998, 304p., Volume Two: Fates 1943-1998, 1999, 448p.,Volume Three: Biographies & Appendices, 2008, 640p.
An immensely detailed trilogy recording the individual fate circumstances and career details of nearly 4900 New Zealand airmen and women, including a number mentioned in this book.

Nancekivell, Arthur H.
"Recollections of a West Coast pioneer aviator" in Aviation Historical Society of New Zealand, Journal Volume 23, Nos. 3 and 4 (Combined), Winter 1980, p.48-49.
Nancekivell writes about his early flying experiences on the West Coast.

Nolan, Desmond Joseph
Haast: Unpublished Papers. c1998.
Reminiscences by Des Nolan (1920-2001), a well known West Coast identity. Includes early West Coast flying days from his eye-witness account, as a boy, of 'Mac' McGregor and 'Tiny' White landing at Mussel Point in 1931, through to the demise of the South Westland air service in the late 1960s.

Nolan, J.P (Ed)
A SAGA OF THE SOUTH. A short history of a West Coast family – the Nolans.
West Coast: Nolan Reunion Committee, c1970s, 107p, illus.
Interesting family stories, includes Des Nolan's contribution, 'Aviation in South Westland' (p 71-75) where he describes his experience of the pioneering flying from the 1930s.

Mackie, Andrew J.
REPORT INTO THE LOSS OF AIR TRAVEL (NZ) LTD'S DRAGON AIRCRAFT ZK-AHT ON THE SLOPES OF MOUNT HOPE FRIDAY 30TH JUNE 1944
Paper prepared for the Open Polytechnic of New Zealand and the Murchison & Districts Museum and Historical Society. September 1993.
Comprehensive essay report covering the crash of the Air Travel (NZ) Ltd Dragon.

Pascoe, John
THE HAAST IS IN SOUTH WESTLAND.
Wellington: A.H.& A.W. Reed, 1966, 116p., illus.
An early history of the Haast area from Maori and early Pakeha beginnings to the opening of the Paringa-Haast section of the new highway in November 1965. Written at the height of the excitement of the new road being completed, the historical and social significance of the air service is hardly touched on with only brief mention of Mercer's era and nothing of the NAC and West Coast Airways years.

Peat, Neville
CASCADE ON THE RUN. A season with the whitebaiters of South Westland
Christchurch: Whitcoulls, 1979, 126p., illus.
Refers to a number of early pilots flying out the whitebait, including Geoff Houston (later with West Coast Airways) and a fatal Auster accident.

Riding, Richard (Editor)
DE HAVILLAND – THE GOLDEN YEARS 1919-1939
England: I.P.C Transport Press Ltd, 1981, 221p., illus.
A significant collection of contemporary technical descriptions and drawings reproduced from various issues of "Flight" and "The Aeroplane" covering most of the de Havilland Aeroplane Company's aircraft designs from 1919 to 1939, including all the types seen in New Zealand.

Roxburgh, Irvine
JACKSONS BAY. A Centennial History
Christchurch: Cadsonbury Publications, 1997, 198p., illus., maps.
Originally published by Reeds in 1976 this book concentrates on the Jackson Bay story, and also contains basic information about the South Westland air service, including many pilot names. One chapter is titled, "A Highway Opened: A Skyway Closed".

Rudge, Chris
MISSING. Aircraft Missing in New Zealand 1928-2000.
Christchurch: Adventure Air, 2001, 313p., illus.
A detailed record of missing aircraft which gives prominence (second longest chapter) to the fate of Dragonfly ZK-AFB "… one of New Zealand's greatest aviation mysteries". The author notes his interest in writing the book was sparked by his 1995 purchase of the spare propeller of ZK-AFB.

Sheehan, Paul
THE AIRCRAFT OF AIR NEW ZEALAND AND ITS AFFILIATES SINCE 1940
Wellington: Transpress NZ, 2003, 235P., illus.
Lists all the aircraft operated by Air New Zealand, its predecessors and subsidiary companies up to 2003 with comprehensive details of each aircraft.

Simons, Graham M.
DH84 DRAGON.
England: International Friends of the DH89, c1988, 34p., illus.
A brief history of the type with short paragraph descriptions of each of the aircraft produced.

Simons, Graham M.
DH89 DRAGON RAPIDE
England: International Friends of the DH89, 1986, 48p., illus.
A brief history of the type with short paragraph descriptions of each of the aircraft produced.

Simons, Graham M.
DH90 DRAGONFLY.
England: International Friends of the DH89, 1987, 28p., illus.
A brief history of the type with short paragraph descriptions of each of the aircraft produced.

Sinclair, Roy
JOURNEYING WITH AVIATORS IN NEW ZEALAND.
Auckland: Random House New Zealand Ltd, 1998, 290p., illus.
Recounts some of the adventures of pioneer and contemporary aviators, including Gerald Grocott, and aircraft restorers Colin and Maeva Smith of the Croydon Aircraft Company. Several South Westland air service photographs and references are included, with a prominent account of how DH83 Fox Moth ZK-ADI was purchased by Gerald Grocott and returned to New Zealand in 1996.

Sinclair, Roy
NEW ZEALAND AVIATION YARNS.
Wellington: Grantham House, 1994, 196p. Illustrations by Simon van der Sluijs.
Stories, rather than historical accounts, from a range of people involved in aviation, including reminiscences from Dick Ferguson who was an apprentice engineer with Air Travel (NZ) Ltd from April 1942.

Stapleton, James A.
THE NEW ZEALAND AIRMAIL CATALOGUE.
Christchurch: The Air Mail Society of New Zealand Inc, 1994, 81p.
Includes information on first day covers relating to a variety of Air Travel (NZ) Ltd, NAC and West Coast Airways flights on the South Westland air service.

Stapleton, Doug
WANDERINGS IN WESTLAND: TRIPS DOWN MEMORY LANE.
Hokitika: D. Stapleton, 2007, 143p.
A series of short historical reflections that originally were published as "Musings" in the West Coast Times. Includes a chapter on "Aviation – The Great Pioneers."

Stevens, Bob
FLYING HOME. A History of Aviation in Nelson.
Nelson: Nelson Mail Promotions Ltd, 1985, 108p., illus.
Contains brief references to Air Travel (NZ) Ltd operations in the early period.

Waugh, Brian
TURBULENT YEARS. A Commercial Pilot's Story. Edited by Richard Waugh.
Christchurch: Hazard Press, 1991. 229p., illus., map.
An autobiographical account of Waugh's aviation career from wartime Lancaster bomber pilot flying with No. 75 (NZ) Squadron to extensive DH89 Rapide/Dominie flying in England and New Zealand, including his long stint as Chief Pilot of West Coast Airways 1959 to 1967. Waugh was the last of the South Westland air service pilots and started flying before the Haast Pass and Paringa to Haast Roads were opened. Written in Nelson during the early 1980s it is a valuable pilot's account of small airline operations in New Zealand during the 1950s and 1960s.

Waugh, Brian
"WHATEVER HAPPENED TO MY COBBER … CHADWICK?" in New Zealand Wings magazine, February 1982, p.28-29.
A feature article, written by a friend of Brian Chadwick, for the 20th anniversary of the disappearance of Dragonfly ZK-AFB. The aircraft was on a Christchurch to Milford Sound scenic flight. ZK-AFB was Mercer's first Dragonfly.

Waugh, Richard
"DRAGONFLY MYSTERY" in Classic Wings Downunder magazine, Volume 4, No.4 October-December 1997, p.42-43.
Written at the time Dragonfly ZK-AYR (G-AEDT) arrived in New Zealand, the first of its type seen in New Zealand since ZK-AFB in 1962.

Waugh, Richard (Editor)
EARLY RISERS. The Pioneering Story of Gisborne and Hawkes Bay Aviation. Contributing authors: John King and David Phillips and Richard Waugh.
Auckland: East Coast Air Service Celebration Committee, 1997, 92p., illus., map.
Concentrates on the pioneering years and devotes two chapters to the operations of East Coast Airways Ltd, which began services at a similar time to that of Bert Mercer's Air Travel (NZ) Ltd. The airline used DH84 Dragons, one of which later became ZK-AHT and was used by Air Travel (NZ) Ltd for a short time in 1944. East Coast Airways was the first licensed airline in New Zealand and the second to commence services, four months after Air Travel (NZ) Ltd.

Waugh, Richard (Editor)
ELECTRA FLYING. The Lockheed 10 Electra in New Zealand and the Pioneering of the Main Trunk Air Service. Contributing authors: Richard Waugh and David Phillips.
Auckland: Project Electra Committee, 1998, 120p., illus., map.
The best source of New Zealand Lockheed 10A Electra history, with many rare photographs of international significance. Gives some information about the integrated nature of pre-war and early post war air services with some references to the operations of Air Travel (NZ) Ltd.

Waugh, Richard
LOST … without trace? Brian Chadwick & the missing Dragonfly.
Invercargill: The Kynaston Charitable Trust in conjunction with Craig Printing Co Ltd, 2005, 215p., illus., maps.
A detailed account of the disappearance of Captain Brian Chadwick and four passengers in Dragonfly ZK-AFB, on 12 February 1962, while on a Christchurch to Milford Sound scenic flight. ZK-AFB was purchased new by Air Travel (NZ) in October 1937 and operated extensively on the West Coast until being sold to the Canterbury Aero Club in September 1946. The book also contains a feature on the loss of Dragonfly ZK-AGP on 21 December 1942.

Waugh, Richard
"Nelson flight ended tragically" in *Nelson Evening Mail*, June 30 1994, p.6.
Feature article about the crash of Air Travel (NZ) Ltd Dragon ZK-AHT on June 30 1944.

Waugh, Richard with Bruce Gavin, Peter Layne & Graeme McConnell
TAKING OFF. Pioneering Small Airlines of New Zealand 1945-1970.
Invercargill: The Kynaston Charitable Trust in conjunction with Craig Printing Co Ltd, 2003, 228p., illus, map.
A comprehensive history of all small post-war regional airlines, including a chapter on West Coast Airways, outlining the many challenges and struggles these airlines faced. Other West Coast related airlines covered or mentioned include: Coast Aviation and Buchanan Enterprises, Phoenix Aviation and Golden Coast Airways.

Waugh, Richard & Peter Layne
SPANZ. South Pacific Airlines of New Zealand and their DC-3 Viewmasters.
Invercargill: Craig Printing Co Ltd, 2000, 148p., illus, map.
SPANZ was a popular yet politically controversial private enterprise airline operating during the 1960s. It flew regular scenic flights to South Westland and Fiordland and also briefly operated a scheduled service through Hokitika.

Waugh, Richard (Editor)
STRAIT ACROSS. The pioneering story of Cook Strait Aviation. Contributing authors Graeme McConnell, David Phillips and Richard Waugh.
Auckland: Cook Strait Air Service Celebrations Committee, 1995, 80p., illus, map.
Covers the history from the first flight across Cook Strait in 1920 to mid 1990s developments, with a focus on the pre-war pioneering operations of Cook Strait Airways (CSA). CSA operated a West Coast service from February 1937 using DH89 Rapides, connecting with Air Travel (NZ) Ltd flights at Hokitika, until the outbreak of World War II.

Waugh, Richard with Peter Layne & Graeme McConnell
NAC. The Illustrated History of New Zealand National Airways Corporation 1947-1978.
Invercargill: The Kynaston Charitable Trust in conjunction with Craig Printing Co Ltd, 2007, 320p., illus, maps.
Containing more than 500 photographs and reproduced memorabilia, with extensive text, this large book includes a detailed airline chronology from 1942 to 1978 and a history of all aircraft flown by the airline. Included is a variety of South Westland air service information and photographs, related to the NAC era 1947-1956.

Waugh, Richard (Editor)
WHEN THE COAST IS CLEAR. The Story of New Zealand's first and most unique licensed air service – South Westland 1934-1967. Contributing authors John King, Paul Beauchamp Legg and Richard Waugh.
Invercargill: Craig Printing Co Ltd, 1994, 80p., illus, map.
Published for the 60th anniversary in December 1994. Extensive history in text and many rare photographs of the South Westland air service, a de Havilland biplane operation of international significance. The Air Travel (NZ) Ltd chapters written by John King.

Wearne, Max
THE LIFE OF GUY MENZIES. The forgotten flyer.
Australia: Max Wearne, 2005, 160p., illus.
An account of the life and exploits of Guy Menzies who on 7 January 1931 flew the first solo crossing of the Tasman Sea, crash landing his Avro Avian in a swamp near Hari Hari in South Westland.

White, Leo
WINGSPREAD. The Pioneering of Aviation in New Zealand.
Auckland: Unity Press, 1945 (Revised), 192p., illus.
A reprint of a 1941 edition with valuable first-hand stories and accounts of Kiwi aviation pioneers by aviation journalist and early historian Leo White. Probably the first book published with an account of Mercer's work on the West Coast with Air Travel (NZ) Ltd.

Wigram, Henry F.
THE FIRST HUNDRED PILOTS.
Christchurch: The Canterbury (N.Z.) Aviation Co. Ltd, 1918, 11p., illus.
Includes brief mention of Bert Mercer, the seventh pilot to be trained.

Williams, Havelock
WITH MY CAMERA FOR COMPANY. Adventures and Images of a Pioneering New Zealand Photographer. Edited by Diana Rhodes.
Christchurch: Hazard Press, 2003, 232p., illus.
Includes a valuable first-hand account of Williams (1884-1968) being a passenger aboard Maurice Buckley's first flights over South Westland in January 1924 (see pages 160-171). Williams took the first aerial photographs of Hokitika and South Westland, and his account of the pioneering flights are historically valuable and well written.

Williams, Robin and Tom
GREYMOUTH AERO CLUB (INC) Golden Jubilee 1933-1983.
Greymouth, James Printing Service, 1983, 40p., illus, maps.
A brief illustrated history of the first 50 years of the Greymouth Aero Club with references to other aviation events relevant to Greymouth.

Woodhall, Derek
"De Havilland Gipsy Moth ZK-AAI" in Aviation Historical Society of New Zealand. Journal Vol. 6, No. 10, November 1963, p.199-200.
A brief history of Gipsy Moth ZK-AAI which engaged in a range of pioneering flights from 1929. On 20 November 1933, piloted by Jack B. Renton, with passenger J.D. Lynch (former Mayor of Greymouth) it crashed on Mt. Turiwhate killing both occupants. The registration was used on a rebuilt aircraft which was later written off in a crash at Hokitika in 1937.

Woodhall, Derek
"The De Havilland DH83 Fox Moth" in Aviation Historical Society of New Zealand. Journal Vol. 15, Nos. 3-12, April-December 1972, p.66-70, 90-96, 126-130, 150-159, 174-178, 198-202, 222-226, 246-250, 270-272.
An early detailed account of Fox Moth operations, including much Air Travel (NZ) Ltd history, by an experienced aviation historian, who did extensive newspaper research as well as exploring many other primary sources. A valuable resource.

Woodhall, Derek
"The Spartans" in Aviation Historical Society of New Zealand, Journal Vol. 12, Nos. 7-9, August-October 1969, p.159-165, 183-189, 207-215.
A comprehensive account of Simmonds Spartan aircraft which did much pioneer flying in New Zealand, including early West Coast flights, and describes the early charter work by Arthur Nancekivell with ZK-ABU of West Coast Airways 1932-1934.

OTHER:
AIR MINISTRY. PILOT'S NOTES FOR DOMINIE 1 & C11.
England: Air Data Publications, 1946, 19., illus and diagram.
The official service pilot's notes for the operation of the Dominie aircraft type. Air Publication 1763A & B – PN.

GUY MENZIES DAY. 7th January 2006.
Harihari: Guy Menzies Committee, 2006, 30p., illus.
A useful booklet produced for the 75th anniversary of Menzies flight – the first solo flight across the Tasman Sea.

NEW ZEALAND WINGS AIR DIRECTORY (various issues)
Christchurch: New Zealand Wings Ltd and Urbane Media Group
Comprehensive reference publication. Contains concise summaries of New Zealand's civil aviation operators, clubs, societies, etc. Updated and published annually. Previously published as 'Whites Air Directory' from 1947.

STORIES OF THE FOX-PARINGA-HAAST ROAD
Hokitika: Fox Glacier-Paringa-Haast Road 30th Anniversary Committee, 1995, 95p., illus, map.
An important collection of stories, by many of the original participants of the mammoth task of building the final highway through South Westland, culminating in the opening in November 1965. Includes some references to the South Westland air service and a detailed account of the January 1965 air ambulance landing of West Coast Airways Dominie ZK-AKS at the hastily prepared Whakapohai airstrip.

The Dictionary of New Zealand Biography, Volume Four 1921-1940
Auckland: Auckland University Press, Department of Internal Affairs, 1998, 650p.
Contains a biography of James Cuthbert Mercer (1886-1944) by John King, p.348.

The Dictionary of New Zealand Biography, Volume Five 1941-1960
Auckland: Auckland University Press, Department of Internal Affairs, 2000, 679p.
Contains a biography of Brian Kynaston Waugh (1922-1984) by Richard Waugh, p.547-548.

Journals of the **Aviation Historical Society of New Zealand**. Reference material and helpful information from various journals.

New Zealand Wings magazines from 1933 to 1948.

Various newspaper references from the ***Greymouth Evening Star, Greymouth Star, Hokitika Guardian**, Nelson Evening Mail, South West Scene. The Dominion, The Press* and the ***Westport News***.

Various extracts from correspondence related to the South Westland air service. Also the Brittenden Collection and J.C. Mercer Collection at the Canterbury Museum.

Audio Tapes held by the Department of Conservation archive, Hokitika, include a number of interviews with people about South Westland aviation e.g. Bert Barley (recovery of Fox Moth from Franz Josef Glacier), Jack Cox (flying with Bert Mercer), Charlie Eggeling (about the start of the air service), Des Nolan (early flying), Kevin Nolan (flying with Bert Mercer).

Videos/DVDs
FLYING THE COAST
Christchurch: Vidpro (NZ) Ltd, 30min, 1995.
A professional video about the 1994 60th anniversary South Westland air service celebrations including interviews with key people, airshow coverage, plaque unveilings and air-to-air of Fox Moth ZK-AEK and Dominie ZK-AKY.

HOKITIKA AIRSHOW. 50th Anniversary of the opening of Hokitika Airport.
Riverton: South Coast Productions, 45min, 2002.
A video record of the commemorative 50th anniversary air show at Hokitika in December 2001. Includes interviews with a number of people connected to the South Westland air service, Fox Moth replica and air-to-air of Fox Moth ZK-ADI and Dominie ZK-AKY.

LOST ... Without trace? A pictorial look at the book of the same name written by Richard Waugh.
Nelson: Video Wings Limited, 90min, 2006.
Filmed at the time of the launch of the Lost book at Christchurch in February 2006 on the 44th anniversary of the disappearance of Dragonfly ZK-AFB. Includes interviews with people involved and has excellent air-to-air of Dragonfly ZK-AYR.

NAC: The 60th Anniversary Tour.
Nelson, Video Wings Aviation Production, 350min (2 DVD), 2007.
A comprehensive and professional record of the New Zealand National Airways Corporation anniversary tour around New Zealand in March 2007 flying a DC-3 and joined for part of the route by DH89 Dominie ZK-AKY. The Dominie landed at Haast to celebrate the NAC era of the South Westland air service, and to commemorate the 40th anniversary of the close of the historic air service. The DVD covers the visit, including air to air of the Dominie over Haast and an interview with Allan Cron about his father's influence on Bert Mercer.

THE FLIGHT OF THE DRAGONFLY. A 10 minute trip down memory lane aboard the DH90 Dragonfly ZK-AYR.
Nelson: Video Wings Limited, 10min, 2006.
Narrated by Dragonfly pilot Ryan Southam, this short film covers a Christchurch to Nelson flight in February 2006 with Rev Jean Waugh (Brian Waugh's widow) as a special passenger.

WEST COAST REMEMBERS
Wellington: Ian Crosland, 80min, 1995.
A privately and competently produced video of the 1994 60th anniversary South Westland air service celebrations. Covers most aspects in detail; including the Warbirds DC-3 flight from Auckland, Kawatiri Memorial service and plaque unveiling for Mercer, celebration dinner at Hokitika, airshow, and Southside plaque and information plaque unveiling.

HIGHLY RECOMMENDED READING

TAKING OFF.
Pioneering Small Airlines of New Zealand 1945-1970. By Richard Waugh with Bruce Gavin, Peter Layne and Graeme McConnell.

TURBULENT YEARS.
A Commercial Pilot's Story. By Brian Waugh. Edited by Richard Waugh.

WEST COAST MEMORIES.
Volume One. By Paul Beauchamp Legg.

WHEN THE COAST IS CLEAR.
The Story of New Zealand's first and most unique licensed air service - South Westland 1934-1967. Edited by Richard Waugh: with contributing authors John King, Paul Beauchamp Legg and Richard Waugh.

Index

Bold figures indicate illustrations

Abel Tasman Aviation Ltd 142
Addington School, Christchurch 73
Admiral Scheer 104
Aerial Sowing Ltd 118, 143
Aero Commander 500 ZK-CTM 133
Agnew, Lindy (L.) 130
Ahaura Helicopters Ltd 143
Air Navigation and Trading Company 104
Air Charter 71
Air Contracts Ltd, Masterton 41
Air Nelson Ltd 136 – 138
Air New Zealand Link 125, 136 – 138, 140
Air New Zealand Ltd 94, 117, 127, 133, 136, 138
Air Safaris and Services (NZ) Ltd 142
Air Services Licensing Authority 91, 134, 139
Air Travel (Hokitika) Ltd 115, 127
Air Travel (NZ) Ltd 12, 18, 25, 27, 32, 33, 36, 39 – 41, 43 – 46, 49, 53 – 55, 57, 64, 65, 67, 70, 72, 73, 75, 77, 86, 91, 97, 114, 115, 118, 122, 124 – 126, 129, 131, 132 , 142
Air West 142
Air West Coast Ltd 140, 142
Air West Helicopters Ltd 143
Aircraft Engineering Ltd, Wellington 71
Aircraft Hire Ltd 133
Airsow Westport 143
Airspeed Horsa glider 104
Airspeed Oxford 57, 77, 104
Airspeed Oxford NZ1243 53
Airspeed Oxford NZ1257 53
Albert Glacier 110
Aldridge, Mr (Postmaster) 65
Alexander Helicopters Ltd 143
Allard, 'Bert' (A.) 130
Allard, Miss **75**
Allen, Fred (F.C.) 56
Almer Hut 62
Alpine Adventures and Fox and Franz Heli Services 143
Alpine Deer Group Ltd 43
Alpine Enterprises Ltd 143
Alpine Helicopters Ltd 143
Amberley 31
Anderson Helicopters Ltd 141, 143
Anderson, Jean (J.) **86, 87,** 91, 130
Anderson, Kevin (K.) **141**
Anderson, 'Bob' (R.A.L.) 134
Andrews, 'Ted' (E.) **17**
Andrews, Noel (N.) **37**
Andy's Glacier 38
Ansett Transport Industries Ltd 134
Anti-Aircraft Flight, Mangere 85
Aoraki Mount Cook Skiplanes Ltd 142
Arahura 97
Arahura Pa 18
Arahura riverbed 43
Arawata Aerodrome 33
Arawata campsite **27**
Arawata River 38
Ardmore Aerodrome, South Auckland 86, 97, 135
Armstrong-Siddeley Genet IIA 20
Arrow Aviation Company 8
Ashburton 31, 94, 140
Ashburton Air Services Ltd 140
Ashwell, 'Ted' (A.E.) 85
Atkinson, Sheila (S.) **134**
Auckland 13, 21, 31, 32, 66, 134
Auckland Aero Club 32
Auster aircraft 104, 142
Auster ZK-AUO **92,** 104, 106, 127
Auster ZK-AWZ 133
Auster ZK-AYB 93
Auster ski-plane ZK-BDX 135
Australia 10, 22
Australian National Airways 70
Automobile Association reliability trials 31
Avro 504K H1970 10
Avro 504K H5241, G-NZAO *Blazing Arrow* **8,** 10
Avro Anson 77, 91
Avro Avian G-ABCF *Southern Cross Junior* **10,** 12,
Avro Avian G-ABCF *Southern Cross Junior* replica 23
Avro Lancaster 54, 104
Avro Lancaster LL888 54
Avro Lancaster R5611 54
Avro Lancaster R5750 54
Ayson, Don (D.F.) 80

BAe Jetstream 138
Baedeker 104
Baines, Arthur (A.) 47, **50,** 57, 58, 60 – 62, **62,** 72, 129
Baring Square Methodist Church 31
Barltrop, Ron (R.) 129
Barnard, Spencer (S.) 63
Barnett, Graeme (G.) 76, 130
Barnhill, Charlie (C.) 14
Barnhill, Jean (J.) 14
Barry, Alister (A.) 117, 119
Batchelor's Paddock, North Revell Street, Hokitika 9
Batten, Jean (J.G.) **37**
Bealey River 22
Beban, A.B. 22
Beechcraft D18S ZK-BQE 104
Belgian Congo 43
Belgium 43, 104
Bell 47
Bell 206A Jet Ranger ZK-HPP 143
Bell 206B Jet Ranger ZK-HSG **141**
Bert Mercer Wing 51
Betley, Captain Roland (R.) 55
Big Bay 41, 85, **124,** 139
Bishop, 'Norm' (N.G.) **119,** 138
Blackball 127
Blaketown Beach 92
Blanchfield, Hugh 'Paddy' MP 133
Blechynden, Alex. (A.) 41
Blenheim 17, 132, 135
Bluff 25
Bombardier DHC-8 Q300 138
Borthwick, F. 87
Bowen Falls, Milford Sound **88**
Bowes, Murray 142
Bowman, Gordon (G.) **40, 47,** 50, 54, 114
Bradshaw, Arthur (A. J.) 49, 71, 93, 109, 130, 142
Brazier, 'Bill' **19**
Breccia Creek **112,** 113
Bremen, Germany 104
Brigade of Guards Flying Club 33
Brighton, England 55
British and Inter-Colonial Exhibition 10
Broady, Bruce (B.) 44, 127
Broken Hill, N.S.W. 70
Brown Walters 77
Brown, Allan (A.) **94**
Brown, Doug. (D.)
Browning Range **92**
Bruce Bay 21, **25,** 26, 34, **36, 37,** 46, 56, **58,** 50, 99
Brunell, Geoff (G.) 61
Buchanan Enterprises 134
Buchanan, Gloria (G.) **105**
Buchanan, Heather (H.) **105**
Buchanan, Henry (H.) 134
Buchanan, John (J.) 128, **128**
Buchanan, Rosalie (R.) 80
Buckley, Maurice (M.) **9,** 10, 12, 31, 117
Buller District 131, 133, 134, 142
Buller Hospital 67
Bullock Creek bridge **60**
Bullock Island 10
Burrell, 'Sam' (H.B.) 12
Busch, Jack (J.J.) 17, 22

Cambrai, France 55
Cameron, Sir Houghton 21
Cane, 'Jimmy' (J.F.) 75, 130
Canterbury 77, 143
Canterbury (N.Z) Aviation Company Ltd 10, 31, 54
Canterbury Aero Club 17, 21, 22, 23, 26, 27, 32, 33, 44, 53
Canterbury Automobile Association Rooms, Worcester Street, Christchurch 23
Capital Air Services Ltd 135
Carmine, Phil. (P.) 82, **87,** 91, 130
Carroll, Jack (J.) **47,** 129
Cascade Waterfall 38
Castle Flat 102
Caudron biplane 31
Caversham 31
Cessna Crane 77
Cessna 150 139
Cessna 152 Aerobat 139
Cessna 172 135, 139
Cessna 172M ZK-DHS 142
Cessna 177 Cardinal ZK-DIH 139
Cessna 180 135, 142
Cessna 180 ZK-BJW 106, **108**
Cessna 180 ZK-BJY 94, **94,** 142
Cessna 180 ZK-BVQ 134
Cessna 185 135
Cessna 185 ZK-CAK 133
Cessna 185 ZK-CEW 110
Cessna 185 ZK-CKP **136**
Cessna 207 ZK-DSE 142
Cessna 207 ZK-EJD 139
Cessna 337 Skymaster 135
Cessna 402 135
Cessna 402A ZK-DHW 138, **138**
Cessna 404 Titan ZK-NDY 140
Cessna U206F ZK-PCS 142
Chadwick, Brian (B.G.) 71, 104, 105, 127
Chaffey, Simon (S.) 111
Changi, Singapore 104
Chapman, George (G.H.) 54, 65
Cherbourg, France 55
Childs, Rev. H.A. 68
Chorley, Lancashire, England 54
Christoffels, Albert (A.) 73
Christchurch 10, 17, 27, 34, 66, 69, 79, 82, 83, 104, 110, 127, 128, 133 – 136, 138 – 140
Christchurch International Airport 71, 105, **134**
Christchurch Technical College 73
Christie, Hume (H.D.) 27
Civil Aviation 66, 68, 76, 87, 133, 140
Clark, Ronnie (R.) **37**
Clarke, Maurice (F.M.) 70
Classic Flyers' Museum, Tauranga Airport **85,** 86, 89
Clifford, Aroha (A.) 32
Coast Air (operated by Coast Air Charter Ltd) 140
Coast Air Charter Ltd 139, 142
Coast Aviation 134, 142
Coastair (operated by Ashburton Air Services Ltd) 140
Coastwide Helicopters Ltd 143
Collingwood 18, 63
Collyer, Frank (F.) 99
Como Holdings Ltd 140
Condon, Fay (F.) **25**
Condon, Jack (J.) **25**
Conradson, S.J. 26, 33
Cook Strait 86, 135
Cook Strait Airways Limited 52, 53, 65, 69, 85, 86, 97, 131, 132
Cook, Peter (P.) 55
Copeland Valley 102
Cornwall, Margaret (M.) **62,** 63
Cosford, England 104
Cowan, J. 21
Craigieburn 43
Cromwell 17
Cron, Allan (A.) 22, **27, 28,** 29
Cron, Allan Jnr (A.)**114**
Cron, Jack (J.) **27,** 29
Cron, John (J.) **11**
Cron, Myrtle (M.) **11, 79,** 82, **92, 99**
Cron, Nora (N.) **11, 27,** 29, **93**
Cron, Reg (R.) **11, 27**
Cron Homestead, Haast **19, 38, 99**
Cronin, Maurice (M.) 130
Cropp, 'Bill' (W.) 109, 122
Croydon Aircraft Company 41, 43
Croydon Aviation Heritage Trust 41, 85, 88, 124

Daniel, Rob (R.) 125
Daniell, Rex (R. D.) 134
Dawe, Maurice (M.) 67, 68, 72, 123
de Castro, S.K. 21
de Havilland Aircraft Co Ltd, Hatfield, England 26, 44, 46, 71, 97
de Havilland Aircraft Company of New Zealand 43, 44, 53, 65, 66, **72**
de Havilland Canada DHC-6-300 Twin Otter ZK-OTR **139,** 140
de Havilland DH9 D3139, G-NZAM 31
de Havilland DH60G Gipsy Moth ZK-AAH **12, 13, 15,** 22
de Havilland DH60G Gipsy Moth ZK-AAI **12 - 15,** 17, 18, **18,** 22
de Havilland DH60G Gipsy Moth ZK-AAR, NZ519 37
de Havilland DH60G Gipsy Moth ZK-AAS **11**
de Havilland DH60G Gipsy Moth ZK-AAW **12, 13, 15**
de Havilland DH60G Gipsy Moth ZK-ABQ **12, 15, 16,** 22, 23
de Havilland DH.82A Tiger Moth 104
de Havilland DH.82A Tiger Moth ZK-AFW 141
de Havilland DH.82A Tiger Moth ZK-AFY 141
de Havilland DH82A Tiger Moth ZK-AGX, NZ712 73
de Havilland DH82A Tiger Moth ZK-AJQ 141
de Havilland DH82A Tiger Moth ZK-ALP 141
de Havilland DH82A Tiger Moth ZK-AND 141
de Havilland DH82A Tiger Moth ZK-ARY, NZ798 73
de Havilland DH83 Fox Moth 22, 76, 77, 94, 132
de Havilland DH83 Fox Moth ZK-ADH **19, 20,** 23, **24, 27,** 33, 34, 44, 46
de Havilland DH83 Fox Moth ZK-ADI, NZ566, ZK-ASP *Mimiro*, N83DH, G-ADHA, **25,** 26, **26,** 27, **28,** 29, 33, 34, **34 – 36, 38, 40,** 41, **41, 45,** 46, **48, 49, 57,** 63, 76, 77, **83,** 117 – 119, 121, **124,** 125, **125,** 126
de Havilland DH83 Fox Moth ZK-ADI replica 51, 78, **120,** 125
de Havilland DH83 Fox Moth ZK-AEK *Mohua*, *Duke*, G-ACAJ, G-ACDD, OO-ENC, VQ-FAT, C-FYPM **32,** 34, **35,** 38, **38,** 39, **42, 43, 46, 50, 62,** 63, 65, 77, **78, 79, 83, 121,** 124
de Havilland DH83 Fox Moth ZK-AEK replica 51, 126, **152**
de Havilland DH83 Fox Moth ZK-AEK model **122**
de Havilland DH83 Fox Moth ZK-AGM *Matuhi* 44, **44,** 47, **52, 66,** 75 – 77, **83, 87, 127**
de Havilland DH83C Fox Moth ZK-APT 102, 134
de Havilland DH84 Dragon G-ACGG 43
de Havilland DH84 Dragon ZK-ADR, ZK-AER, NZ551, ZK-AHT 64, 65, 67, **67, 69,** 72, 86, 97, 123
de Havilland DH89A Dragon Rapide 104, 132
de Havilland DH89A Dragon Rapide G-AFMF 104
de Havilland DH89A Dragon Rapide ZK-ACO *Tainui* 37
de Havilland DH89A Dragon Rapide ZK-AEC *Mercury* **131**
de Havilland DH89A Dragon Rapide ZK-AHS, NZ558, ZK-AGT *Neptune, Mokai* **65,** 69, **70, 74,** 76, 77, 88, 91, **92,** 93, **96,** 97, **97,** 101, **105,** 106, **107, 108,** 110, **112,** 113, **113,** 114, 118, **118,** 121, 122, 126, **131**
de Havilland DH89B Dominie 77, 78, 132, 133, 142
de Havilland DH89B Dominie ZK-AKS 75, 109, **109**
de Havilland DH89B Dominie ZK-AKT *Tareke* 75, 77, 91, 93, **96, 98, 99,** 101, 104, **104**
de Havilland DH89B Dominie ZK-AKU *Tawaka* 77, 85, **85,** 86, 89, **89, 119**
de Havilland DH89B Dominie ZK-AKY *Tui* **76,** 77, 85, **85,** 86, 87, 89, **119,** 121, **124, 125,** 127, 128, **128**
de Havilland DH89B Dominie ZK-ALB 77, 85
de Havilland DH89B Dominie ZK-BAU 85, 99
de Havilland DH89B Dominie ZK-BCP 115, 118, 136, **136**
de Havilland DH90A Dragonfly ZK-AFB *Kiwi Rover* 9, **39, 40,** 45, **45, 52, 55,** 56, 58, **58, 59,** 62, 69, **70,** 71, **71, 77,** 93, 105
de Havilland DH90A Dragonfly ZK-AGP 47, 50, **52,** 54, **57,** 58, 60, **60,** 61, **61,** 62, 71, 72, **72**
de Havilland DH98 Mosquito NZ2324 **81**
de Havilland Technical School 44
de Jong, Basil (B.) 96, 130
Defiance Hut 50
Delahunty, James (J. R.) 26
Denmark 104
Denniston 61
Department of Conservation, Visitor Centre, Haast Junction 114
Devlin and Wilding Ltd 140
Dickie, Norman (N.) **16**
Dillmanstown 17
Dini, Bill (W.S.) 69, 129
Diserens, Percy (P.) 68
Doig, Brian (B.) 94
Dominie/Dragonfly hangar 88
Dornier Do228-202 ZK-VIR 140
Douglas Dakota 104
Douglas DC-3 77, 94, 133
Douglas DC-3 ZK-DAK 127
Douglas DC-3 Skyliner ZK-BEU *Westport* 118, **132**
Douglas DC-3 Viewmaster 134
Douglas DC-10 94
Douglas Neve landing strip102
Dovey, Rex (R.) 130
Dowd, 'Shem' (E.P.M.) **119,** 130
Dowell, Malcolm (M.) **76,** 87
Dowell, Max (M.) **76,** 87, **120,** 125
Dowell, Phillip (P.) **76**
Drummond, Andy (A.) 129
Drummond, Constable 18
Dublin, Ireland 104
Duggan, Malcolm (M.) **96**
Duke of Gloucester 29
Dunedin 31, 37, 50, 95
Dunn, Merv. (M.) 134
Dusseldorf, Germany 53
Duthwaite, Bill **38**

Eagle Airways Ltd 136, 138
East Coast Airways Ltd 42, 64
Eden, Ken (K.) 93, 95, 96, **101,** 130
Eggeling, Clifford (C.) 74, 128, **128**
Eggeling, Dorothy (D.) **16**
Eggeling, Betty (E.) **74**
Eggeling, Kerry (K.) 128, **128**
Eggeling, Margaret (M.) **105**
Eggeling, Peter (P.) 128, **128**
Eggeling, Roger (R.) 128, **128**
Eggeling, 'Dick' (R.) **16**
Egypt 43
Ellsworth, Lincoln (L.) 22
England 10, 21, 39, 47, 54, 65, 77, 86
Epitaph Rift **111**
Essendon Airport, Melbourne 70
Evans, A. J. 41
Evans, Bill (W.) 133

Fairchild Argus 104
Fairchild- Swearingen SA 227AC Metroliner III 136, 138
Fairchild- Swearingen SA 227AC Metroliner III ZK-NSI **137**
Fairchild- Swearingen SA 227AC Metroliner III ZK-NST **137**
Fairy the horse **25**
Falcon Airways 37
Ferguson Brothers 139
Ferguson, 'Dick' (R.) **74, 78, 81,** 129, 130
Fielden, Flt Lt E.H. 43
Fiennes, Roger (R.) 43
Fiji 43
Finch, Noel (N.) 78
Findlay, Captain J.L. 32
Finny, Ivan (I.) 16
Fiordland 54
Fiordland National Park 110
Five Fingers Mountains 38
Fletcher FU-24 143
Fletcher, Dorothy (D.) **119**
Flight Corporation Ltd 142
Flynn, John (J.B.) 21
Fokker F-27 Friendship 115, 117, 133, 134, 136
Fokker F27-100 ZK-BXC *Kerangi* **132**
Fokker F27-100 ZK-BXF *Karuwai* **137**
Fokker F27-100 ZK-NAF *Korimako* 117
Fokker F-28 Fellowship PH-MOL 118
Fokker F.V11B VH-USU *Southern Cross* 32
Forbury Park Racecourse 96
Forsyth, Malcolm (M.) 134
Fox Glacier 34, 55, 76, 85, 95, **98,** 107, 119, 135, 142
Franklyn, Jack (J.) 87, 130
Franz Josef 10, **14, 18,** 17, 22, 23, 34, 58, 63, 76, 78, 82, 85, 89, 95, 109, 113, **113,** 118, 119, 122, **136,** 142, 143
Franz Josef Glacier 10, 21, 27, 38, **48,** 50, **62,** 94, **97,** 102, **103, 105,** 106, 135
Franz Josef Hostel 82
Franz Josef Hotel 82
Franz Josef Motor Camp **103**
Fraser, Dr. 18
Fyfe, Colin (C.) 31

Gael 43
Garden City Helicopters Ltd 143
Garnier, Terry (T.) 44
Gatineau Airport, Canada 43
Geerds, Henuri (H.F.) 84
George, G. 18
Gibbons, Sidney (S.) 73
Gibson, Wing Com. Guy (G.P.) 54
Gilbert, J. 117
Gillespies Beach 32
Gisborne 104
Glacier Helicopters Ltd 143
Glacier Heliventures 143
Glacier Southern Lakes Helicopters Ltd 143
Glenbeg 85
Glenhope 67
Gloriavale Christian Community 140
Glubb, David (D.) 128, **128**
Godwit Club 86
Gold Band Taxis 110
Golden Bay 69
Golden Bay Air Ltd 142
Golden Bay Aviation Ltd 142
Golden Bay Cement works 69
Golden Coast Airlines (1965) Ltd 115, 133 – 135, 142
Golden Coast Airlines Ltd 133, 134, 142
Golden Coast Airways Ltd 133, 142
Goodwin Chichester Aviation Company 37
Gore 85
Gowan Bridge 67
Gowan Bridge Store 68
Graham, 'Gar' **123**
Graham, Alexander (A.C.) 26, **45**
Graham, Peter (P.) 10, **16,** 26
Graham, Rose (R.) 26
Graham's Creek 23
Graham's Glacier Hotel 10, 22, 23, **36**
Granity 67
Grant, Ross (R.) 129
Grantham, Elmer (E.) 32
Grave Creek **112**
Gray, David (D.W.) 86
Green's Beach 107
Grey River 18
Greymouth 10, 16, 20, 21, **45, 71,** 72, 76, 77, 82, 83, 93, 117, 119, 131 – 135, 138, **138,** 139, 140, 142
Greymouth Aero Club 102, 134, 141
Greymouth Aero Club Flight Centre 142

Greymouth Technical High School 77, 105
Greymouth Hospital 18, 139
Greymouth Hospital Board 113
Grocott, Gerald (G.) 41, 125
Groom, F. 87

Haast 22, 26, 29, **29,** 33, **38,** 44, 50, 54, **74,** 58, 76, 78 – 80, 82, 83, **83,** 85 – 87, 91, **92,** 93, 94, 97, 98, **99,** 101, 102, **105,** 106, **107, 109,** 110, 113, 114, 119, 124, 127 – 129, 131
Haast Aeradio 95
Haast Beach 95
Haast Bridge **100**
Haast Highway 22
Haast Pass 9, 80, 101
Haast Pass Road 39, **93,** 101, 102, **111**
Haast River **15, 90**
Haast School 127
Haast Ticket Office **99,** 114
Haast Valley 40
Hadfield, Rev K.A. 68
Hale, Lawrence (L.) 55
Hallaran, Frank (F.) 139
Hall-Jones, Rod (R.) 41
Halton, England 104
Hamilton 133
Hamilton Airways Ltd 11
Hamilton, 'Bill' (C.W.F.) **30**
Handley Page Hampden 77
Hanlon, E. 86
Hansez, Guy (G.) 43
Harihari 23, 127
Harper, Jim (J.) 99
Harrington, 'Bill' (W.J) **9,** 10, 117
Harris, Tom (T.) 56, 71, **79, 81,** 91, 93, 129, 130
Hawea 101
Hawker Hurricane Mk1A ZK-TPK **125**
Heaphy Track 135, 142
Heaphy, Philip (P.) 139
Hearty, Michael (M. J.) 60, 61
Helicopter Charter Karamea (2006) Ltd 143
Heliventures Ltd 143
Hende family 26
Hende, 'Bill' (W.) 130
Hendon, England 43
Hewett, 'Jim' (J.D.) 34, **35,** 39, 43, **45,** 47, 53, 66, 97, 129
Hewett, LAC James (J.D.) 53
Hewett, Linda (L.) 39, **45**
Hexham, Northumberland, England 104
Hill, Cecil (C. M.) 31
Hinemoa **25**
Hobsonville 73, 85
Hochstetter Forest 141
Hogg, Doctor 93
Hokitika 8 – 10, 16 – 24, 26, 27, 30, 41, 43 – 47, 50, 54 – 57, 60, 64 – 73, 75, **76,** 77 – 80, 82, **82,** 83, 85 - 89, 91, 95 – 97, 101, 104, 108 – 111, 113, 114, 117, 119, **119,** 121, 124, 126 – 128, 131 – 136, **137,** 138 – 143
Hokitika Aeradio **40, 52,** 78
Hokitika Aero Club 15, 21, 23, 93, 141
Hokitika Airport Committee 122
Hokitika Airport Terminal 89, 114, 117, 125, **125,** 126, **137**
Hokitika Aviation Heritage Trail 124
Hokitika Borough Council 104
Hokitika Boys Brigade Hall **122,** 124
Hokitika Cemetery 68, 72, **103**
Hokitika Court 61
Hokitika District High School 54
Hokitika Post Office 57
Hokitika Primary School 54, 77
Hokitika River Bridge 51
Holden, Des (D.) **87,** 118, 119, **119,** 130
Holyoake, Keith (K.J.) **112**
Hope Saddle 67, 68
Hope-Cross, David (D.) 122
Hotel Westland 54
House of Travel 127
Houston, David (D.) 107
Houston, Geoffrey (G. M.) 72, 101, 102, **103,** 105 – 108, 130
Houston, Kelvin (K.) 107
Houston, Noeline (N.) 102, 107
Howaldt Works, Germany 104
Howard, Harry (H.) **74,** 75, **81,** 129, 130
Hughes, Arthur (A.) 68
Humber Ambulance 95
Humphries, Jack (J.) 91, 93, 94, 130
Hungerford, England 44, 127
Hunter, Nadine (N.) 129
Hupmobile cars 31
Hutchison, Helen (H.) 105, 115, 130
Hutchison, Paul (P.) 119

Ikamatua 20
Inchbonnie 27
Inchbonnie Aerodrome 33
India 37
Ingham, Arnold (A.) 130
Inglis, Robert 136
Inter Colonial Exhibition 10
Invercargill 13, 21, 31, 50, 54, 134
Iringatau Villa **103**
Isle of Man 104

Jackson Bay 34, 41, **42,** 43, 46, 58, 75, 82, 86, 95, 101
James Aviation Ltd 135
James, Harry (H.) 111
Jamieson, Jim (J.) 118, **119, 137**
Jenkins, Harry (H.) 135
Jenny the horse **36**
Jever, Germany 54
John Burns & Co Ltd 73
Johnston, J. 21
Johnson, Albert (A.) 58, 60, 61
Jones, Hon. Frederick. (F.) 54, 68
Judge, Phillip (P.) 95
Junkers Ju88 54

Kahaurangi Point 63
Kaipaki 73
Kakapo 60
Kaniere 93, 125
Karamea 10, 12, 20, 131, 133, 135
Karamea Heaphy Air Charter Ltd 142
Karangaroa 102
Karoro Aerodrome/Greymouth Airport **20,** 132
Kawatiri Aerodrome/Westport Airport 97
Kawatiri Junction 67, 68, 72, 86
Kawatiri Junction memorial plaque 72, **73,** 86, 123
Kay, Cyril (C.E.) 39
Keenan, Michael (M.) 122
Kelly, G.W. 21
Kennedy, Jim (J.) 57, 68 – 70, 129
Kent, James (J.B). MP 80
Kerang, Victoria, Australia 70
Kere, Parata Pita (aka 'Friday' Kelly) **40**
Kiel, Germany 54, 104
Kilian, John (J.). 91, 130
King, John (J.) 41, 117, 119, 123, 124
King, Ross (R.) 54, 56, 58, **74,** 75, **79,** 81, 129, 130
King, Sister 93
King, Roy (K.) **96**
King, Unice (U.) 111
Kingsford-Smith, Sir Charles 10, 32
Kirkup, Ron (R.A.) **47**
Knight's Point 111, **112**
Kokatahi Helicopters 2000 Ltd 143
Korari Street, Riccarton, Christchurch 23
Kortegast Brewery **11**
Kumara 18

La Fontaine swamp, Harihari **10,** 12
Lake Brunner 142
Lake Ellesmere 31
Lake Haupiri, Grey Valley 140
Lake Ianthe 96
Lake Kaniere Yacht and Power Boat Club 93
Lake Mahinapua 10
Lake Mapourika **45,** 96
Lake Paringa 96
Lake Wahapo 96
Lake, A. 34
Lands and Survey Department 18
Landsborough Aerodrome 33,
Lawler, Joy (J.) 94
Lawler, Karen (K.) **94**
Leech, Jack (J.J.) 130
Legg, Paul Beauchamp (P.B.) 93, 94, **96, 98,** 101, 102, **123,** 124, 130
Leslie, Jack (J.) **47**
Leuna Oil Refinery, Merseburg, Germany 104
Levin 54, 55
Lewis Pass 22
Lewis Pass Road 42
Lewis, Cliff (C.) 41, 45 – 47, 53, 129
Lewis, Colin (C.) 58, 63, 67, 68, 79, 130
Lilico, Dave (D.K.) 41, 117, 118
Lister, Doug (G.D.) 78, **79,** 118, **119,** 130
Lister, Jean (J.) **86**
Little, Bill (W.) 129
Lockheed 10A Electra 77, 132
Lockheed 10A Electra ZK-AFE *Kereru* **52**
Lockheed 10A Electra ZK-BUT 104
Lockheed Hudson 57, 77
Lockheed Lodestar 18-56 77, 133
Lockheed Lodestar 18-56 ZK-AKW *Kopara* 80, **82**
Lockheed Ventura 55, 77
London - Sydney Air Race 86
Long, Monsignor James (J.) **134**
Lucas, 'Popeye' Fred (F.J.) 91, 94, **101,** 130
Lynch, 'Jimmy' (J.D.) 17, **18,** 23

Macduff's, Wellington 67
MacRobertson Air Race 1934 37
Mahitahi River Mouth Aerodrome 33, **45**
Mahuika, Ben (B.) **37**
Mahuika, Pat (P.) **25, 37**
Mahutu 61
Makarora 101
Makawhio Point **36**
Marker, S.M. 41
Markland, Edward (E.) 54
Markland, Esther (E.) 54
Markland, Roy (E. R.) **47,** 54, **54,** 55, 129
Mark Range **92**
Marshall, Alf (A.) 87
Marshall, Dot (D.) 87
Marshall, Kaye (K.) **76**
Marshall, Murray (M.) **76**
Marshlands, Christchurch 22
Maruia Springs 93
Masterton 71, 85
Matheson, 'Bob' (R.) 17, 21
Mayne, Alan (A.) 101
McBride, 'Doll' 16, **16**
McBride, Geoffrey (G. C) 60, 61
McCallum, J.A. 21
McConnell, Graeme (G.J.) 72, 114, **126**
McCook, Bryan (B.) 43, 91, 130
McCormack Ross Trish (P.) 80
McDonald, C. 87
McDonald, David (D.) 109, 130
McDougall, Thora (T.) 78
McDowell, A. J. 22
McEwan, Alex. (A.) **25**
McEwan, Cyril (C.) **25**
McEwan, Letti (L.) **25**
McEwan, Margaret (M.) **25**
McGovern, M. 38
McGregor, 'Mad Mac' Malcolm, (M.) **11,** 15
McIntosh, J. J. 21
McIntyre, 'Dick' (R.) **38**
McKay, Rev Father 16
MacKay, Horatio 11, 14
McLaren, Archie (A.) **37**
McLaren, 'Jimmy' (J.) **25, 37**
McLean, Dr 'Mac' (D.) 80
McLean, Dr Jean (J.) 80, **80,** 86, 119
McLellan, Hugh (H.) 139
McLellan, Malcolm 139
McLernon, Jock (J.S.) 39, **119,** 130
McQuitty, Clare (C.) **62,** 63
Melbourne 37
Melbourne Cup 66
Menzies, Guy (G.) 10, 12, 23
Mepal, Cambridgeshire, England 104
Mercer, 'Bert' (J.C.) 9, 12, 13, **15, 16,** 17, 18 – 20 , 22, 23, 25, **25,** 26, 27, 29, 31, **31,** 32, **32,** 33, 34, **35 – 37,** 38, 41 – 45, **45,** 47, **47,** 50, 53, 54, **55,** 56, **56,** 58, **60,** 65, 66, 68 – 72, 75, 77, 85, 99, 105, 109, 112, 114, 115, 118, 121 – 129
Mercer, 'Bert' (J.C.) mannequin **121**
Mercer, Billee Jean (B.J.) 31, **47,** 121, 125, 129
Mercer, Bruce (B.) **56**
Mercer, Jane (J.) 31, **36,** 69
Mercer, Marie (M.) 31, **36, 39,** 72, **120,** 121, 122, **122,** 125, 129
Methodist Church 104
Midget the horse **36**
Mildura, Victoria, Australia 70
Miles Gemini ZK-AQO *Mokai* 79, **79**
Miles Magister 104
Miles, 'Bill' (G.W.) 76
Milford Sound 47, **49,** 50, 71, 76, 87, 89, 102, 104, 105, 110, 127
Millar, F. 80
Minaret Creek 44
Minarets **105**
Ministry of Works, Greymouth 80, 101
Moll, (A.P.) 118
Molloy, Emma (E.) 77
Molloy, Frank (F.) 16, 39, 72, **74,** 75, 77, **78,** 80, 82, 85 – 87, **87,** 89, 119, 123, 129
Molloy, Gavin (G.) 77, **119**
Molloy, James (J.) 77
Molloy, June (J.) 77, **123**
Molloy, Keith (K.) 77
Molloy, Phillip (P.) 77
Molloy, Richard (R.) 77
Moltke Spur **8**
Moran, Vincent (V.) 130
Morrison, C. 18
Mosquito Hill **38**
Motueka 63, 135, 136
Mount Aspiring **14**
Mount Aspiring National Park 110
Mount Cook 22, 23, 31, 32, **36,** 38, 95, 96, 104, 138
Mount Cook Air Services Ltd 110, 135, 136, 142
Mount Cook Airlines 85, 97, 115, 117, 118, 121, 122, 136, 138, 143
Mount Cook and Southern Lakes Tourist Company Ltd 135
Mount Hope 67
Mount Mark 92
Mount Moltke 10
Mount Soho **109**
Mount Tasman 32, **36,** 96
Mount Turiwhate 18
Mount Turiwhate Memorial Cairn 23
Mount Warren 92
Mountain Helicopters 143
Murchison 67
Murchison Earthquake 12
Murdoch, J.A. 21
Murie, R. 31
Museum of Transport and Technology, Auckland (M.O.T.A.T.) 88, 97, 108, 114, 118, 121, 126
Mussel Point (Lower Okuru) Aerodrome **11, 13,** 14, **16,** 17, **18, 30,** 33, **40,** 43, **44,** 75, 119

NAC (New Zealand National Airways Corporation) 41, 43, 44, 70, 71, 73, 75, 77, 78, 83, 85 - 89, 91, 97, 98, 110, 114, 115, 118, 126, 127, 132 – 136, 142
Nairn Aviation Ltd 142
Nairn, Don (D.) 43
Nancekivell, Arthur (A.) 13, 14, 16, 17, 21, **21,** 22
Napier 41
Neale, Maureen (M.) 129
Neame, W. 18
Neave, John (J.) **41,** 43, 47, 53, 65, 69, 70, 129
Neils Beach **40**
Nelson 17, 18, **52,** 53, 54, 63, 67, 72, 75, 82, 97, 104, 110, 119, 131 – 136, 140, 142, 143
Nelson Aero Club 86, 135, 142
Nelson-West Coast Road 67
New Plymouth 133
New Zealand Aero Transport Company 31
New Zealand Airways Ltd 11, 22
New Zealand Forest Service 100
New Zealand Historic Aircraft Trust 86, 89
New Zealand Lotteries Board 125
New Zealand National Airways Act 75
New Zealand Navy 54
New Zealand Permanent Air Force 12, 31, 37
New Zealand Railways 139
New Zealand Territorial Air Force 17
New Zealand Tourist Air Travel 85, 97, 98, 110
Newcastle-upon-Tyne 104
Newman, H.C. 26
No. 1 E.F.T.S., RNZAF 73
No. 3 E.F.T.S., RNZAF 54
No. 3 School of General Reconnaissance, Squires Gate, England 77
No. 3 Lancaster Finishing School 55
No. 3 Wireless School, Winnipeg, Canada 55
No. 4 Squadron, NZAF 17
No. 4 S.F.T.S., Saskatoon, Canada 77
No. 5 O.T.U., RAF, Megaberry 77
No. 6 A.F.U., RAF, Little Rissington 54
No. 8 Bombing and Gunnery School, Leithbridge, Alberta, Canada 55
No. 16 O.T.U., RAF 53
No. 23 Fighter Squadron, RAF France 35
No. 27 Air School, South Africa 104
No. 34 O.T.U., Pennfield Ridge, New Brunswick, Canada 55
No. 42 Squadron, RNZAF. 41, 53, 73, 85, 86, 98
No. 48 Squadron, RAF 104
No. 75 (NZ) Squadron Mepal, Cambridgeshire, England 55, 104
No. 76 Maintenance Unit, RAF 85
No. 106 Squadron, RAF 54
No. 487 RNZAF Squadron, Norfolk, England 55
No. 1407 (Met) Flight, Iceland 77
No. 1525 B.A.T Flight, Docking 77
No. 1653 Heavy Conversion Unit 104
No. 1654 Conversion Unit 54
Nolan, Ann (A.) **11**
Nolan, Des (D.) 15, 21, 80, **119,** 125
Nolan, Dini (D.) **11, 28**
Nolan, 'Eddie' (E.) **11**
Nolan, Johanna (J.) **11**
Nolan, John **124**
Nolan, Kevin (K.) **11**
Nolan, Maria (M.) **11**
Nolan, Mary (M.) **11, 28**
Nolan, Mrs 93
Nolan, Robert (R.) **11, 28**
Nolan 'Bill' **11**
Norfolk Island 104
North Atlantic 77
Northern Group Communications Flight 85
Northern Ireland 77
North Shore Airfield 86
Nossiter, 'Bob' (R.) **81,** 130

O'Brien, Bill (W.) **86, 87**
O'Brien, Hon. James (J.) MP **28,** 54, 66
O'Neil, Grif (G.) 129
Oamaru 17
O'Brien, 'Billy' 99
Okarito **8,** 10
Okarito Lagoon 10, **96**
Okuru 17, 21, 22, 26, 29, 30, 34, 46, 58, 78, 79
Okuru Hall 79
Okuru River 15, 92
Old Mandeville Airfield 41, 85, 88, 124
Oldstead Aircraft Company 104
Olson, Jon (J.) 125
Openshaw, 'Ozzie' Orville (O.D.) 43, 56, 60, 61, **62,** 63, 64, **66,** 70, 129
Opuku Cliff 107
Orakei, Auckland 37
O'Reilly, Merv (M.) **100**
Oshkosh Air Show 43
Otira Tunnel 117
Overell, 'Rocky' (R.E.) 75
Overton, Ross (R.) 125

P & D Duncan Foundry, Christchurch 73
Palmerston North 77, 94
Paraparaumu 79, 82, 135
Paringa 44, 86, 102, 109, 111
Paringa river 106
Paringa riverbed **38**
Parry, Horace (H.T). 16, 20, 21, 58
Parry, Lloyd (L.) 57
Pascoe, Pat (P.) 138
Patchett Tours 86
Patea 60, 72
Paterson, Des (D.) 57, 129
Paterson, Nell (N.) 67
Patterson, Dick (R.W.) 117
Penman, Margaret (M.) **70, 75, 81,** 129
Percival P.28 Proctor 91, 142
Percival P.28 Proctor V ZK-AQZ **119**
Perry, Bruce (B.) 67, 68
Perry, G.A. 18
Phoenix Airways 133, 134, 142
Picton 17, 142
Pilgrim, Marilyn (M.) **127**
Pinckney, George (G.) 111
Piper PA.23-160 Apache ZK-BLP 102, 133 – 135
Piper PA.23-160 Apache ZK-BYB 133, **134**
Piper PA-23-250 Aztec ZK-CEU 135
Piper PA-25 Pawnee 143
Piper PA-31-310 Navajo 140
Piper PA-31-350 Navajo Chieftain 136
Piper PA-31-350 Navajo Chieftain ZK-VIP 140
Piper PA-32 Cherokee 6 ZK-ECV 138
Piper PA-34 Seneca ZK-KAE 140
Pitt Island, Chatham Islands 73
Polbury, Miss 129
Port Chalmers 85
Port Fairy 26, 41
Port Huon 98
Post and Telegraph Department 66
Preston, Hugh (H.B) 16, 21
Preston, S.J. 21, **22**
Prince of Wales (later King Edward VIII) 33, 43
Provis, Norma (N.) 87
Public Works Department **40,** 45, 66, 68, 80, 95
Public Works Department camp **28,42**
Pukutuaro 117

Queenstown 85, 94, 97, 98, 102, 104, 114, 121
Quinn, Roy (R.) 129

Radio 3ZA 104
Rae, R.N. 41
RAF (Royal Air Force) 34, 104
RAF Vickers Valiant 86
Railway Hotel, Hokitika 21
Rangitata 97
Rangitiki 47
Raytheon/Beech 1900D ZK-EAA **125,** 138
Red Hills, South Westland 139
Reefton 20, 127, 139
Reid, M.E. 44
Remote Adventures Ltd 142
Renton, Jack (J.B.) **12,** 13, 14, 17, **17,** 19, 22, 23, 72, **119**
Renton, Mary (M.) 17
Renton, Paul (P. E. L.) 17, 18, 25, 26, **39,** 127
Renton, Paul (P.) Senior 17, 66
Rex Air Charter 135
Rex Aviation (NZ) Ltd 135
RFC (Royal Flying Corps) 34
Rieux Communal Cemetery, France 55
Rieux, France 55
Ritchie Air Services 85
RNZAF (Royal New Zealand Air Force) 41, 55, 64, 73, 77, 85, 93, 97, 127, 132
RNZAF Band 122
Roberts, Neil (N.) **96**
Robertson 'Bill' **30**
Robertson, Myles (M.P.) 41
Robertson, Neil (N.) 43
Robinson Redwing G-ABMV, ZK-ADD 20, **20, 77**
Robson, Eric (E.) **94, 95**
Rongotai, Wellington 47, 53, 64, 65, 69, 86
Rope Construction Company camp **42**
Rosel, Emil (E.) 56, 129
Ross (South Westland) 20
Rothmans Masterton to Christchurch air race 109
Rotorua 41, 73, 85
Rotorua Aero Club, 86

The Author – REV RICHARD WAUGH

Growing up in Hokitika, the third child of Brian Waugh, the last of the South Westland air service pilots, Richard has a life-long interest in West Coast aviation history. He was a young passenger on the final West Coast Airways Dominie flight in 1967.

Richard's academic study has included New Zealand history, religious studies, theology, and business administration. While researching and writing this book he was completing doctoral studies from Asbury Theological Seminary in the United States.

Over the past 20 years Richard has done extensive research, writing and organising for a range of New Zealand aviation historical subjects, including being Organiser of the 1994 South Westland air service 60th anniversary celebrations. Since 1998 he has served as Honorary Chaplain to the Guild of Air Pilots and Air Navigators (New Zealand Region) and in the 2007 Queen's Birthday Honours was awarded the Queen's Service Medal for services to aviation history and the community. In 2009 for the 75th anniversary of Bert Mercer's pioneering airline efforts he initiated and helped organise celebrations at Hokitika and Haast.

In addition to his voluntary aviation work, Richard is a well known evangelical Church leader, Senior Minister of East City Wesleyan Church in Auckland (www.ecw.org.nz), and National Superintendent of the Wesleyan Methodist Church of New Zealand (www.wesleyan.org.nz). Richard is married to Jane, an architect, and they have three children.

Richard Waugh with the Fox Moth ZK-AEK replica at MOTAT, Auckland, July 2009. (Theresa Waugh)

Rowan, John **126**
Rowan, Louis (L.) 127
Rowley Aviation Ltd 118, 143
Rowling, 'Bill' Wallace (W.E.) MP 133
Royal Aero Club 31
Royds, John (J.) 139
Rudnick Helicopters Ltd 107
Rumsey, Mervyn (M.) 98, 105, **107**, 110, 113, 130
Runnymede Memorial, Middlesex, England 54
Rural Aviation Ltd 94
Russell, Eva (E.) 67

SAAB SF340 138
Sage War Cemetery, Oldenburg, Germany 54
Sage, Doctor 98
Salter, Alan (A.) 129
Savage, Jerry (J.) **136**
Saville, Elwyn (E.) 127
Saville, Valerie (V.) 127
Saxton, David (D.) 128
Scenicland Helicopters 143
Sea Gull 54
Seaview Hospital **103**
Seddon, (T. E. Y.) 21, 29, 117, 118
Seddon, Sir Richard John 29, 117
Shallcrass, Dick (R.) 16
Shell Oil 77
Shiels, Darrell (D.) 127
Short Stirling 55
Short Sunderland Flying boat 57
Shotover River 98, 104, **104**
Shrewsbury, Shropshire, England 104
Silver Fern 73
Simmonds Spartan ZK-ABU *Lovebird* **11, 13, 14**, 15 -17, 19, **19**, 20, **20, 21**, 22, **22**
Sleeman, Major J.L. 31
Smith, 'Tex' **101**, 130
Smith, Blatchford (B.) 130
Smith, Colin 43, **124**, 125, 126
Smith, Nikki (N.) 136
Snow Commander 143
Sockburn 31, 32
Somme, France 34
Sounds Air Tourism and Travel Ltd 142
South African Air Force 104
South Beach 92
South Island Airways 104
South West Helicopters Ltd 143
Southam, Ryan (R.) 127
Southern Alps 9, 10, 17, 22, 26, 38, 45, 71, 91, 96, 101, 138
Southern Lakes Helicopters Ltd 143
Southern Scenic Air Services Ltd 83, 86, 87, 91, 94, 97, 104, 110, 142, 143
Southland Airways 49, 142
Seaview Aerodrome (Hokitika) 75, 80, **82, 88, 103**, 133
Southside Aerodrome (Hokitika) **11**, 14, 15, **15**, 17, 18, 29, 33, **35, 37**, 38, **39, 46, 47, 49, 52**, 55, 57,
57, 65, **70, 74**, 75, 76, **76**, 77, **78**, 80, **81**, 88, **90**, 97, 117, 118, **121**, 124, 126, 132
Southside Memorial Plaque and Information Panels **49**, 51
Spalding Airways 104
SPANZ (South Pacific Airlines of New Zealand Ltd) 134
Spencer-Bower, Simon (S.) **119**
Sport and Vintage Aviation Society 85
Spreydon, Christchurch 73
Spring Plains, New South Wakes, Australia 70
St Clair School 96
St Mary's Primary School, Hokitika 105
St Mary's Catholic Church, Hokitika 18
St Mary's Catholic School 55
State Highway 6
Staines, Joy (J.) **87**, 91, 130
Stevenson, Dave (D.) **47**
Stewart Island 50
Stewart, Frank (F.) 39
Stinson Model A VH-UYY 70
Stoke Aerodrome, Nelson 97
Stoop, Jean (J.) **70, 81**, 129
Stopforth, W.H A. 21
Straight, A. 18
Stratmore, George (G.) 67
Stuart, Jack (J.) 16
Sullivan, Jim (J.) 34
Supermarine Spitfire ZK-XVI **119**, 124
Suttie, Alexander (A.) 73
Suttie, Jemima (J.) 73
Suttie, Jill (J.) 73
Suttie, John (J.) 73
Suttie, Nancy, (N.) 73
Suttie, Norm (N.A.) 44, 69, 73, **75**, 76, **77**, 79, 129, 130
Sweney, Ray (R.) 43
Swissair 41
Switzer, John (J.H.) 41
Sydney, Australia 12, 104
Syron, Lesley (L.) 126
Syron, Matthew (M.) 126

Tahunanui, Nelson 10
Taieri 73, 77, 96
Takaka 63, 135
Taramakau 18
Tasman Sea 9, 10, 12, 37, 39
Tauranga 62
Taurau, Nash (N.) 139
Taylor, 'Mick' (M.) **96**
Taylorville 77
Te Kinga 21
Te Koeiti, 'Dan' Taane, (T.) **40**
Te Marie Villa **103**
'*Te Parae*', Masterton 85
TEAL – Tasman Empire Airways Ltd 94
Teen, T. 418
Teichelmann, Dr Ebenezer (E.) 10, 17, 21, **39**, 114
Teichelmann's Bed and Breakfast 114
Templeton, Owen (O.) 39, 45, 47, **47**, 56, 129
The Air Survey and Transport Co. Ltd 47
The Hague 104
The Hermitage, Mount Cook 135
The Press 26, 33, 78
The Radio Service 66
The Weekly News **27**
Thomas, R. 17
Thompson, Diane (D.) 130
Timaru 17, 31, 96, 140
Tofua 43
Toohey, Alexandra (A.) 55
Toohey, Cornelius (C.) 55
Toohey, Edward (E.W.) **54**, 55, 129
Topliss, Barry (B.) 91, 98
Totara Stream 10
Tourist Air Travel and Transport Service Ltd 16, **16**, 22, 25
Trans Island Airways 104
Transport Co-ordination Board 33, 34
Transport (Nelson) Ltd 68
Treacy, M. 18
Troon, Russell (R.) **101**, 130
Trowsdale, Rod (R.F.) 117
Truman, Doug (D.) 139
Tuck, Lew (L.) 92
Turbulent Years – A Commercial Pilot's Story 104, 119
Turiwhate 17, 18
Turley, Murray (M.) 135
Turnbull River 92
Turner, J.L. 21

Union Airways 52, 53, 85
Upper Okuru (Nolans') Aerodrome 21, **28**, 33, 75
Urewera National Park 110

Valenciennes, France 55
Vickers Viscount 119
Vickers Wellington 53
Vintage Wings of Canada 43
Von Haast, Julius 9
Waghorn, 'Bert' (B.L.) 139
Waiho 17, 22, 23, 27, 38, 39, 46
Waiho (Franz Josef Glacier) **32**
Waiho (Franz Josef) Aerodrome **20, 28**, 33, **35**, 43, 44
Waiho River 38, 122
Waikari 31
Waikato Aero Club 73, 79
Wairoa 41
Wakeman, Keith (K.) 41, 43
Walker, 'Johnny' (H.C.) 80
Wall, A.J. 59
Wallis, Sir Tim (T.) 43, 119, 124
Walters, Albert (A.) 60, 61
Waltham Railway yards, Christchurch **19**
Wanaka 9, 77, 101, 113, **126, 127**
Wanganui 113
Wanganui Aero Work Ltd 44
Warbirds over Wanaka Airshow 126
Ward, Nell (N.) **62**, 63
Waugh, Alec (A.K.) 104, 109
Waugh, Brian (B.K.) 39, 92, 93, **94, 96, 96**, 98 – 102, 104, 105, **105**, 106 -110, 112 – 114, **118**, 119, 124, 128, 130
Waugh, (nee Kynaston) Helen (H.) 104
Waugh, Jean (J.M.) **2**, 104, 107, **123**
Waugh, Kathryn (K.L.) 104
Waugh, Lesley (L.H.) 104
Waugh, Michael (M.G.) 104, 107
Waugh, Noah (N.) **128**
Waugh, Richard (R.J.) 72, 104, 114, **120**, 122, 124, **126, 152**
Waugh, Walter (W.) 104
Waziriston Field Force 37
Weheka (Fox River) Aerodrome 33, 41, 44
Weheka Airstrip (Fox Glacier) **27**, 33
Welcome Flat landing strip 102
Weld Street, Hokitika 89
Wellington 11, 34, 60, 67, 97, 110, 132, 133, 135, 138, 140, 142
Wellington Aero Club 135
Wells, Ashley (A.). 86
Wells, Jean (J.) 119, 130
Wells, Pat (P) 86
Wells, Phillip (P.) 86
Wessex Aviation 41
West Coast Air Charter 142
West Coast Airways 21, 22
West Coast Airways Ltd 87, 88, 91, 93 – 97, 101, 102, 104, 106, 107, 110, 111, 113, 118, 127, 134, 142, 143
West Coast Airways Ltd steps 96, **118, 122**
West Coast Historical Museum 122
West Coast Table Tennis Association 104
West Coast United Aero Club 13, 77, 141
Westair Flying Ltd 142
Westhaven, 63
Westland Aero Club 17
Westland Air Charter Ltd 142
Westland Air Ltd 135, 142
Westland County Council 40
Westland District Council 120, 122, 125
Westland Flying Services Ltd 138, 142
Westland Hospital 34, 39, 111, 114
Westland Savings Bank 127
Westland Transport Ltd 70, 142
Westport 10, 12, 20, 47, 54, 58, 62, 63, 67, 71, 72, 75, 76, 82, 85, 86, 119, 132 – 136, 138 – 141, 143
Westport Aeradio 58, 68
Westport Aero Club 143
Westport Air Show 1997 41, 124, 126
Westport Airport (see Kawatiri Aerodrome) **70**, 72, **78**, 110, **131**
Westport breakwater 60
Westport memorial plaque 72, **73**
Westport News 135
Whakapohai River 113
Whataroa 20, 41, 93, 110
When the Coast is Clear 124
Whiley, Peter (P.) 87, **87**, 130
Whirl-Wide Helicopters Ltd 143
White, Irene (I.) **47**
White, Leo (L.L.) 47
White, 'Tiny' (T.W.) **11**, 14, 54
Whitebaiters' Ball 78
Wickes, Laurie (L.) 95
Wigley, Harry (H.R.) 135
Wigley, Rodolph (R.L.) 31
Wigram Aerodrome, Christchurch **12, 17, 18**, 22, 41, 44, 45, 73
Wigram, Lady Agnes 54
Wild, Wilkinson and Dawe 68
Wilderness Wings Ltd 94, 142
Wilding, Peter (P.) 111
Wilhelmshaven, Germany 54
Wilkes, T.M. 18
Williams, Darrell 143
Williams, Havelock (H.) 8
Williams, Tom (T.C.) 85
Williamson, F. 66
Wilson, Iris (I.) **25**
Wilson, Molly (M.) **62**, 63
Win, Joan (J.) **86**, 130
Winged Hunters Ltd 143
Winter Brothers 77
Wio Villa **103**
Woodbourne, Blenheim 53
Woodford, Brian 41
Woodhen Bend 68, **68**
World War I 31
World War II 70, 74, 132, 142
World War II Memorial, Hokitika 55
Wornall, C.A. 43
Worrall, 'Harry' (H.) 25 – 27, 70
Worthington family 103, 106
Wright, 'Buster' Robert (R.) 127
Wright, Vivien (V.) 127
Wright, Desmond (D.R.) 72, 92, 102, 106, 107, 115, 121, 127, **127**, 130
Wright, J.G. 59,
Wright, Raeoni (R.) 127
Wyn-Irwin, J. 34

Ypres, France 34

Text: 9.5/13 Stone Serif
Paper: 128gsm matt art
Layout by Craig Printing Co. Ltd (from typesetting supplied)
Book design: Ellen van Empel
Printed by Craig Printing Co. Ltd, Invercargill, New Zealand.